Positioning Theory and Strategic Communication

In public relations, people talk about positioning an idea, a persona, a political ideal, an ideology – but what are they talking about? Why do some positions taken by organizations crystallize in the minds of audiences, while others fail?

Whilst positioning is not something new in public relations, this book is the first to explicate what it involves, how it works and how to do it. This is the first in-depth exploration of the possibilities of Positioning Theory for the public relations field. It adds a new perspective to the growing body of multidisciplinary work in this rich theoretical area, moving the discussion away from the traditional communication plans of previous decades, which fail to accommodate the changing media and opinion landscapes. The author pulls together various strands of socio-cultural theory into an analytical framework, providing readers with a tool to analyze the organizational implications of public relations decisions, to guide strategic decision making through realistic scenario planning.

This thought-provoking book provides an alternative path to studying communication in increasingly complex environments and as such, will be vital reading for researchers and educators, advanced communication and public relations students, and for senior public relations practitioners.

Melanie James is senior lecturer in communication at the University of Newcastle, Australia. She is a national-award-winning practitioner, having held senior roles in public relations and marketing communication. She has published in public relations journals and authored Australia's first public relations careers book.

Routledge New Directions in Public Relations and Communication Research

Edited by Kevin Moloney

Routledge New Directions in Public Relations and Communication Research is a new forum for the publication of books of original research in PR and related types of communication. Its remit is to publish critical and challenging responses to continuities and fractures in contemporary PR thinking and practice, and their essential yet contested role in market-orientated, capitalist, liberal democracies around the world. The series reflects the multiple and inter-disciplinary forms PR takes in a post-Grunigian world; the expanding roles which it performs; and the increasing number of countries in which it is practised.

The series will examine current trends and explore new thinking on the key questions which impact upon PR and communications, including:

- Is the evolution of persuasive communications in Central and Eastern Europe, China, Latin America, Japan, the Middle East and South East Asia developing new forms or following Western models?
- What has been the impact of postmodern sociologies, cultural studies and methodologies which are often critical of the traditional, conservative role of PR in capitalist political economies, and in patriarchy, gender and ethnic roles?
- What is the impact of digital social media on politics, individual privacy and PR practice? Is new technology changing the nature of content communicated, or simply reaching bigger audiences faster? Is digital PR a cause or a consequence of political and cultural change?
- Books in this series will be of interest to academics and researchers involved in these expanding fields of study, as well as students undertaking advanced studies in this area.

Public Relations and Nation Building
Influencing Israel
Margalit Toledano and David McKie

Gender and Public Relations
Critical perspectives on voice, image and identity
Edited by Christine Daymon and Kristin Demetrious

Pathways to Public Relations
Histories of practice and profession
Edited by Burton Saint John III, Margot Opdycke Lamme and Jacquie L'Etang

Positioning Theory and Strategic Communication
A new approach to public relations research and practice
Melanie James

Positioning Theory and Strategic Communication

A new approach to public relations research and practice

Melanie James

Routledge
Taylor & Francis Group
LONDON AND NEW YORK

First published 2014
by Routledge
2 Park Square, Milton Park, Abingdon, Oxon OX14 4RN

and in the USA and Canada
by Routledge
711 Third Avenue, New York, NY 10017

First issued in paperback 2017

Routledge is an imprint of the Taylor & Francis Group, an informa business

British Library Cataloguing in Publication Data
A catalogue record for this book is available from the British Library

Library of Congress Cataloging in Publication Data
Positioning theory and strategic communications : a new approach to public relations research and practice / Melanie James. – First Edition.
pages cm. – (Routledge new directions in public relations & communication research)
Includes bibliographical references and index.
1. Public relations. I. Title.
HD59.J36 2014
659.2–dc23
2013046883

ISBN 13: 978-1-138-49736-8 (pbk)
ISBN 13: 978-0-415-53263-1 (hbk)

Typeset in Times New Roman
by Fish Books Ltd.

To my parents, Joan and Frank Skillen, with much love from "the doc" and to Russell Francis Skillen, one special brother.

Contents

Illustrations

Figures

Tables

Acknowledgements

This book would not exist if not for the faith shown in my work by the series editor, Dr Kevin Moloney. His guidance and understanding throughout the process is very much appreciated. Thanks also to Professor Karen Miller Russell who was so supportive of my effort to first publish my work on the application of positioning theory in public relations in 2009–2010.

I must acknowledge the generous support of the University of Newcastle, Australia. Through the support offered by the university I have been able to spend extended periods of time working firstly on my doctoral thesis and secondly on significantly extending that research for this book. I have been afforded opportunities through the university to travel to present my research to my peers at conferences, a vital part of my ability to move through this project. I especially thank Professor Bill Hogarth, Dr Anne Llewellyn and Professor Tim Roberts for providing guidance and support.

I also acknowledge Associate Professor Marj Kibby, Professor Patricia Gillard and Associate Professor Christine Daymon who have become valued mentors over the past years. A big thank you also to the wonderful academics I've met through the Australia New Zealand Communication Association and the Public Relations Institute of Australia. There are so many of you to thank but I must express my deep gratitude to Associate Professor Jennifer Bartlett, Associate Professor Joy Chia, Dr Gwyneth Howell, Dr Leanne Glenny, Dr Lynette McDonald, Professor David McKie, Professor Jim Macnamara, Dr Amisha Mehta, Professor Judy Motion and Dr Elspeth Tilley. You've all welcomed me to the fold and have encouraged me along the academic path that I just love. I also acknowledge the support and guidance provided in recent years by Professor Anne Gregory and Professor Jacquie L'Etang.

In addition, I must thank all my colleagues in the School of Design, Communication and IT at the University of Newcastle and in particular Dr Janet Fulton, Dr Susan Kerrigan, Ms Christina Koutsoukos, Ms Prue Robson and Dr Judith Sandner, who have supported me personally and professionally through some "rocky patches" in recent years. Thank you also to Professor Mark Balnaves for your guidance at key stages of this project.

Two of my PhD students, Ms Deborah Wise and Ms Andrea Cassin, also must be thanked for their feedback, collaboration and support over the past few years.

As my students, colleagues, and friends, you have made the journey so much richer, not to mention fun. I also appreciate the insightful feedback provided on my work at key points by Dr Maulina Pia Wulandari – *terima kasih*. I also wish to thank all of my students who have challenged me and spurred me on to engage with new techniques and ideas. It always amazes me how much I learn from my students.

Last but absolutely not least, thank you to my husband, Stephen, and to my children, Alexandra and Patrick, for your love and for accommodating the somewhat crazy life of an academic.

Introduction

This book is about "positioning theory" and its application to public relations. Some may wonder why they should engage with a whole book about a theory they may not have heard about. Others who have heard about the theory may be wondering why it is being applied to public relations. The answer lies in defining what is theory. Put simply, "theory is a statement of concepts and their interrelationships that shows how and/or why a phenomenon occurs" (Corley and Gioia, 2011: 12). The phenomenon under examination in this book is that of "positioning". Particularly, it is the phenomenon of positioning in public relations.

Few public relations textbooks mention positioning and there has been relatively little attention given to public relations positioning in the academic literature. This struck me as very strange when, in 2008, I was trying to analyze findings from a large research project that was examining Australian award-winning public relations campaigns. In almost half of the case studies I was analyzing, and in almost all of my interviews with senior practitioners, the word "positioning" kept appearing. In the main, these people were not referring to marketing concepts of differentiating one product from another. They were referring to the way they wanted people to think about something such as a place, an idea, a person, a process, a project, a behavior and so on.

A positioning "gap"

When I turned my attention to public relations academic studies, the field seemed ill-equipped to show how or why this phenomenon occurred. Kilduff states (2006), "the route to good theory leads not through gaps in the literature but through an engagement with problems in the world that you find personally interesting" (p. 252). Given that I was in a situation where there was both a gap and personal interest, I began to look to other areas for a theory that would address the concepts and interrelationships of public relations positioning, and how and why it occurred.

I looked to established, dominant public relations theory and found aspects of all theories that applied in some instances, but not others. I examined critical scholarship in public relations. For example, Motion (1997) in her paper on discursively constructing positions from a personal public relations perspective stated, "positioning may be thought of, from a public relations perspective, as strategic, representational, and promotional" (p. 8). Motion drew on the work of Foucault, and found there was significant relevance to conceptualizing positioning. Again, I didn't see that it provided the whole answer. When talking to many academics in wider communication contexts, the theoretical approach that kept arising was social constructionism. Like in so many academic exercises, you start on a seemingly straightforward path but then find yourself going deeply into fascinating theoretical territory.

It was this process that led me to the foundational book of Berger and Luckmann (1966), *The Social Construction of Reality,* which "is recognized as the leading inspiration for constructionist work in communication" (Foster and Bochner, 2008: 88). Around this same time, Gordon and Pellegrin's (2008) chapter, Social constructionism and public relations, was published. Reading these texts resonated profoundly with my own research and theoretical "grappling". I was trekking through some dense theory forests!

I knew language, text and discourse played a significant role in public relations. However, theoretical approaches that disconnected this from social practice and social science didn't sit comfortably with what I knew. I had never warmed to assertions such as that made by Derrida that there is "nothing beyond the text" (cited in Weinberg, 2008: 33). What made sense in the context of my practice and research was the social constructionist assertion that:

> Reality is a social construction that is created, maintained, altered, and destroyed through the process of human interaction. Social constructionism does acknowledge a physical world independent of human interpretation.
>
> (Gordon and Pellegrin, 2008: 105)

This is a view of the world stemming from theoretical traditions in phenomenology (Balnaves, Donald and Shoesmith, 2009) that sees "experience as subjective interpretation by humans rather than 'objective' reality" (Macnamara, 2012: 55). A leading phenomenologist of the twentieth century, Alfred Schutz (Barber, 2012) was key to defining the idea of social reality. Berger and Luckmann (1966) in the preface to their text, acknowledged the large intellectual debt they owed to the work of Schutz. Schutz stated:

> By the term "social reality" I wish to be understood the sum total of objects and occurrences within the social cultural world as experienced by the common-sense thinking of men living their daily lives among their fellow-men, connected with them in manifold relations of interaction. It is the world of cultural objects and social institutions into which we all are born, within which we have to find our bearings, and with which we have to come to terms. From the outset, we, the actors on the social scene, experience the world we live in as a world both of nature and of culture, not as a private but as an intersubjective one, that is, as a world common to all of us, either actually given or potentially accessible to everyone; and this involves intercommunication and language.
>
> (Shutz, 1954: 261)

The more I engaged with the writings on social constructionism the more it seemed to make sense in terms of public relations theory and practice.

Finding "positioning theory"

From this point, it was a matter of searching the terms "social constructionism" and "positioning", which, I thought somewhat serendipitously, returned the result "positioning theory" (Harré and van Langenhove, 1999). In 2012, Harré defined positioning theory as being:

> ...based on the principle that not everyone involved in a social episode has equal access to rights and duties to perform particular kinds of meaningful actions at that moment and with those people. In many interesting cases, the rights and duties determine who can use a certain discourse mode...A cluster of short-term disputable rights, obligations and duties is called a "position".
>
> (Harré, 2012: 193)

In retrospect, the fact that these search terms delivered the result of "positioning theory" should not have been unexpected, as the theory is described as a social constructionist approach (Harré and van Langenhove, 1999; Kroløkke, 2009). The first applications of positioning theory were focused on the analysis of positions taken in interpersonal encounters such as conversational exchanges, but I immediately saw relevance to public relations and positioning efforts. Others had also made the connection to the theory's possibilities in analyzing positioning in contexts other than interpersonal exchanges. Positioning theory was especially taken up in the early 2000s in education studies, international relations and to a lesser extent, organizational studies.

I applied positioning analytical methods (Harré and Moghaddam, 2003) to my award-winning case study data (James, 2011). I found that the central organizing idea of the theory, the "positioning triangle" (van Langenhove and Harré, 1999: 18), could be applied to each of the award winning case studies in my sample (n=57). As shown in Figure 0.1, the "positioning triangle" is a triangle with three vertices (as from geometry, the three "corners" of the triangle; each "corner" being called a vertex) that are:

> ...occupied by positions, storylines and act interpretations. The constituents of the three vertices mutually determine one another. If any one changes – for example, by a successful challenge to the distribution of rights and duties – then all three change. Change the distribution of rights and duties and the storyline that has been realized thus far may be transformed. At the same time, the meanings of what has been said and done by the actors are also transformed. The future relations between the actors and the subsequent form taken by the unfolding strip of life will be different after changes in any three components of the positioning triangle.
>
> (Harré, 2012: 196)

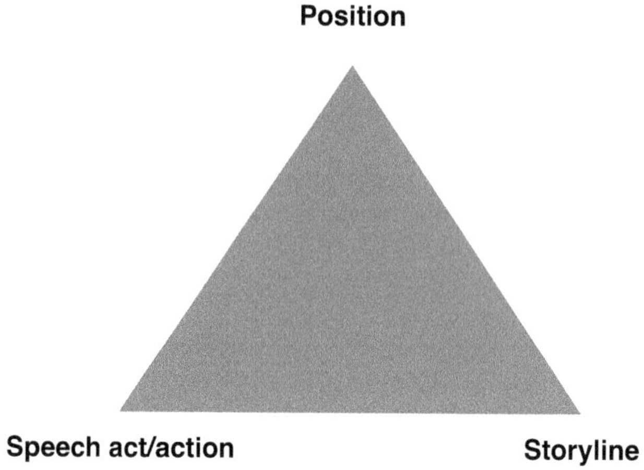

Figure 0.1 A representation of the positioning triangle
Source: adapted from van Langenhove and Harré, 1999.

My positioning triangle analysis showed an alignment of the three positioning triangle vertices in all my sample's 57 case studies. These were the cases reported by their authors as having been successful (hence their "award-winning" status) in achieving their public relations goals. It was clear in all cases that there was alignment between the position that was trying to be achieved by the public relations client/organization; the speech act/actions that had been enacted; and, the storylines used in narratives expressed through constructs such as "key messages". I tentatively concluded that when there was an alignment between the stated desired position, the way it had been enacted, and the way it had been supported through storylines, public relations positioning had been successful. Although the positioning triangle analysis indicated that the "building blocks of meaning: speech acts, positions, and storylines" (Slocum-Bradley, 2007: 637) were clearly present in the case studies, it was clear that there were other factors at play in these and other public relations episodes.

Applying positioning theory to public relations

All public relations activity is undertaken with a purpose to achieve a particular outcome. If this was not the case, one would not undertake public relations. In all cases of the data I was examining, the positioning efforts were strategic in nature, meaning that the public relations episodes were happening in the context of a contested environment. All case studies could be interpreted as public relations situations where the position their client/organization (or its service, idea, product, project etc.) "occupied" was not the one they wanted to be in. All situations required some intentional effort to occupy, or assign to another, a new position.

The contest was around various factors including gaining "share-of-voice" in crowded media spaces, or displacing dominant behaviors or ideas, in order for desired positions to be achieved.

My analysis indicated that the positioning triangle on its own did not fully conceptualize the strategic goal-directed nature of public relations, and this pushed me to explore further. In 2009 I first presented my initial ideas about social constructionism and positions to various local academic conferences (see also James, 2009). Then in 2010, I presented my work at the 17th International Public Relations Research Symposium, BledCom. I did this because as Kilduff (2006: 252) states, "once you have articulated your main theoretical idea, in however preliminary a form, it is time to discuss, debate, and argue with both your supportive and skeptical colleagues". At the same time, the new *Sage Handbook of Public Relations* (Heath, 2010) was released. In this volume, Leitch and Motion (2010) made links between the 1991 positioning theoretical work of Harré and van Langenhove and the work in discursive positioning in public relations critical scholarship over the previous fifteen years. Although the feedback I received from the first "test flights" of my own work on public relations positioning were mixed, my high regard for the work of Shirley Leitch and Judy Motion was such that if they were making such links, I was probably on the right path. I returned to working through van Langenhove and Harré's (1999) four different types of intentional positioning, namely:

- deliberate self-positioning
- deliberate positioning of others
- forced self-positioning
- forced positioning of others.

I found that these four categories could be applied to analyze the type of public relations positioning that had occurred in the award-winning case studies. Interestingly, all cases could be interpreted as a deliberate positioning of "self", that is, the organization/client and/or its offering or proposition. In addition to "self-positioning" there was evidence of each of the other types of positioning in the data (see James, 2011). This was not unexpected as van Langenhove and Harré (1999) had noted, "whenever positioning occurs, several forms of positioning are likely to be occurring simultaneously" (p. 24).

This was an exciting development because it started to raise questions related to which entities had the power to position themselves and others. What kinds of power would be wielded, and by whom, in such situations? These questions related to what has come to be the key differentiator of positioning theory from other theoretical approaches. This differentiator involves the "concepts and principles from the local moral domain, usually appearing as beliefs and practices involving rights and duties" (Harré, Moghaddam, Pilkerton Cairnie, Rothbart and Sabat, 2009: 6). I knew that having a conceptual framework would be potentially useful as: a) a tool to scaffold research, or, b) as a tool for program planning (Smyth, 2004). My research had indicated that there needed to be a domain within the framework that addressed the goal directedness of public relations positioning efforts. I knew I definitely had to include the "positioning type" as one of the domains. I knew there had to be a domain wherein the positioning triangle would sit. The specific development of the framework and its domains are discussed in detail in Chapter 3 of this book. Suffice to say, from this work, I drew together a Provisional Conceptual Framework for Intentional Positioning in Public Relations (James, 2010, 2011).

To provide an overview how it all sits together, the following example may help. Theoretical work of James Grunig has dominated the field of public relations for several decades and has been positioned as the dominant approach. When scholars talk of Grunig's work as dominant, it positions all other work in the field as "not dominant". As a result, for a scholar to question this dominant position, as Gower (2006) did, was an interesting exercise. Using the positioning framework it is evident that Gower's goal was to set out where the public relations field was in terms of research. Gower aimed to articulate an alternative pathway for future research that moved the field away from "the dominant theoretical paradigm in the field—two-way symmetrical communication" (2006: 178). The type of positioning was deliberate positioning of others (i.e. positioning of theories and theorists), a positioning type that raises questions of who holds the right and power to position others in this scholarly space. The strategic prepositioning involved assigning an attribute of sorts to the theoretical field. Gower (2006) told us it was at "the crossroad", a metaphor to illustrate that the field had come to a place where it could branch off onto different theoretical paths than those that had dominated previously.

Within the "positioning triangle domain", we could see the position taken (first vertex) was that the dominant theoretical paradigm was no longer what the field needed. This was asserted (a speech-act) by a scholar with the credentials to make such a claim, that is, Gower had claimed the right to assert the position (second vertex – positioning enactment). This opened access for Gower to fulfill her duty in taking the position, to support it (third pole) through particular storylines the evidence of what was happening in public relations and related fields.

The positioning as described above maps quite closely to what happens in much public relations practice. When someone, or an organization, takes a position on something it opens up possibilities for action. However, taking a position can also close down options for action. Positioning theory provides a way to tease all this out as it is concerned with the way the actions of participants in social interactions are constrained by an understood framework of rights, duties and obligations, a moral order (Tan and Moghaddam, 1999). It can serve to define the nature of constraints and possibilities for participants in public relations episodes and assist in both researching past practice and in future program design. It can provide a method for analysis as entities establish, maintain and even transform their relationships (Tan and Moghaddam, 1999). Applying positioning theory to public relations provides a new way to practice strategic public relations that aligns with the increasing complexity of the twenty-first century.

This book

Since 2010 I have been working to apply and test the rigour of the Framework, and to explore the further application of positioning theory to public relations. This book is the culmination of that work. I have set out my understanding of positioning theory and how it relates and can be further adapted to public relations. The book aims to take readers on a journey of sorts. Section 1 (Chapters 1–3) starts with understanding the theory and what it can offer, and proceeds to the latest iteration of the Framework for Intentional Positioning in Public Relations. Section 2 takes readers through a deeper application of key aspects of the theory such as the central organizing "positioning triangle". Section 3 presents detailed accounts of how the theory and Framework can be applied as a public relations analytical tool and also as a public relations program design tool.

Specifically, Chapter 1 introduces positioning theory, its central ideas, and why it is relevant to public relations. The chapter also examines how positioning has been addressed in the public relations academic literature, primarily through critical scholarship and discussions of discursive positioning, and also through framing theory. Chapter 2 discusses the key concept of rights and duties conferred in positioning and the local moral orders that are in operation. The chapter discusses the possibilities for further linking positioning theory concepts to Bourdieu's ideas of field and habitus. Given the theoretical lineage back to the work of Schutz of both positioning theory and much of Bourdieu's work (Thompson, 1991) it is surprising that this linkage has not been further examined in the context of the application of positioning theory. I have drawn on how, e.g., Ihlen's work (2009) on applying Bourdieu's social theory to public relations can strengthen understanding. In Chapter 3, I report on the development and application of the latest iteration of the Framework for Intentional Positioning in Public Relations.

Chapter 4 sees an exploration of how positions in public relations can be determined: the first vertex of the positioning triangle. It draws on other public relations theories and proposes scenario planning as an effective exercise in developing positioning strategy. In Chapter 5 I examine how positions are enacted at the second vertex of the positioning triangle through speech acts. There has been much criticism of speech act theory (e.g. Bourdieu, 1991). However, within the context of positioning theory, speech acts are conceptually embedded in socio-cultural environments through the "positioning triangle" and are no longer theoretically disembodied in the social sense. The third vertex of the positioning triangle, storylines, is the topic of Chapter 6. I draw deeply on the narrative theory of Gergen (2005) and apply the concept of storyline through this approach to positioning in a public relations sense.

I outline in Chapter 7 the public relations positioning analyses that have been published at the time of writing. An approach to conducting a positioning analysis in a public relations context, based extensively on the method proposed by Harré and Slocum (2003), is also proposed. Chapter 8 sees this method applied to a public relations positioning analysis in which the discursive efforts of government politicians and officials to position one another in a public diplomacy context are examined. In Chapter 9 the Framework for Intentional Positioning in Public

Relations is applied in response to an actual communication brief and details how the Framework can guide the development and implementation of a public relations positioning program.

In Chapter 10, I summarise where things stand for positioning theory in public relations and suggest pathways for future research. I also speculate on how this theory will be useful for guiding future practice in the changing world where the expansion of social media technologies, and the increased use of big data and networked approaches to communication, will continue.

This book is primarily designed for academic researchers and educators, postgraduate communication and public relations students, and for senior public relations practitioners. Though many of us engage with language and words generally, in this text it is presumed that most readers would not have a background in linguistics. In discussing such things as discourse, aspects of language, speech acts, narrative and so on, it is necessary to be clear on the theoretical assumptions on which the discussion is based. Without this the positioning processes and techniques being examined will appear *ad hoc* and lacking theoretical foundation. To this end, this text looks at language from an integrationist point of view, which Harré, Brockmeier and Muhlhausler say is one that regards the primary function of language as being:

> to enable human beings to develop communication processes that are intrinsically open-ended and necessarily involve nonverbal as well as verbal components. These processes take the form of integrated sequences of activities (both physical and mental) contextualized by the participants themselves.
>
> (Harré, Brockmeier and Muhlhausler, 1999: 43)

This view is consistent with the social constructionist epistemology within which the concept of positioning in public relations sits; the meanings constructed through public relations efforts are co-created by practitioners and audiences and publics. Thus meanings created in particular situations can be seen as negotiations involving the way language is used and distributed by public relations professionals; what is expected within the site of public relations; and, the meaning systems that are used personally by individuals and that are applied to the situation they have encountered (Bazerman, 2013).

The book provides insights into positioning theory and considers some of the ways it can guide research, analysis, education and program design. I have tried to use examples and scenarios from around the world but inevitably, because I am based in Australia and much of my own positioning research work has been conducted in this country, there may be more Australian examples than readers would like. However, I believe, based on my experiences living, working and travelling around the world, that such examples are readily translatable to most contexts within which public relations operates. I certainly look forward to researchers from around the world investigating the possibilities that positioning theory opens up in their own contexts, and would welcome opportunities to collaborate on international projects.

This is the first in-depth exploration of the possibilities of positioning theory for the public relations field and as such, adds to the growing body of multidisciplinary work on this rich theoretical area.

Definitions of key terms used throughout this book

It is acknowledged that definitions in the fields of public relations, especially those pertaining to the concept of publics, and related terms, are contested (Chia, 2009; Tindall and Vardeman-Winter, 2010: n.p.). I will use the following definitions in this book:

- **Audience/s:** any individual or group who might receive or listen to campaign messages but may not be a stakeholder or specific public (Chia, 2009: 6).
- **Organization/s:** used throughout this book "in its broadest sense" in line with previously published scholarly work (Hallahan, Holtzhausen, van Ruler, Verčič and Sriramesh, 2007: 4) to refer to for-profit and not-for-profit organizations, corporations, clients of public relations agencies and consultants, activist groups, nongovernment organizations, social change organizations, political entities, and government organizations and agencies.
- **Public/s:** any group of people who share common interest or values in a particular situation (Chia, 2009: 5).
- **Publics and audiences:** a broad reference to those people who organizations interact with through communication programs and campaigns (Chia, 2009: 6).
- **Public relations:** "involves all those deliberate efforts to formally communicate with individuals or groups and includes management or internal communication, marketing and advertising, and public relations. Public relations itself covers media (traditional, online and social), corporate communication, public affairs, community relations and investor relations. These disciplines are converging with each using the channels of the other and the drive for a more unified voice makes it sensible pragmatically to bring them together. Communication is the word often used to describe these collective specialist functions, but we will use the phrase public relations because it best describes what happens: the organization builds relationships in public and with these various publics" (Gregory and Willis, 2013: 11).
- **Stakeholder/s:** a group or individual who can affect, or is affected by, the achievement of an organization's objectives (Freeman, 1984).

References

Balnaves, M., Donald, S., and Shoesmith, B. (2009) *Media Theories and Approaches: A global perspective.* Basingstoke: Palgrave Macmillan.

Barber, M. (2012) Alfred Schutz. In E. N. Zalta (ed.) *The Stanford Encyclopedia of Philosophy* (Winter 2012 edn). Retrieved from http://plato.stanford.edu/archives/win2012/entries/schutz/

Bazerman, C. (2012) Genre as Social Action. In J. Gee and M. Handford (eds) *The Routledge Handbook of Discourse Analysis.* London: Routledge, pp. 226–38.

Berger, P. and Luckmann, T. (1966) *The Social Construction of Reality: A Treatise in the Sociology of Knowledge*. London: Penguin.

Bourdieu, P. (1991) *Language and Symbolic Power*. Cambridge: Polity Press.

Chia, J. (2009) Understanding twenty-first century public relations. In J. Chia and G. Synott (eds) *An Introduction to Public Relations: From theory to practice*. South Melbourne: Oxford University Press.

Corley, K. G., and Gioia, D. A. (2011) Building theory about theory building: what constitutes a theoretical contribution? *Academy of Management Review*, 36(1): 12–32.

Foster, E. and Bochner, A. P. (2008) Social constructionist perspectives in communication research. In Holstein, J. and J. Gubrium (eds) *Handbook of Constructionist Research*. New York: Guilford, pp. 85–107.

Freeman, R. (1984) *Strategic Management: A stakeholder approach*. Boston, MA: Pitman.

Gergen, K. (2005) Narrative, moral identity, and historical consciousness: a social constructionist account. In J. Straub (ed.) *Narration, Identity, and Historical Consciousness*, New York: Berghahn, pp. 99–119.

Gregory, A. and Willis, P. (2013) *Strategic Public Relations Leadership*. London: Routledge.

Gordon, J. and Pellegrin, P. (2008) Social constructionism and public relations. In T. Hansen-Horn and B. Neff (eds.). *Public Relations: From theory to practice*. Boston, MA: Pearson.

Gower, K. K. (2006) Public relations research at the crossroads. *Journal of Public Relations Research*, 18(2): 177–190.

Hallahan, K., Holtzhausen, D., van Ruler, B., Verčič, D., and Sriramesh, K. (2007) Defining strategic communication. *International Journal of Strategic Communication*, 1(1): 3–35.

Harré, R. (2012) Positioning theory: moral dimensions of social-cultural psychology. In J. Valsiner (ed.) *The Oxford Handbook of Culture and Psychology*. New York: Oxford University, pp. 191–206.

Harré, R., Brockmeier, J., and Mühlhäusler, P. (1999) *Greenspeak: A Study of Environmental Discourse*. London: Sage.

Harré, R. and Moghaddam, F. (2003) Introduction: the self and others in traditional psychology and in positioning theory. In R. Harré and F. Moghaddam (eds) *The Self and Others: Positioning individuals and groups in personal, political and cultural contexts*. London: Praeger, pp. 1–11.

Harré, R., Moghaddam, F., Pilkerton Cairnie, T., Rothbart, D. and Sabat, S. (2009) Recent advances in positioning theory. *Theory and Psychology*, 19(1): 5–31. doi: 10.1177/0959354308101417

Harré, R. and Slocum, N. (2003) Disputes as complex social events: on the uses of positioning theory. In R. Harré and F. Moghaddam (eds.). *The Self and Others: Positioning individuals and groups in personal, political and cultural contexts*. London: Praeger, pp. 123–36.

Harré, R., and van Langenhove, L. (1991) Varieties of positioning. *Journal for the Theory of Social Behaviour*. 21(4): 393–407.

Harré, R. and van Langenhove, L. (1999) *Positioning Theory: Moral contexts of intentional action*. Oxford: Blackwell.

Heath, R. L. (ed.) (2010) *The Sage Handbook of Public Relations*. Thousand Oaks, CA: Sage.

Ihlen, O. (2009) On Bourdieu: public relations in field struggles. In O. Ihlen, B. van Ruler and M. Fredriksson (eds) *Public Relations and Social Theory: Key figures and concepts*. London: Routledge, pp. 62–82.

James, M. (2009) Getting to the heart of public relations: the concept of strategic intent. *Asia Pacific Public Relations Journal*, 10: 109–22.

James, M. (2010) The use of intentional positioning techniques in government agencies' communication campaigns. In D. Verčič, and K. Sriramesh (eds). *Government Communication: Proceedings of the 17th International Public Relations Research Symposium BledCom*. Bled, Slovenia, Ljubljana: Pristop, pp. 140–7. Retrieved from www.bledcom.si/uploads/ppt2010/bledcom 2010 proceedings hi.pdf

James, M. (2011) A provisional conceptual framework for intentional positioning in public relations. *Journal of Public Relations Research*, 23(1): 93–111. http://dx.doi.org/10.1080/1062726X.2010.505120

Kilduff, M. (2006) Editor's comments: publishing theory. *Academy of Management Review*, 31(2): 252–5.

Kroløkke, C. (2009) Positioning theory. In S. Littlejohn, and K. Foss (eds) *Encyclopedia of Communication Theory*. Thousand Oaks, CA: Sage, pp. 765–7. doi: http://dx.doi.org/10.4135/9781412959384.n289

Leitch, S. and Motion, J. (2010) Publics and public relations: effecting change. In R. Heath (ed.) *The Sage Handbook of Public Relations*. Thousand Oaks, CA: Sage, pp. 99–110.

Macnamara, J. (2012) *Public Relations: Theories, practices, critiques*. Frenchs Forest, NSW: Pearson.

Motion, J. (1997) Technologising the self: an art of public relations. *Australian Journal of Communication*, 24(2): 1–16.

Schutz, A. (1954): Concept and theory formation in the social sciences. *The Journal of Philosophy*, 51(9): 257–73.

Slocum-Bradley, N. (2007) Constructing and de-constructing the ACP Group: actors, strategies and consequences for development, *Geopolitics*, 12(4): 635–55. doi:10.1080/14650040701546095

Smyth, R. (2004) Exploring the usefulness of a conceptual framework as a research tool: a researcher's reflections. *Issues in Educational Research*, 14(2): 167–80.

Tan, S. and Moghaddam, F. (1999) Intergroup positioning. In R. Harré and L. van Langenhove (eds) *Positioning Theory: Moral contexts of intentional action*. Oxford: Blackwell, pp. 178–94.

Thompson, J. (1991) Editor's Introduction. In P. Bourdieu (ed.) *Language and Symbolic Power*. Cambridge, UK: Polity, pp. 1–31.

Tindall, N. and Vardeman-Winter, J. (2010) *Call for Papers: Segmenting publics*. Retrieved September 22, 2010, from www.prismjournal.org/segment_cfp.html

van Langenhove, L. and Harré, R. (1999) Introducing positioning theory. In R. Harré and L. van Langenhove (eds) *Positioning Theory: Moral contexts of intentional action*. Oxford: Blackwell, pp. 14–31.

Weinberg, D. (2008) The philosophical foundations of constructionist research. In Holstein, J. and Gubrium, J. (eds) *Handbook of Constructionist Research*. New York: Guilford, pp. 13–39.

Part I

Public relations and positioning theory

1 Positioning in public relations

Much of the public relations effort exerted by organizations aims to move people towards a position where they share with the organization a way of thinking, knowing, acting or speaking about an aspect of the world. Such "organizations" include corporations, small businesses, not for profits, trade unions, activist groups, individuals, celebrities, government agencies and more. Sometimes these public relations efforts are used for "good", such as moving new parents to a point where they seek to have their babies immunized. There are public relations practitioners that work to position immunization as the "right thing to do". They do this in an effort to get parents to act in the way the public health officials want them to act. At other times the same techniques are used for less ethical reasons. We know that some people in the public relations industry work to position smoking as fashionable behavior, in attempts to attract young people to take up the habit. Both are positioning exercises, both draw on strategies and techniques that aim to have people construct meaning in certain ways in certain social contexts.

This book is premised on the assumption that public relations is a strategic undertaking underpinned by techniques or processes that help organizations achieve their goals. As Heath (2001) said, "public relations is called to action when an organization's routine activities fail to produce the desired results" (p. 33). When organizations engage public relations they often do this with the strategic intent to move themselves, or another entity from one position to another. Once so positioned, organizations also use public relations to maintain and secure those positions for strategic purposes (James, 2011).

Positioning is often used in public relations contexts but it has been very under-researched given its ubiquitous use in practice (James, 2009, 2011). Public relations practitioners often refer to positioning until recently little had been written to explore what was meant by the concept outside a marketing context. In the first edition of The Encyclopedia of Public Relations, positioning was defined as something that "depends on how a consumer compares a product to the competitor's product" (Pompper, 2004: 629). In the most recent edition, it is becoming clear that the field is starting to give more consideration to the concept of positioning. Pompper (2013, p. 663) acknowledges that "the posiiton-positioning process is a deeply complex one that depends on context and orientation" and, that "while public relations practitioners and academics may not offer formal operationalizations for position and positioning, they nonetheless imply its significance in relationship building". However, it is within the marketing literature that discussion of positioning predominates, and this primarily relates to brand and product positioning or to identity, profile and image (e.g. Butler and Harris, 2009; Egan, 2007; Holm, 2006; Knox and Bickerton, 2003; Porter, 2008). This concept of positioning in marketing is most often centered on the "4 Ps" of marketing, namely: product, place, price and promotion (Egan, 2007).

A better understanding of positioning in public relations contexts is needed for several reasons. Firstly, practitioners may want to know how to design more effective positioning strategies for their clients and organizations. Secondly, people may want to understand the mechanisms and thinking behind strategic positioning to facilitate understanding of how organizations wield and concede power. Thirdly, others may want to gain insights into the way elements of practice such as language use and stakeholder engagement come together to shape the meanings that circulate in our societies.

In 2008, I was conducting a large research project wherein positioning had emerged as a key aspect of Australian award-winning public relations practice. I was trying to make sense of my findings when I encountered "positioning theory". In 2012, Harré defined positioning theory as being:

> ...based on the principle that not everyone involved in a social episode has equal access to rights and duties to perform particular kinds of meaningful actions at that moment and with those people. In many interesting cases, the rights and duties determine who can use a certain discourse mode...A cluster of short-term disputable rights, obligations and duties is called a 'position'.
>
> (2012: 193)

Moghaddam and Harré (2010: 2) state that positioning theory is about "how people use words (and discourse of all types) to locate themselves and others". These definitions immediately struck a chord. Intentional positioning in public relations could be seen to be about how organizations used words (and discourses of all types) to locate themselves and others in particular ways, in order to achieve specific outcomes. Although the theory originally was applied to how individuals positioned themselves and others in unfolding episodes such as a conversation (van Langenhove and Harré, 1999), I saw immediate relevance for public relations. In a conversation, the ebb and flow of exchanges means that positions can be constructed by individuals but also challenged by other conversational participants. In public relations episodes, when an organization takes and enacts a particular position, it also is open to challenges and attempts by others to reposition in different ways.

Since the late 1990s, positioning theory has been seen to allow "for a very natural expansion of scale, from the analysis of person-to-person encounters to the unfolding of interactions between nation states" (Harré, Moghaddam, Pilkerton Cairnie, Rothbart and Sabat, 2009: 6). Although originating in the field of social psychology it has had widespread application over the last decade or so (Moghaddam and Harré, 2010). This has included research in areas as varied as anthropology (e.g. Handelman, 2008), journalism (e.g. Miller, 2013; Weizman, 2008) midwifery (Phillips and Hays, 2008), organizational change studies (Zelle, 2009), political identity studies (e.g. Slocum-Bradley, 2008), and recently, public relations (e.g. James, 2010, 2011, 2012; Leitch and Motion, 2010; Tsetsura, 2012; Wise and James, 2013).

At a basic level, positioning refers to a process by which certain characteristics are attributed to an individual, group or some other entity (Baert, 2012). However positioning theory moves beyond this and is "based on the principle that not everyone involved in a social episode has equal access to rights and duties to perform particular kinds of meaningful actions at *that* moment and with *those people*" (Harré, 2012: 193). This idea resonates with public relations practice in that not all organizations are able to position themselves or others in particular ways, at certain times. An organization's ability to undertake any type of positioning will depend on who else is involved with the actual or potential episode. For example, take a leader of a company whose employees have recently been involved in corrupt practices. He or she may be seen by some as not having the right to position the management team as being trustworthy; at least not until trust had been re-established in some way.

Public relations practitioners may be involved in devising a strategy to help position the company as being trustworthy after such an incident. In this instance, it could be that a public has undertaken a specific act in order to position the company management team as untrustworthy. For example, a group of shareholders may have undertaken a public relations program of their own, publishing an open letter in a newspaper, regularly "tweeting", and starting a Facebook page detailing their views on the situation. Undertaking a positioning analysis could help the public relations manager to determine a course of action that would assist the company to respond appropriately in the circumstances. Of course, the shareholder group could also undertake a positioning analysis to guide their own campaign to achieve better management practices.

What is a position?

The concept of "position" has not been explored thoroughly outside of the marketing discipline. The word itself is often used in public relations and strategic communication as if everyone knows what it means. Within positioning theory literature, the term "position" is "somewhat ambiguous" (Slocum-Bradley, 2010: 88). However definitions center on a position being a "cluster of rights and duties that limits the repertoire of possible social acts available to a person or person-like entity (such as a corporation)" (Moghaddam, Harré and Lee, 2008: 294). Louis (2008) states, a position defines what is "socially possible without incurring reprobation or punishment" (p. 22). In a public relations context Motion (1997) and Berger (1999) both defined positioning. Motion stated:

> ...positioning is a subjectifying process of locating and being located within discourse sites or spaces...involves the struggle to create what may be known

> and how it may be known....Positioning may be either a strategic manoeuvre or ploy by an individual, or the result of the discourses one is situated within as a subject of particular institutional relations, power relations, and social relations.
>
> (1997: 7)

Berger (1999: 195) described positioning as a:

> ...simple but particular representation of events, a company-constructed worldview, which subsequently would anchor and frame all...communications (e.g. news releases, advertisement, medical and governmental presentations, and interviews).

These definitions and subsequent small amount of academic work on public relations positioning were not widely taken up by the field. It is notable that position is sometimes used almost interchangeably with the word "stance", but when viewed through the lens of positioning theory, the words mean quite different things. Myers (2010) stated that generally stance-taking is seen as a "'public act' of taking a point of view...[and] does not just involve having an opinion on a topic; it involves using that opinion to align or disalign with someone else" (p. 264). Stance in public relations is most often discussed in the context of contingency theory and has been defined as:

> The general way in which management in an organization approaches conflict. Stances range from accommodative, a willingness to make concessions, to advocacy, a willingness to persuade others to your position.
>
> (Coombs, 2010: 484)

Stance in contingency theory has been operationalized as the position an organization takes in decision making, which is supposed to determine which strategy to employ (Pang, Jin and Cameron, 2010: 25).

It is evident that a "stance" differs from a "position" in regards to the attribution of rights and duties. This will be explored more fully in Chapter 2 but Harré (2006) summarizes here:

> It seems that what people are taken to mean by what they say and do is partly a matter of what the various people involved in a social episode believe that persons of this or that category are entitled to say and do. Such entitlements are called "positions"...Everyone does not have equal access to the local repertoire of meaningful actions. Some members of a group are more advantageously positioned than others. Some categories of persons are accorded rights and duties distinct from those of others in the same episode. In many cases, people are satisfied with their rights. In other cases, the distribution of rights and duties can be challenged (Davies and Harré, 1999). Revealing the subtle patterns of the distributions of rights to speak and act in certain ways can open

> up the possibility of their transformation. At the same time, analysis of patterns of meaningful actions in terms of story lines can bring to light previously unnoticed presumptions about what is going on in an episode.
>
> (2006: 229)

Positioning theorists have stated that positions are "related both to the storylines realized in the unfolding of episodes and to the acts that are the meanings of the intentional actions of the people who take part" (Harré, 2012: 194). Moghaddam, Harré and Lee (2008: 294) define "strategic positioning" as the "attributions of rights and duties that are to the advantage of the person who performs the positioning acts". However this does not account for the specific strategic context of public relations in all cases. Neither does it account for situations where public relations, while still being goal directed, is actually being undertaken to advantage key publics, such as in emergency situations or in charitable fundraising. Motivation and goal directedness of positioning efforts in strategic public relations is a key component of practice. It is also the point at which issues of power come into play, and ethical considerations should be accounted for.

Taking account of the work of Berger (1999) and Motion (1997), together with the perspectives of positioning theory, I propose that the definition of a public relations position is: a point of intentional representation discursively constructed for the purposes of achieving an intended outcome, and from where possibilities for action are established, or in some cases denied, in terms of the local moral order/s wherein the public relations activity is taking place. Positioning comprises the actions taken to achieve the position.

How do positioning theory and public relations work together?

Positioning theory is a social constructionist approach (Kroløkke, 2009; Slocum and van Langenhove, 2003) that began to emerge in the 1980s primarily in the area of gender studies:

> One of the first scholars to illustrate the workings of positioning theory was psychologist Wendy Hollway, who demonstrated how people take up and negotiate their gender-related places in conversations. Social psychologists Jonathan Potter and Margaret Wetherell, psychologists Rom Harré and Bronwyn Davies, and sociologist Luk van Langenhove are most often seen as the founders of positioning theory. They share a social-constructionist approach to how communication shapes identity.
>
> (Kroløkke, 2009: 765)

Slocum-Bradley (2010) states, "if we understand how we construct social reality, we can construct more consciously to sustain norms that promote the ends we profess to desire" (p. 81). This relates to how public relations practitioners work to construct versions of social reality through positioning. If social realities could be constructed more consciously by public relations practitioners, they could better sustain those practices that are achieving desired outcomes for their clients/organizations.

The dimension of positioning theory that has the most profound relevance for public relations is the concept of rights and duties that are associated with positions. Moghaddam and Harré (2010) state "it is with words that we ascribe rights and claim them for ourselves and place duties on others" (p. 3). Positioning has direct moral implications, such as some person or group being located as 'trusted' or 'distrusted', 'with us' or 'against us', 'to be saved' or 'to be wiped out'" (Moghaddam and Harré, 2010: 2). This has been touched on in more recent work on positioning in public relations (James, 2010, 2011; Leitch and Motion, 2010) but this book expands such work, and examines what it means for the field and how it can be used (and potentially abused) in practice.

Taking a social constructionist perspective of communication, it is accepted that there can be more than one way of describing aspects of the world we live in (Balnaves, Donald and Shoesmith, 2009). This is the point where the formulators of such descriptions need to be taken into account. Whose description of a social phenomenon is to be believed or even heard? How have such descriptions come into play at all? What underpins such descriptions? Is it scientific knowledge or some other proof? Or is it that one formulator of descriptions has exclusive access to an audience, that is, is it a situation where only one description is available? Many public relations efforts can be seen as a discursive struggle to champion particular descriptions of things in the world over others. This is where the concept of positioning comes into play.

The rise of positioning as a concept relevant to public relations

Some four decades ago, Ries and Trout (1981) began to define positioning from an advertising and marketing perspective. Interestingly, although starting from the idea of a product, they saw a product as being anything from a piece of merchandise, a service, a company, an institution, or even a person or oneself. Key to their ideas about positioning was that it was not something you did to a product but what you did "to the mind of the prospect. That is, you position the product in the mind of a prospect" (p. 2). They stated further that the basic approach of positioning was not to "create something new and different, but to manipulate what's already up there in the mind, to retie the connections that already exist" (p. 5). van Langenhove and Harré (1999) drew on this marketing idea, along with ideas of military positioning, to inform the development of positioning theory.

The marketing literature on positioning is extensive, most often drawing from the original propositions put forward by Ries and Trout (1981), but focusing almost exclusively on increasing sales of products and services. Definitions of marketing positioning have not changed much over the last two decades. For example, Boone and Kurtz (2013) state that positioning is "placing a product at a certain point or location within a market in the minds of prospective buyers" (p. 301). Stanton, Miller, Layton and Rix (1995) state that "a position is the image that a product or organization occupies in a consumer's mind relative to other products in the same category" (p. 92). Rossiter and Bellman (2005) state, "brand positioning is an attempt to create and maintain a unique representation of the brand in customers' minds, a representation that is expected to stimulate choice of that brand" (p. 42). It is evident that there are some alternative views emerging in the marketing literature, e.g. semiotic approaches to marketing positioning, but these remain very much in the minority (e.g. de Burgh-Woodman and Brace-Govan, 2007; Baines, Fill and Page, 2008; O'Shaunessy and Baines, 2009). While there is some surface applicability of mainstream marketing views of positioning for some public relations activities, they fail to provide a useful conceptualization for the field as a whole.

Another interesting view of positioning that could relate to some specialist areas of communication is Chew's (2005, 2009) work on the role of strategic positioning for not-for-profit organizations. This work focuses on the need for differentiation from other organizations in the quest for funds. Seeing a lack of guidance for her sector in the literature, Chew (2005) put forward a model "comprising of three interrelated components: choice of target audience/segments to serve, choice of generic positioning strategy, and positioning dimensions to differentiate the organization/offerings from other service providers" (p. 6–7). She identified positioning dimensions as including a unique combination of quality service, benefits, responsiveness, speed to market and low price. Although of interest to the charitable fundraising sector its relevance to the wider public relations field appears limited.

It is notable that there is a small but significant body of work that relates to positioning in public relations contexts (e.g. Berger, 1999; Hallahan, 1999; Motion, 1997; Motion, 2000; Motion and Leitch, 1996; Roper, 2005; Tilley, 2009; Wang, 2007; Waymer and Heath, 2007; Wu, 2007). In 1996, critical public relations scholars Motion and Leitch discussed the link between public relations and discursive positioning:

> As Moffitt asserts, the notion that multiple and changing images may be held by a single individual is not generally accepted in public relations theory. Critical discourse theory would explain this phenomenon in terms of multiple discursive positionings. Fairclough, drawing on Foucault, suggests that individuals are, in part, constituted as subjects in and through discourse and thus that individuals occupy multiple subject positions within the multiple discourses in which they participate. Public relations practitioners attempt to gain acceptance of particular organizational images or particular policy proposals by achieving an articulation between these images and proposals and particular subject positions occupied by members of key publics.
>
> (Motion and Leitch, 1996: 300)

Motion (1997: 1), drawing on Foucault's "technologies of the self", identifies discursive positioning as "a crucial public relations technology for commodifying and promoting the subject" (p.14). She states, "discursive positioning involves the struggle to create what may be known and how it may be known… Discourse constraints, limiting the places or sites one may occupy within a discourse, are imposed upon subjects as a condition for qualifying them to act as subjects" (p. 7). It is evident that there is much commonality between Motion's 1990s work on discourse and personal public relations positioning and with the social psychology positioning theorists who were working to develop their theory throughout the same decade. For example, the idea that positions are discursively constructed and that there are constraints on this process are common to both. The constraints are named by Motion as "discourse constraints" (p. 7) and by positioning theorists as the constraints of the local moral order (Moghaddam, Harré and Lee, 2008: 294). These are seen to restrict or facilitate the discourse construction processes, and how discourses become known. It is evident that work relating to subject positioning within a "field" (Bourdieu, 1991) was also being developed around the same time. Bourdieu had also identified such constraints on this process. These included the amount of "symbolic capital" (1991: 106) one possessed, that is, the "socially recognized power to impose a certain vision of the social world"; or whether one's "habitus" enabled or disabled one's ability to be able to position within the field. Although from different disciplines, we can see that the concept of "position" is common across the work that was happening at the time. Although not specifically defining position, it was Sless who said that:

> Position is a central concept in our field of communication. The concept of position provides us with the best hope of integrating our diverse interests and methods into a unified point of view from which to develop the future of our subject.
>
> (Sless, 1987: 1)

One of the most significant features of the logic of positions put forward by Sless (1987) is that it:

> ...straddles both critical and applied interests. It has the capacity to address our profound concerns about changes occurring in our society. Position is not simply a conceptual device; it grows out of a deep concern for our geographical and social position.
>
> (Sless, 1987: 24–25).

The connections between this "critical" work and positioning theory are becoming clearer, and they provide a strong foundation for future positioning research and the situating of public relations firmly in the wider discipline of communication. Motion and Leitch pursued scholarship in positioning throughout the 2000s but moved away from publishing in public relations journals into publications focusing on discourse or policy (e.g. Motion and Doolin, 2007; Motion and Leitch, 2009). Roper was one of the few scholars who further examined discursive positioning. She undertook an examination of identity and positioning in a political context and found that political parties and candidates were constantly altering their identities and that voters were "identifying themselves with the discursive constructions of their potential representatives" (Roper, 2005: 142). Roper stated that the evidence in her study "strongly proposed that discursive repositioning is a key function of public relations" (2005: 145). Roper's work specifically explored the political sector, but she did propose that it had broader application:

> If a market place were to be theorized as having the same attributes as a political field, a public relations professional would do well to consider the range of positions available within that marketplace and the extent to which consumers can identify with and thus legitimize a position taken.
>
> (Roper, 2005: 146).

Although Roper (2005) herself did not make the specific connection, it can be seen that her analysis indicates that public relations practitioners are working within the broad parameters of a local moral order, and that this is constraining what can be said and done once a particular position is taken. Practitioners can be seen to be working to align the meaning they want audiences to take up with the "zones of meaning" (Berger and Luckmann, 1966: 55) that are operating within the local moral order:

> The discourse technologists who construct political discourses use data from opinion polls, focus groups and demographic sciences to articulate campaign messages with voter discourses and concerns.
>
> (Roper, 2005: 142)

Moffitt's (1994) discussion of Stuart Hall's articulation model of meaning is helpful in further understanding Roper's statement, in that meaning is not only determined by someone's position in terms of social, political or gender factors but is also determined by multiple factors (that could include race, class, work and family, various environmental, cultural and historical factors, etcetera) intersecting or articulating. This then creates the possibility at each intersection of a factor over-determining the others to impact on what the meaning is at any moment. Roper (2005) states that practitioners must be aware of the positions taken, or those that are likely to be taken, by opposition parties or candidates. Reports of public relations practice outside of political sectors indicate that this is what practitioners are often doing in terms of environmental scanning (James, 2009, 2011).

Outside of critical scholarship, the main area where positioning has been addressed is in discussion of framing in public relations contexts. Hallahan (1999) made the link between framing and positioning in that framing focuses attention on the elements within the frame, effectively "delimiting the subject matter" (p. 207). He describes framing as a process not just of inclusion but also of exclusion, and of adding emphases to specific elements. This shows the strategic nature of positioning and sheds light on some of the ways that public relations works to co-construct meaning through the use of messaging techniques. For example, Wang's (2007) work on the effects of priming, framing and positioning on corporate social responsibility activities (CSR), although not examining positioning as such, suggests public relations practitioners could work more strategically to position publics in relation to a wider scope than CSR. Wang states, "public relations practitioners must assure that the structure of the communications themselves are primed or framed properly to facilitate favorable attitudes" (2007: 141). He states that the "strategic uses of priming, framing, and position are perhaps the most important strategic choices made in a public relations effort" (p. 141). Wang's work relates to trying "to manipulate what's already up there in the mind, to retie the connections that already exist" (Ries and Trout, 1981: 5). It also aligns with attempts by practitioners to construct "zones of meaning" (Berger and Luckmann, 1966: 55) wherein actions are undertaken to support positioning. These are undertaken in ways that are interpretable by audiences in terms of narratives that are operating in the communities into which the messages are being sent (Heath, 2001: 47–8).

This idea of working with "zones of meaning" (Berger and Luckmann, 1966: 55) again can be seen in the work of Wu (2007). He reported on a model "to identify the stakeholders and position them into a dynamic public relations context". He suggests that the underlying reason for stakeholder analysis is to identify, position, understand and predict those conflicting and often contentious relationships among various constituents. He states further, "one of the real objectives of stakeholder analysis should be to construct and position the interrelations and interactions of different stakes as well as their holders" (Wu, 2007: 417). This highlights to the practitioner the need for a positioning strategy and underpins why research should always be the starting point of public relations planning.

In another example of the type of positioning that cannot be adequately explained by marketing conceptualizations, Waymer and Heath's (2007) work identified framing as a tool used both in positioning an issue and repositioning opposing views, even if those with opposing views didn't want to be repositioned. They made a link between the position taken, the framing of an issue, and the ability to reposition others, thus enabling other story frames to be heard and other actions to be taken. The way framing works in strategic positioning is further examined in Chapter 5.

Viewing public relations through the positioning lens

Strategic positioning in public relations can be conceptualized as a discursive struggle or as "a kind of bargaining dialogue" where "the various parties adapt their roles to meet (or preempt) the perceived positions of other parties involved" (Murphy, 1991: 117). Such practice is dynamic and the limitations of functional approaches to planning and accommodating such dynamism are clear. Working in a control paradigm where efforts are exerted to tightly control messages and meaning as a way of engineering defined outcomes for organizations no longer works, if it ever did (Macnamara, 2010). Public relations can be conceptualized as a process whereby discursive positions are actively negotiated and achieved, rather than as a prescriptive technique where a pre-existing position is merely occupied. From here, the dynamic processes involved can be both examined from an academic standpoint and also adapted to practice.

It would be helpful to everyone to be able to prescribe a set of failsafe steps to successfully undertake strategic positioning but this ignores the complexity of public relations practice. The complexity stems from many sources, and their interplay and articulations, but it seems that much of what public relations is about is the strategic construction of meaning; more accurately, the strategic co-construction of meaning between audiences, publics and organizations in their widest sense (James, 2009). What positioning theory brings to public relations is the idea of rights and duties, and how the local moral order influences what can be said and done. Positioning analysis can indicate to organizations when their desired positions are likely to be achieved and when they are not. Such analysis will indicate what an organization would need to do, in each of the various environments in which they operate, to earn or construct the right to position in a certain way.

It is evident that much effort is expended by organizations trying to position things in the minds of target publics and audiences, but that rights and duties are rarely considered. This can especially be seen in campaign-style work. According to Danowski (2008), most campaign scholarship is concerned with "media coverage effects on audiences" (p. 287) but campaigns can be viewed through a positioning lens as well. For example:

- A campaign was designed to strengthen concepts of a nation and its religious faith, and public relations activity was conceptualized as a combination of relationship management and promotional strategies (Tilson, 2006). This could also be seen as a campaign to try and position religious faith as an inherent part of national identity. Spain could be seen by many, given its history, to have the right to position in this way and use the related storylines to strengthen such positioning.
- Efforts to ensure ongoing global sales of a sleeping tablet (Berger, 1999) described public relations as an effort to construct a certain ideology/world view favorable to the pharmaceutical manufacturing company. Berger also noted it was a campaign to position the medicine as being safe in spite of some research stating otherwise. The company could be seen to have constructed a "right" to position the medicine as safe, but then of course had the related duty to ensure that it was in fact safe.
- Building a favorable public opinion against terrorism and the removal of Saddam Hussein (Jo, Shim and Jung, 2008) saw "the war against Iraq [as] a global public relations campaign allowing the US administration to build a favorable public opinion" (p. 64). This could also be conceptualized as an effort by the US administration to position the United States of America as a force against evil. The fact that such positioning was unsuccessful in some countries was linked to the US not being perceived as having the right to take such a position in those countries.
- A promotional campaign for breast self-examination amongst women in the Arab Emirates (Al Khaja and Creedon, 2010), could readily be seen as one that tried (unsuccessfully) to position breast examination as a desirable and normal

activity amongst local women. This lack of success could be linked to campaigners not having positioned in accordance to the local moral order in operation in that country.

- A campaign to encourage teenage girls to be vaccinated with the anti-cervical cancer drug, Gardasil (Vardeman-Winter, 2010), showed a public relations campaign as having not sufficiently considered the particular cultural context of the target public. This can be viewed as a case where vaccination was not successfully positioned as a worthwhile activity for the target public. From a positioning theoretical perspective, the duties of the young women being positioned as needing the vaccination were not aligned to the local moral order in which they operated.
- A campaign where fans were advised that the National Hockey League (NHL) was back after a period of lock-out (Batchelor and Formentin, 2008) used public relations and marketing techniques to construct a promotional campaign that would "prod" (p. 160) fans to watch the sport. This could be recast as an effort to position/reposition the game as one worth watching again. The NHL could be seen to work hard to earn back the right, in the eyes of the audiences, to again position the game positively.
- A positioning approach can also be used to look at public relations efforts to restore the tarnished national image of Saudi Arabia in the post-9/11 era (Zhang and Benoit, 2004). Although categorized as an image restoration campaign, the positioning aspects of the Saudi government's campaign can be seen to have accommodated the local moral order in operation in the US. That is, the Saudi Government determined a desired position, enacted it through public relations techniques and supported it through appropriate storylines.
- An issues management campaign designed to oppose genetic engineering (GE) in terms of GE testing and the importing of genetically modified foods (Henderson, 2005), used "discursive strategies...to obtain public consent and influence public policy" (p. 133). This can also be seen as a campaign that claimed the right to position GE in a negative way in the minds of consumers and elected representatives of the government.

The above examples show that positioning theory offers another way of examining and planning public relations activities. It enables us to look at public relations as both a phenomenon in our societies and also as a suite of techniques and processes related to the management of meaning and communication. For public relations, it offers a way of conceptualizing the field as it is practiced and as it could be practiced, moving beyond setting normative models as the bar to be reached. A significant amount of public relations takes place in situations where there is no possibility or desire to deliver mutually beneficial outcomes, or to seek symmetry in communication or relationships (e.g. Stokes and Rubin, 2010). There is a need to understand all types of public relations activity, not just normative models or practice that is framed as excellent or award-winning.

In conflict situations, positioning theorists have eschewed "the naïve idea that conflict resolution comes about by negotiation and the development of mutual respect among the parties" (Moghaddam, Harré and Lee, 2008). They have instead acknowledged that in some situations, the best that can be achieved is to present a positioning analysis to the conflicted parties so that areas of misunderstandings can be pointed out. They note situations in which such action has resolved conflict, but note others such as stand offs between nations that remain unresolved. Their other point worth acknowledging in its relevance to some public relations practice is that there are times when parties seek to escalate, amplify or even create conflict:

> Just as Socrates remarked that doctors make the best murderers so Positioning Theorists who understand the source of many conflicts in positioning incompatibilities have the skills to bring conflicts to the boil. They should be the best agents provocateurs.
>
> (Moghaddam, Harré and Lee, 2008: 18)

We can see this when organizations seek to position themselves in one way and seek to position others in different ways, sometimes negatively. For example, political parties (we're for the common people, the other party is for the elites); competing companies (we offer best value, the others do not); nations (we are the protectors of peace, they are warmongers); sporting teams (we deserve your support, the other teams do not); sporting codes (rugby is the best game, soccer is a "wannabe"); and even celebrities (Madonna deserves to be in the hall of fame; Lady Gaga does not). This positioning can be very strategic in its planning and execution. If one organization acts preemptively on positioning another, the audiences who engage with messages, and co-construct meanings from this and other information, may be primed to view the other organization from the first one's perspective.

We know that this type of strategy is not always successful and can of course backfire in that the first organization's efforts may only serve to position them more negatively. How could this happen? Did they underestimate the power of other organizations? Did they underestimate community sentiment or knowledge levels? Were they ignorant of other things happening in the environment, such as a similar organization behaving badly etcetera? Engaging with positioning theory and analysis can help answer such questions. Public relations programs have been too often viewed as "set and forget" or, as Pieczka (2007) found, as presented in public relations award entry case studies, as linear and systematic. Anyone who has worked in the industry for a time knows this is not how it works. The processes within public relations programs are dynamic. Practitioners often want responses to their efforts that help move things towards the achievement of their client/organization's goals. However, some responses to practitioners' actions don't turn out as expected, and then what?

A traditional campaign plan such as taught to public relations students, e.g. "research, planning, communication and evaluation", "RACE", or "PIE – Planning, Implementation and Evaluation" (Bobbitt and Sullivan, 2014: 17–18) often will not effectively accommodate this dynamism. Such approaches also may not suit experienced practitioners who are able to anticipate likely scenarios and to read emerging situations. The application of a positioning theory approach, as I've incorporated into a Framework for Intentional Positioning in Public Relations, offers one way of addressing the changing landscapes within which public relations programs are designed and delivered. The Framework, which is explained in Chapter 3, is goal directed in its approach but accommodates the central organizing idea of positioning theory, the "positioning triangle" (van Langenhove and Harré, 1999: 18). As such the Framework offers a different way of thinking about public relations planning and implementation than is currently presented in many public relations texts. It is also potentially a way forward in translating to practice more co-constructionist approaches that have been explored in academic contexts.

Interviewing senior award-winning practitioners during my research fieldwork highlighted the challenges faced by many of them in educating chief executives and other senior decision-makers about alternative approaches to public relations. They spoke of the difficulties in getting resources and support for cultivating relationships with publics and stakeholders, and moving on from a media relations and campaign focus for their activities. However, some also spoke of how once CEOs "got it" they often became their biggest supporters. My research to date indicates that applying the positioning framework in practice may assist with this internal education and explanatory process.

A deeper look at positioning theory and public relations

When an organization makes a declaration about itself, e.g. that it's a community-minded organization, it then must work to make such a declaration known. However, it must also know when it is appropriate to say such a thing and to anticipate what may happen once it has been declared. Communication outcomes will only be possible if people have certain skills and know the "rules" (Harré and van Langenhove, 1999: 4). It is only "because people have some knowledge of rules, and have expectations, that meaningful communication is possible" (ibid: 4).

Public relations practitioners work with a level of discursive skill. They rely on targeted publics and audiences also possessing such skill, in order to jointly construct meaning that will advance the agenda of their client/organization. Practitioners can be seen to work to try to engage people in episodes within which there are opportunities to create particular meanings. Episodes are a sequence of happenings involving visible behaviors, thoughts, feelings, intentions and plans of all those who participate (Harré and van Langenhove, 1999: 5). While episodes are defined by the participants they are also shaped by what those participants say and do (ibid: 5). We know that a wedding is different to a football match or a job interview. In a public relations episode, such as the launch of a new project, it could be anticipated that there would be a running list of planned activities, invited guests, key speakers and so on. However we know that such an episode can be disrupted if uninvited people turn up who wish to say and do things that do not align with the intended goals of the launch event. So we can see that practitioners may attempt to define an episode but will also bring into account contingency plans to deal with people attempting to redefine it through not playing by the "rules".

In their exploration of the skills and rules of discursive processes, Harré and van Langenhove (1999: 5) state that the assumptions made by people about the nature of the episode in which they are participating has a profound influence on what people will say and do. It is evident that people's past history must also be taken into account. If their past history includes negative experiences with particular types of organizations, the assumptions about the nature of the next episode may influence the way it could unfold. Similarly, an organization may have prior experiences with specific audiences or publics and may assume rightly or wrongly that the way those people acted before will be the way they will behave in future encounters.

Looking at episodes "as structured sequences of act-actions" (Harré and van Langenhove, 1999: 5), positioning theory aims to assist us in understanding the dynamics involved in such episodes. In public relations contexts, organizations may decide to, or be forced to, engage in some way with particular publics. No matter what the reason behind such engagement, the organization will approach such an episode with some kind of goal or objective, otherwise it wouldn't be involved. Organizations and the people with whom they engage may plan for such engagement and draw on past experiences with each other, or on past encounters with similar parties. However, Harré and van Langenhove (ibid: 6) tell us that in such episodes knowledge of the past encounters must be augmented with insight into the current unfolding situation. Even then there "is something that makes it impossible to predict what will happen next in the episode" (ibid: 6). Practitioners can try to plan for the unexpected, and positioning theory can help in that it offers a means of understanding interactions and public relations episodes in detail, and even in real time. Drawing heavily on the work of Harré and van Langenhove (ibid: 6) there can be seen to be three basic features in understanding and explaining much of what goes on in public relations episodes. These are:

- the "moral positions" of the participants and the rights and duties they have to say certain things;
- the history of engagement between parties and the sequence of things already being said and done; and,
- the actual sayings of each of the parties with their power to shape certain aspects of the social world, namely the public relations episode.

These features have been incorporated into the Framework for Intentional Positioning in Public Relations. The Framework was developed by overlaying the strategic context within which public relations is employed by organizations onto the work of Harré and van Langenhove (1999). One dimension considered in the Framework is who or what is trying to position something. For example, is a company trying to position another company or is a political party trying to position an individual in some way? On another dimension what matters is whether an individual or organization reflexively positions itself/themselves, or whether they/it is being positioned by some other entity. In public relations, we can see that in a strategic positioning context these dimensions will impact on how an organization acts and what it says, both as a corporate entity and through its spokespeople, employees or members.

An experienced practitioner would recognize that each situation requires the deployment of different skills and techniques. For example, in a situation of deliberate self-positioning, your organization might be working on a new project with a lead-time of months before launch. Imagine however, that a previously unknown group becomes active on social media platforms regarding some aspect of your organization's operations. Your organization may be in a situation where it feels forced to self-position in order to maintain normal operations, or to protect its reputation, and this might need to happen within a short time frame such as a week, a few days or even within the hour. Both episodes involve strategic positioning but require the deployment of quite different skills and processes over two very different time frames.

Organizations can be conceived as having personas of sorts (Harré and van Langenhove, 1999: 8), which can be seen as publicly presented repertoires or clusters of behaviors that are constructed through discourse (p. 7). Some organizations have several personas and any one could dominate depending on the particular context. For example, a company might position as community-minded in a civic forum; as maximizing return on investment at a shareholders' meeting; or as environmentally responsible to government regulators. In each instance what is presented as the persona in terms of actions and words is different in order to accommodate the differences in the situations. All positions taken might be with the view to achieving the same overall goal or mission. One can see that it may cause problems for an organization if the inappropriate persona was presented in a particular situation, that is, that the positioning was not in accordance to the local moral order which determines what is right to do and say. According to Harré and van Langenhove (1999), it is through the interactions of parties that personas are manifested:

> It is in the constant interplay of mutual recognition of one's own and the other's position that the particular version of public self appropriate to the occasion is constructed.
>
> (Harré and van Langenhove, 1999: 9)

Such a statement could describe what expert public relations practitioners undertake as part of their everyday work; in a nutshell, the expert practitioners' "habitus" (Bourdieu, 1991: 51); that set of skills and ways of acting that are often taken for granted, and which are acquired through the activities and experiences of being a practitioner who is travelling, or has travelled, the path of novice to expert. This is all very well for seasoned practitioners who monitor the moment-to-moment vacillations of the positions of their clients, stakeholders and publics as second nature, but what of the novices? Taking a positioning theoretical approach may assist in articulating the subtleties of advanced practice so that practitioners become more effective more quickly. Applying the Framework could help articulate a substantial amount of the work undertaken by senior practitioners. Such work previously may have been difficult to present to clients as taking time and effort, and this may assist agencies to bill clients more accurately and transparently.

Summary

This chapter discussed that although positioning was ubiquitous in public relations practice, it was rarely examined outside of a marketing conceptualization. Positioning theory was introduced as a way of better conceptualizing public relations positioning. Positioning theory is a social constructionist approach (Kroløkke, 2009; Slocum and van Langenhove, 2003) that began to emerge in the 1980s primarily in the area of gender studies. Positioning theory is about "how people use words (and discourse of all types) to locate themselves and others" (Moghaddam and Harré, 2010: 2).

The dimension of positioning theory that has the most profound relevance for public relations is the concept of rights and duties that are associated with positions. Moghaddam and Harré (2010) state "it is with words that we ascribe rights and claim them for ourselves and place duties on others" (p. 3). Drawing on positioning theory, and on the work of Motion (1997) and Berger (1999), I defined a public relations position as: a point of intentional representation discursively constructed for the purposes of achieving an intended outcome, and from where possibilities for action are established, or in some cases denied, in terms of the local moral order/s wherein the public relations activity is taking place. Positioning is what we call the actions taken to achieve the position. When public relations is conceptualized as a process whereby discursive positions are actively negotiated and achieved, rather than as a prescriptive technique where a pre-existing position is merely occupied, the dynamic processes involved can be both examined from an academic standpoint and also adapted to practice.

In some ways positioning theory shows the futility of trying to position in a way that an organization knows is unsupportable. It can serve to guide practitioners in their advice to their clients/employers as to what positions are available to them at particular times and in particular contexts. In the next chapter, the concept of rights, responsibilities and power in public relations positioning is examined in more detail.

References

Al Khaja, M. A. W., and Creedon, P. (2010) Evaluating the effectiveness of the first breast cancer awareness campaign in the United Arab Emirates: lessons learned and next steps. *Public Relations Review*, 36(4): 386–8.

Baert, P. (2012) Positioning theory and intellectual interventions. *Journal for the Theory of Social Behavior*, 42(3): 304–24, doi: 10.1111/j.1468-5914.2012.00492.x

Baines, P., Fill, C. and Page, K. (2008) *Marketing*. Oxford: Oxford University Press.

Balnaves, M., Donald, S. and Shoesmith, B. (2009) *Media Theories and Approaches: A global perspective.* Basingstoke, UK: Palgrave Macmillan.

Batchelor, B. and Formentin, M. (2008) Re-branding the NHL: building the league through the "My NHL" integrated marketing campaign. *Public Relations Review*, 34(2): 156–60.

Berger, B. (1999) The Halcion affair: public relations and the construction of ideological world view. *Journal of Public Relations Research*, 11(3): 185–203.

Berger, P. and Luckmann, T. (1966) *The Social Construction of Reality: A treatise in the sociology of knowledge*. London: Penguin.

Bobbitt, R. and Sullivan, R. (2014) *Developing the Public Relations Campaign: A team based approach* (3rd edn). Boston, MA: Pearson.

Boone, L. and Kurtz, D. (2013) *Contemporary Marketing Update* (15th edn). Mason, OH: Cengage.

Bourdieu, P. (1991) *Language and Symbolic Power*. Cambridge: Polity Press.

Butler, P. and Harris, P. (2009) Considerations on the evolution of political marketing theory. *Marketing Theory*, 9: 149–64.

Chew, C. (2005) Strategic marketing planning and positioning in voluntary non-profit organizations: empirical findings and implications for British charitable institutions. *Aston Business School Research Paper RP0506*. Birmingham: Aston University.

Chew, C. (2009) *Strategic Positioning in Voluntary and Charitable Organizations*. London: Routledge.

Coombs, W. T. (2010) Crisis communication: a developing field. In R. Heath, (ed.) *The Sage Handbook of Public Relations*. Thousand Oaks, CA: Sage, pp. 477–88.

Danowski, J. (2008) Short-term and long-term effects of a public relations campaign on semantic networks of newspaper content: priming or framing? *Public Relations Review*, 34, 288–90.

de Burgh-Woodman, H. and Brace-Govan, J. (2007) We do not live to buy: why subcultures are different from brand communities and the meaning for marketing discourse. *International Journal of Sociology and Social Policy*, 27(5/6): 193–207.

Egan, J. (2007) *Marketing Communications*. London: Cengage Learning EMEA.

Hallahan, K. (1999) Seven models of framing: implications for public relations. *Journal of Public Relations Research*, 11(3): 205–42.

Handelman, D (2008) Afterword: Returning to cosmology – thoughts on the positioning of belief. *Social Analysis*, 52(1): 181–95.

Harré, R. (2006) Positioning theory. In V. Jupp (ed.) *The Sage Dictionary of Social Research Methods*. Sage, pp. 229–30. Retrieved from http://srmo.sagepub.com/view/the-sage-dictionary-of-social-research-methods/SAGE.xml

Harré, R. (2012) Positioning theory: moral dimensions of social-cultural psychology. In J. Valsiner (ed.) *The Oxford Handbook of Culture and Psychology*. New York: Oxford University, pp. 191–206.

Harré, R., Moghaddam, F., Pilkerton Cairnie, T., Rothbart, D. and Sabat, S. (2009) Recent advances in positioning theory. *Theory and Psychology*, 19(1): 5–31. doi: 10.1177/0959354308101417.

Harré, R. and van Langenhove, L. (1999) *Positioning Theory: Moral contexts of intentional action*. Oxford: Blackwell.

Heath, R. (2001) A rhetorical enactment rationale for public relations: the good organization communicating well. In R. Heath (ed.) *The Sage Handbook of Public Relations*. Thousand Oaks, CA: Sage, pp. 441–4.

Henderson, A. (2005) Activism in "paradise": identity management in a public relations campaign against genetic engineering. *Journal of Public Relations Research*, 17(2): 117–37.

Holm, O. (2006) Integrated marketing communication: from tactics to strategy. *Corporate Communications: An International Journal*, 11(1): 23–33.

James, M. (2009) Getting to the heart of public relations: the concept of strategic intent. *Asia Pacific Public Relations Journal*, 10, 109–22.

James, M. (2010) The use of intentional positioning techniques in government agencies' communication campaigns. In D. Verčič and K. Sriramesh (eds). *Government communication: proceedings of the 17th International Public Relations Research Symposium BledCom* Bled, Slovenia, Ljubljana: Pristop. 2010, pp. 140–7. Retrieved from www.bledcom.si/uploads/ppt2010/bledcom 2010 proceedings hi.pdf

James, M., (2011) A provisional conceptual framework for intentional positioning in public relations. *Journal of Public Relations Research*. 23(1): 93–111. http://dx.doi.org/10.1080/1062726X.2010.505120

James, M. (2012) Autoethnography: the story of applying a conceptual framework for intentional positioning to public relations practice. *Public Relations Review*, 38(4): 555–64. http://dx.doi.org/10.1016/j.pubrev.2012.05.004

Jo, S., Shim. S. and Jung, J. (2008) Propaganda or public relations campaign? International communication on the war against Iraq. *Public Relations Review*, 34, 63–5.

Knox, S. and Bickerton, D. (2003) The six conventions of corporate branding. *European Journal of Marketing*, 37(7/8): 998–1016.

Kroløkke, C. (2009) Positioning theory. In S. Littlejohn and K. Foss (eds) *Encyclopedia of Communication Theory*. Thousand Oaks, CA: Sage, pp. 765–7. doi: http://dx.doi.org/10.4135/9781412959384.n289

Leitch, S. and Motion, J. (2010) Publics and public relations: effecting change. In R. Heath (ed.) *The Sage Handbook of Public Relations*. Thousand Oaks, CA: Sage, pp. 99–110.

Louis, W. (2008) Intergroup positioning and power. In F. Moghaddam, R. Harré, and N. Lee, (eds) *Global Conflict Resolution through Positioning Analysis*. New York: Springer, pp. 21–40.

Macnamara, J. (2010) Public relations and the social: how practitioners are using, or abusing, social media. *Asia Pacific Public Relations Journal*, 11(1): 21–39.

Miller, D. (2013) The Morality Play: Getting to the heart of media influence on foreign policy. In J. Hamilton & R. Lawrence (eds) *Foreign Correspondence*. London. Routledge, pp. 89–104.

Moffitt, M. (1994) Collapsing and integrating concepts of 'public' and 'image' into a new theory. *Public Relations Review*, 20, 159–170.

Moghaddam, F. and Harré, R. (2010) Words, conflicts and political processes. In F. Moghaddam and R. Harré (eds) *Words of Conflict, Words of War: How the language we use in political processes sparks fighting*. Santa Barbara, CA: Praeger.

Moghaddam, F., Harré, R. and Lee, N. (2008) Positioning and conflict: an introduction. In F. Moghaddam, R. Harré, and N. Lee, (eds) *Global Conflict Resolution through Positioning Analysis*. New York: Springer, pp. 3–20.

Motion, J. (1997) Technologising the self: an art of public relations. *Australian Journal of Communication*, 24(2): 1–16.

Motion, J. (2000) Personal public relations: the interdisciplinary pitfalls and innovative possibilities of identity work. *Journal of Communication Management*, 5(1): 31–40.

Motion, J. and Doolin, B. (2007) Out of the laboratory: scientists' discursive practices in their encounters with activists. *Discourse Studies*, 9(1): 63–85.

Motion, J., and Leitch, S. (1996) A discursive perspective from New Zealand: another world view. *Public Relations Review*, 22(3): 297–309.

Motion, J. and Leitch, S. (2009) On Foucault: a toolbox for public relations. In O. Ihlen, B. van Ruler and M. Fredriksson (eds) *Public Relations and Social Theory: Key figures and concepts*. London: Routledge, pp. 83–102.

Murphy, P. (1991) The limits of symmetry: a game theory approach to symmetric and asymmetric public relations. *Journal of Public Relations Research*, 3(1–4): 115–31.

Myers, G. (2010) Stance-taking and public discussion in blogs, *Critical discourse studies*, (7)4: 263–275. http://dx.doi.org/10.1080/17405904.2010.511832

O'Shaughnessy, N. and Baines, P. (2009) Selling terror: the symbolization and positioning of Jihad. *Marketing Theory*, 9, 227–41.

Pang, A., Jin, Y., and Cameron, G. (2010) Strategic management of communication: insights from the contingency theory of strategic conflict management, in R. L. Heath, (ed.) (2010) *The Sage Handbook of Public Relations*. Los Angeles, CA: Sage, pp. 17–34.

Phillips, D. and Hayes, B. (2008) Securing the oral tradition: reflective positioning and professional conversations in midwifery education. *Collegian*, 15(3): 109–14.

Pieczka, M. (2007) Case studies as narrative accounts of public relations practice. *Journal of Public Relations Research*, 19(4): 333–56.

Pompper, D. (2004) Position and positioning. In R. Heath (ed.) *Encyclopedia of Public Relations*. London: Sage, pp. 629–31.

Pompper, D. (2013) Position and positioning. In R. Heath (ed.) *Encyclopedia of Public Relations*. (2nd edn) London: Sage, p. 662–4.

Porter, M. (2008) *On competition*. Boston: Harvard Business.

Ries, A. and Trout, J. (1981) *Positioning: the battle for your mind*. New York: McGraw-Hill.

Roper, J. (2005) Organisational identities, identification and positioning: learning from political fields. *Public Relations Review*, 31(1): 139–48.

Rossiter, J. and Bellman, S. (2005) *Marketing Communications: Theory and practice*. Frenchs Forest, NSW: Pearson.

Sless, D. (1987) A matter of position. *Australian Journal of Communication,* 18(3): 9–28.

Slocum, N. and van Langenhove, L. (2003) Integration speak: introducing positioning theory in regional studies. In R. Harré and F. Moghaddam (eds) *The self and Others: Positioning individuals and groups in personal, political and cultural contexts*. London: Praeger, pp. 123–36.

Slocum-Bradley, N. (2008) Discursive production of conflict in Rwanda. In F. Moghaddam, R. Harré, and N. Lee, (eds) *Global Conflict Resolution through Positioning Analysis*. New York: Springer, pp. 20–26.

Slocum-Bradley, N. (2010) The positioning diamond: a transdisciplinary framework for discourse analysis. *Journal for The Theory of Social Behaviour*, 40(1): 79–107. doi: 10.1111/j.1468-5914.2009.00418.x

Stanton, W., Miller, K., Layton, R. and Rix, P. (1995) *Fundamentals of Marketing Essentials*, (2nd edn). Sydney: McGraw Hill.

Stokes, A. and Rubin, D. (2010) Activism and the limits of symmetry: the public relations battle between Colorado GASP and Philip Morris. *Journal of Public Relations Research*, 22(1): 26–48.

Tilley, E. (2009) Strategy and planning. In J. Johnston and C. Zawawi (eds) *Public relations: theory and practice*. Crows Nest, NSW: Allen and Unwin.

Tilson, D. (2006) Devotional-promotional communication and Santiago: a thousand-year public relations campaign for Saint James and Spain. In J. L'Etang and M. Pieczka (eds) *Public Relations: Critical debates and contemporary practice*. Mahwah, NJ: Lawrence Erlbaum, pp. 167–86.

Tsetsura, K. (2012) A struggle for legitimacy: Russian women secure their professional identities in public relations in a hypersexualized patriarchal workplace. *Public Relations Journal*, 6(1): 1–21. Retrieved from www.prsa.org/intelligence/prjournal/documents/2012tsetsura.pdf

van Langenhove, L. and Harré, R. (1999) Introducing positioning theory. In R. Harré and L. van Langenhove (eds). *Positioning Theory: Moral contexts of intentional action*. Oxford: Blackwell, pp. 14–31.

Vardeman-Winter, J. (2010) Using the cultural studies approach to understand health decision-making among a teen public. *Public Relations Review*, 36(4): 383–5.

Wang, A. (2007) Priming, framing, and position on corporate social responsibility. *Journal of Public Relations Research*, 19(2): 123–45.

Waymer, D. and Heath, R. (2007) Emergent agents: the forgotten publics in crisis communication and issues management research. *Journal of Applied Communication Research*, 35(1): 88–108.

Weizman, E. (2008) *Positioning in Media Dialogue: Negotiating roles in the news interview.* Amsterdam: John Benjamin.

Wise, D. and James, M. (2013) Positioning a price on carbon: applying a proposed hybrid method of positioning discourse analysis for public relations. *Public Relations Inquiry*, 2(3): 327–53.

Wu, X. (2007) Stakeholder identifying and positioning (SIP) models: from Google's operation in China to a general case-analysis framework. *Public Relations Review*, 33, 415–25.

Zelle, G. (2009) *Exploring the Application of Positioning Theory to the Analysis of Organisational Change*. Australian and New Zealand Academy of Management Conference. Adelaide, Australia: Australian and New Zealand Academy of Management.

Zhang, J. and Benoit, W. (2004) Arab image: message strategies of Saudi Arabia's image restoration campaign after 9/11. *Public Relations Review*, 30(2): 161–7.

2 Rights, duties and power in public relations positioning

A new conceptual approach to all aspects of public relations can be seen in the application of positioning theory. That is a large claim to make, but it is rare that one theory can provide such an array of applications for a field. If you are a practitioner, this approach offers a new way to undertake highly strategic public relations. Through understanding the concept of rights and duties that are integral to positions taken, or assigned to others, program design can be fine tuned. Strategic relationships can be forged and fostered using the principles of positioning theory; whilst on the other hand, a conflict can be escalated for strategic purposes using the same approach. The theory can guide the most ethical practice, or could inform a highly abusive program that sought to disempower people through the application of malevolent positioning techniques. A positioning analysis of a situation can readily indicate where positioning efforts could be challenged, and can thus inform decision making at the highest level. It is evident that some practitioners struggle to make connections between much of the current public relations theory, ethical guidelines and "real world" strategic practice. Applying positioning theory to practice may prove to be an effective way of drawing these aspects together to better guide practice, but to also further develop theory.

For researchers, positioning theory guides analysis of public relations from macro-level sociocultural aspects of practice through to micro-tactical levels of individual programs. In this book I have provided examples across this range. For example, I have applied the theory to determine the positioning possibilities for a coal mining advocacy association who saw its industry as under attack from environmental groups. I developed possible scenarios based on a small document analysis, and presented a potential way forward based on the concept of rights and duties associated with each of the positioning options (see Chapter 3). Later in the book, I provide an in-depth analysis of the public relations positioning of two countries, Indonesia and Australia, whose governments disagree about the way people who are seeking asylum are treated. The analysis indicates how Indonesia maintained a consistent position through its public communication but also shows where Australia was unsuccessful in positioning in a coherent way (see Chapter 9). These are just some of the ways that the theory can be applied to research. Positioning theory provides links into the wider field of communication, and potentially other academic areas, and can therefore foster multidisciplinary approaches to research projects.

In order to situate positioning both in a public relations context and in the wider discipline of communication, the issue of how one conceptualizes or defines public relations and strategic communication emerges as one that needs to be addressed. This is because "language which communicates common understanding is needed as the basis for meaningful discussion" (Jaques, 2009: 280). According to Hallahan, Holtzhausen, van Ruler, Verčič and Sriramesh (2007), the definition of strategic communication involves an organization communicating purposefully to advance its mission. Such a definition could readily be applied to public relations as it is practiced by many practitioners across the world. Such a definition is congruent with the notion of an organization undertaking strategic positioning activity to achieve its goals. It can be argued that public relations is more than communication, and it could be argued that public relations positioning is more than strategic communication however, when one examines the processes and techniques used in all facets of public relations, it is hard to find any that do not sit in the wider context of communication theory.

It is clear that public relations has "multiple meanings and muddied, conflicting interpretations" (Berger, 1999: 185) and does not have anything approaching consensus on the purpose for which public relations is employed. Jaques states that in many areas within public relations an "agreed taxonomy is both elusive and illusory" (2009: 280). Galloway (2013: 156) concludes "PR may be not only 'unseen' but also ultimately 'unknowable' in the apophatic sense: a phenomenon whose essence is elusive but whose behaviors can be assessed and evaluated". In not having "one set of unquestioned presuppositions that provides an intellectual framework", public relations can be said to be "still in an evolutionary state, redefining itself, which affects its teaching, research and practice" (McDonald, 2008: 3). This is not a new state of affairs, with debates over defining public relations active as far back as the immediate post World War II period (L'Etang, 2006). The development on an agreed definition still has not transpired, in spite of concerted efforts by various professional bodies across the world. This situation presents a challenge for discussing positioning in public relations, especially in terms of power and ethics. This is because if one defines public relations in one way, some techniques and practices may seem to exercise power in a particular way and this will raise a suite of ethical questions. However, if one defines public relations in some other way, a different set of questions relating to power and ethics may arise.

The myriad of views on the definition of public relations can be conceptualized along a continuum of sorts; one that plots definitions in terms of who the beneficiaries of public relations are, or, to whose advantage is public relations practiced. At one end of the continuum there are those who tell us that public relations is about "achieving mutually beneficial relationships" (Heath 2001: 36), that "its major role is to empower those with less power" (Grunig, 2006: 165), or that the public relations function is to ensure the "inclusiveness of all voices that are affected by the organization and thereby benefiting the publics as well as the organization itself" (Holtzhausen, 2002: 255).

These could be defined as normative theoretical approaches in that they focus on ideals that inform prescriptions of how things should be rather than on explaining or predicting activities (Smith, 2008). These normative approaches to public relations theory and research have not "dealt well with dilemmas offered by concepts of propaganda, dialogue or the public sphere, nor [...] produced extensive and convincing explanations of the actual practice" (Pieczka, 2002: 322). At the other end of the continuum there are scholars who state that "modern PR is competitive communications seeking advantage for its principals" (Moloney, 2006: 165), and that "above all, it is communication designed to further the interests of its principals...they would not invest in PR if it were otherwise" (Moloney, 2006: 168). Or, that public relations can be understood as the strategic attempt to control the agenda of public discussion and the terms in which discussion takes place. In these terms public relations practitioners are complicit in the attempt to gain, or maintain, social, political, and/or economic power for the organizations that they represent (Weaver, Motion and Roper, 2006).

At this end of the continuum, public relations is viewed as a tool "for the maintenance of hegemony" (Weaver, Motion and Roper, 2006: 17), as a means for an organization to advocate for a particular view or position in the court of public opinion (Mayhew, 1997), or as the means by which a particular ideological world view is constructed (Berger, 1999). L'Etang (2006) and Moloney (2006) both put forward that public relations is a form of propaganda, with both scholars outlining how the adoption of the term public relations was designed to distance the profession from the negative associations propaganda had with war communication. At this end of the continuum, especially when considering the views of critical scholars who situate public relations within "a world of organizations bent on dominating those of lesser power" (Toth, 2009: 53), one could question how anyone with a degree of social conscience could ever work in a public relations role.

On this continuum, the key question is to whose benefit or advantage is public relations employed. Given that public relations is undertaken by entities such as businesses large and small, trade unions, governments and public sector agencies, not-for-profit organizations, individuals and activists, it is impossible to define the nature of a singular advantage or benefit that would be applicable across this spectrum. A corporation employing public relations may see advantage in positioning itself as the company that returns maximum dividends to shareholders; whereas a publicly-funded health organization employing public relations may see advantage as positioning prostate checks as recommended behavior for all older men. This indicates that the concept of the continuum of definitions based on the question of who benefits from public relations may be flawed.

There is no doubt that public relations positioning is strategic in that much of its practice centers on trying to compete with other entities who are also trying to position their products, services or ideologies in the minds of targeted publics and audiences. From this perspective, Moloney's (2006) definition of public relations as competitive communications seeking advantage for its principals is most appropriate. That being said, it would be hard to argue that a not-for-profit disability organization seeking advantage for its principals (donors; clients with disabilities) would be viewed as unethical. Research in public relations positioning has shown that techniques used by the full spectrum of organizations employing public relations are quite similar (James, 2009). Moloney's (2006) decree that organizations wouldn't invest in public relations if it didn't further their interests is sound.

In the positioning context, if an organization has no need to strive to occupy, assign or maintain a particular position, it does not need to employ public relations. However, it would be hard to find such an entity. The application of positioning theory to public relations, with its focus on rights and duties within the local moral order, seems capable of mapping a way forward for more socially responsible behavior by all organizations. As in much relating to discussions of public relations, it comes back to the issue of intent. If an organization wishes to act ethically, positioning theory can offer a way of conceptualizing practice; but if an organization has another agenda, it can apply positioning theory in a way that is abusive of other parties.

Positioning in public relations: a matter of rights and duties

A key focus of positioning theory is on the rights and duties associated with taking on a position or assigning a position to others. Positions determined, taken up and/or assigned can be seen to constrain what can be meaningfully said and done (Harré and Slocum, 2003). Adapting the work of Harré and Slocum (2003: 140) to public relations it can be seen that the type of participation that is open to any party "involved in the ongoing storyline that is unfolding" in a public relations episode "is limited by a loosely defined set of rights, duties and obligations", and these are determined by the local moral order.

This local moral order is the understood framework of rights, duties and obligations in any social interaction (Moghaddam, Hanley and Harré, 2003). In particular circumstances, "certain kinds of acts are possible and other kinds are ruled out for the participants in the interaction insofar as they are seen as having one set of rights and duties rather than another" (Moghaddam, Hanley and Harré, 2003: 140). According to Harré (2012: 198) the "various and variable" relations between duties and rights are dependent on culture, history, topic and so on, which means that positions can be very complex. In some cases the parties involved in a positioning episode accept each other's understanding of the respective rights and duties of each party, but often there are negotiations, disputes, and continuing reformulations (Moghaddam and Kavulich, 2008).

There are two distinct phases to positioning acts according to Moghaddam and Harré (2010: 9) and they can be readily adapted to public relations positioning. Phase one, which has become known as "pre-positioning" (Moghaddam and Harré, 2010: 9), involves attributing particular qualities to an organization (or a program, person or product). This would be often supported by reports of past behaviors of the organization that supported the possession of such qualities. Such pre-positioning could be part of self-positioning by an organization, e.g. as being an organization that promotes equal opportunity for people with disabilities. That organization would make available past reports, testimonials, awards and so on to support its claim of having this quality. In another instance, a group of people who may not agree with that organization's claim to that quality may try to reposition the organization as one that does not promote equal opportunity for people with disabilities. That group would probably have reports available that dispute that equal opportunities were made available.

The second phase that can be adapted to public relations contexts from Moghaddam and Harré (2010) is that when an organization is "assigned or refused a cluster of rights and duties to perform certain kinds of acts" (p. 9) it constrains what an organization that has been positioned in a particular way can do or say. The examples presented in this book indicate that this seems to be where many organizations tend to go wrong in a public relations sense. A company cannot take a position of being, e.g. customer-focused and then go on to perform acts that demonstrate that they are not focused on customers, as that position would not hold for very long. If this thinking is followed through to its logical conclusion, a company that decided to occupy a particular position viewed as positive by the society within which it operates would have to act in a way that enacted and supported the desired position. This would then lead to a positive change in the organization and the wider society. Thus, there is the potential for a positioning approach to public relations, although highly strategic, to drive positive and ethical behavior by organizations.

Both phases are underpinned by the presumption that there is "a cluster of collectively located beliefs about what it is right and good to do and say" (Moghaddam and Harré, 2010: 10), that is, a local moral order. The analysis of public relations practice within a positioning theoretical context can indicate why what may have worked for an organization in one context, culture or country doesn't work in others. This is because the local moral orders differ and this requires a rethink in some instances of what it is right and good to do and say.

The concept of rights and duties, and the local moral order

Interestingly, Moghaddam and Harré (2010: 17) stated that from the inception of positioning theory, exactly how "the underlying rights and duties existed was not discussed". Theorists has been working with the presumption was "that they existed as part of the systems of beliefs with which people interpreted and managed their lives" (Moghaddam and Harré, 2010, p. 17). They have suggested that some of the literature that provides guidance "in the matter of finding a way for expressing normatively constrained uniformities in people's actions" can assist in our understanding of "how the tacit rights and duties form the relatively stable moral background to ordinary acts of positioning" (p. 16). Moghaddam and Harré suggest the concept of "habitus" (Bourdieu 1990: 54) could be helpful in conceptualizing this aspect of positioning theory but they do not go on to expand this thinking. My reading of Bourdieu supports such an assertion but would also add that Bourdieu's concept of field (1984, 1993a, 1993b), as suggested by public relations scholars such as Roper (2005) and Ihlen (2005), should also be considered alongside "habitus" in positioning theory generally, but especially in a public relations context. Bourdieu (1991) describes the social field as:

> A multi-dimensional space of positions such that each actual position can be defined in terms of a multi-dimensional system of co-ordinates whose values correspond to the values of the first pertinent variables. Agents are thus distributed, in the first dimension, according to the overall volume of the capital they posses and, in the second dimension, according to the composition of their capital—in other words, according to the relative weight of the different kinds of capital in the total set of their assets.
>
> (Bourdieu, 1991: 231)

According to Parmentier, Fischer and Reuber (2013: 375) Bourdieu's fields can be considered "structured networks of social positions within which actors strive to gain access to greater power and control over more resources". They state that:

> Bourdieu argues that actors within fields have shared understandings and ways of acting that include tacitly held attitudes, preferences, and embodied habits of behavior; he refers to these tacit understandings and embodied habits as "habitus", defined as "schemes of perception, thought and action, [which] tend to guarantee the 'correctness' of practices and their constancy over time, more reliably than all formal rules and explicit norms" (Bourdieu 1990: 54). Actors habituated to a field share understandings regarding the value of certain field-specific types of "capital".
>
> (Parmentier, Fischer and Reuber, 2013: 375)

As Ihlen (2005) states, public relations practice "fits this picture if it is regarded as a practice that assists organizational actors in different fields in pursuing their interests with the help of various forms of capital" (p. 493). From the perspective of Bourdieu, Ihlen argues that the "positions of the actors are seen in relation to each other and explained as functions of the types and amounts of capital, the field-specific appreciations of these forms of capital, and the constant attempts to acquire, hold on to, or to convert capital". From a positioning theoretical perspective, having possession of certain rights to position in certain ways according to the local moral order would be part of an entity's "symbolic capital" (Bourdieu, 1991), which is explained by Ihlen:

> Bourdieu's (1986) article on the forms of capital narrows the notion down to three fundamental types: economic capital (money, property, etc.), cultural capital (knowledge, skills, and educational qualifications), and social capital (connections and membership of groups)...these forms of capital may be apprehended as symbolic capital (prestige, honor)...The amount and type of capital that an agent possesses also locates it in the field.
>
> (Ihlen, 2005: 493)

For example, Ihlen (2005) states "capital might be specific to a certain field and relatively worthless in other fields" (p. 493). This can be seen to pertain to positioning theory's ideas around the consequences of trying to position in certain ways when the local moral order does not accord such rights. Rothbart and Bartlett (2008) describe Bourdieu's symbolic capital as "the sociocultural prestige that lends to certain speakers an aura of authority in particular fields of discourse and before the relevant audience" (p. 233). This lends further weight to the concept of the possession of rights and duties in a positioning context as being part of an organization's symbolic capital. It can then be seen that discourse, in these terms, is the mediational means through which speakers are able to realize their embodied symbolic capital as power in action.

Public relations practitioners can be seen to become habituated to a field of practice and, through experience and learning, need to understand the value of field-specific types of symbolic capital. Through the development and management of relationships, practitioners may strive to achieve shared understandings with publics regarding the value of certain field-specific types of capital (Parmentier *et al.*, 2013). Positioning theory suggests that our organizations and clients are not able to simply adopt or assign any position they like, instead, they are only able to position in ways in which their symbolic capital (Bourdieu, 1991) is recognized by others operating within the local moral order (Rothbart and Bartlett, 2008). I adapt some words from Rothbart and Bartlett (2008: 187) and suggest that as public relations practitioners and researchers we can develop an understanding of the complexities of positioning. While understanding that we can never see the whole picture, we might begin to feel it, start to act strategically and, over time, behave intuitively.

How this applies to public relations practice

In public relations the idea can be applied that the first positioning phase (pre-positioning), that is the attribution of qualities, provides the grounding of the second phase, the actual positioning. Moghaddam and Harré (2010) discuss how the same set of qualities can be used to position someone differently in different contexts. In public relations, we can see this happening too. In Australia, Ms. Anna Bligh was the premier of the state of Queensland during the 2010 flood disaster that impacted most of the vast state. She was positioned by media commentators throughout the crisis as being both competent and compassionate in that situation, a position reflected through soaring approval ratings immediately following the disaster. However, the "competent position" did not last beyond the disaster and the government she led lost the next state election in a landslide defeat. Why would this be the case?

During the disaster period Ms. Bligh was seen to take control, call in the appropriate help, provide information, and so on. She self-positioned as being in control of the crisis-response. The behavior she demonstrated was that she was competently handling that particular situation. The storylines meshed with what people were seeing and hearing, hence she was successfully positioned as being competent. Once that disaster had settled, Ms. Bligh was again back to running the state of Queensland. Although she tried to self-position as being competent and in control of the state, she was effectively repositioned by the opposition political party as not being in control. The qualities Ms. Bligh maintained she possessed could not be supported as the opposition had copious evidence to the contrary. There was evidence of budget blow-outs, departmental mismanagement, and loss of business investment confidence. She was successfully positioned by the opposition as being a disastrous leader for Queensland.

The first phase of the opposition's positioning strategy was attributing a set of negative qualities to Ms. Bligh that could be backed up by evidence. The second phase was the assignment of rights and duties to Ms. Bligh according to the local moral order, that is, what is right and good to do and say. The opposition's strategy, of attributing the quality of incompetence to Ms. Bligh, backing it up with evidence that was hard for Ms. Bligh to dispute and then assigning her the rights and duties of being positioned as incompetent, was very effective. Within the context of Western democratic political processes, the duties of someone who is incompetent involve actions such as stepping aside, bringing in people who know what they're doing, trying to fix things and so forth. In spite of Ms. Bligh's attempts to reposition herself, she was unable to do so. In some ways this shows the futility of trying to position in a way that an organization knows is unsupportable. Positioning theory can serve to guide practitioners in their advice to their clients/employers as to what positions are available to them at particular times and in particular contexts. It also demonstrates what materials and other proof points need to be assembled to support a particular position.

If we take a situation, like a company known for its innovation wanting to launch a fabulous new product at an event in a major city like New York, it can be seen that all parties involved would know the "understood framework", that is, the local moral order. For example, at this product launch it is expected by invitees that a new product will be announced and demonstrated in some way. It is expected by guests at the launch that they'll have some chance of exploring the new product, to ask questions and so on. The product will differ, the "bells and whistles" of the event may differ and the questions asked will differ, but everyone generally knows their rights, responsibilities and obligations as "the rules" are clear. The company launching the product has the right to invite people as it has something new to show. If the company invited people on some pretense and indeed had nothing to show, that would be a violation of that right. People who attended would feel duped and their trust in that company would diminish. The company also, in hosting a launch of the new product, has a duty to let those attending have information and ideally a take-home sample or the opportunity to experience the new product. Again, if the company somehow fails to carry out this duty and withholds information or keeps people away from experiencing the new product, people will feel let down. The positioning of the company as being innovative, or for the new product as being worthwhile, may start to falter.

Now imagine what happens when a practitioner is asked to arrange a similar event in a city or country where neither the company nor the practitioner has any previous experience or knowledge. The same event and arrangements may be perfectly appropriate, but they may not be. One of the key issues to be considered is the local moral order. In New York and most Western cities, although the norm would be to give the sample products to attendees, even quite generous offerings, the payment of cash for simply attending the launch would generally not be expected. If however, a practitioner was doing a similar event in a country such as China, payment or some other financial arrangement between the story source and the journalists/editors covering the story may be expected (Chen and Culbertson, 2003). This is an example of different local moral orders in operation. For public relations practitioners operating in an unfamiliar culture, especially on international assignments, this needs to be taken into account. According to Curtin and Gaither (2007) cultural regulations need to be considered alongside regulations pertaining to politics, technology and economy. They conclude that "local public relations advisors are needed in international public relations efforts to help unveil hidden regulators" (p. 65), or from a positioning theoretical perspective, to comprehend and navigate the local moral order.

Understanding the local moral order helps practitioners determine what options may be available to their clients in terms of taking up a position, or assigning positions to others. For instance, if a state passes laws that decree that domestic violence is a crime, it could be that public relations practitioners employed by the responsible government agency may be asked to design a campaign to inform citizens of this change. People who have suffered domestic violence can now be positioned as victims of crime who have a right to assistance and support from police, and have a right to speak out against such violence. They may be ascribed by some as having a duty to report the perpetrators to the police, as perpetrators are now positioned by the new legislation as criminals.

Perpetrators of domestic violence might be shocked if such a campaign portrays their actions as criminal, as they may have previously believed that such actions were a normal part of living with their partners. Being positioned as an actual or potential criminal again brings rights and duties. Perpetrators have a right to know that their actions are now considered to be criminal, and that they have a societal and legal duty not to break the law. Introducing such a law may mean that perpetrators have a right to the opportunity to learn how to manage their anger or to receive a course of counseling. Analyzing the rights and duties associated with each possible position can assist a practitioner to determine the positions to enact through a campaign or other means. It also helps to develop the storylines and key messages that will support the position.

In another instance, a public relations practitioner might be assigned to garner support for paying for an online newspaper's content from a certain date when, prior to that, it had been available to all readers free of charge. Examining the rights and responsibilities associated with the situation, that of the company taking the position that people should pay for their product (the news content), can help the practitioner to identify issues to be addressed. The company has claimed the position that it has the right to charge for content. Readers may position the company as greedy. They feel they have the right to continue to read the content for free as there are advertisements on the pages served to their computer or device, just as in the hard copy paper editions. From this point, the practitioner tries to determine a position that would be acceptable to the company and the readers.

Through research and consultation it could be determined that readers would be prepared to pay a small amount if they received less advertising on their news pages, and/or received more quality content than the current free service. However, it might also be found that many readers will simply stop using the service and find news for free somewhere else. Readers may feel that the company did not have the right to start charging for what had previously been free.

The company, of course, could take the position that because it has been providing the online content at a financial loss it now has the right to start charging. It might have proof in terms of financial statements that would show, to those who cared to look, that the financial losses were real. The company decision-makers might feel that such evidence negates the duty to provide additional or improved content to readers if they introduce a fee. However, what is logical or factual or evident to some may not hold sway with others. Readers may not care about the company's financial losses or understand that what they've been receiving for some time for free came at a cost to the company. All some readers may see is that what they used to have right of access to for no charge now costs money, and people perceive that, rightly or wrongly, as unfair.

This shows how the local moral order is more than just what is legal, logical or evident but is comprised also of social norms and unspoken rules and customs. Indeed Parrott (2003) has analyzed the role of emotions in positioning contexts and argues that they can be used in a highly persuasive and strategic way, "especially when one party's emotion is countered by another party's emotion" (p. 33). By undertaking a positioning analysis of rights and duties of various positions, practitioners can present options and recommendations to the executive management that clearly outlines situations, possible ways forward and associated risks and benefits. Taking an emergent strategic approach (King, 2010) can be helpful here. By monitoring the responses a communication action to position your organization is generating, practitioners can know what type of supporting material and supporting storylines may be needed at a particular time. This can be anticipated if scenario planning is undertaken.

Scenario planning and public relations positioning

Gilpin and Murphy (2006: 388) describe scenario planning as an exercise that encourages managers to think differently and imagine a situation in great detail, "turning it into a sort of future narrative". It is "essentially a way of encouraging executives to leave behind assumptions that normally go unquestioned as a means of learning through mental exploration" (p. 389). Working through different scenarios can demonstrate where there may be holes in the suite of supporting material; or it may even show that a desired positioning is not available to the practitioner's organization or client at a point in time.

For example, the practitioners working for the newspaper company might work through a range of possible scenarios in terms of responding to readers angrily positioning the company as being greedy. Parrott (2003) suggests that there are strategies such as denial and counter-attack, asserting a justification, joining in the anger, admitting to a lesser charge and relabeling emotions, all of which can challenge the moral order that is said to be in operation by other parties to the public relations episode.

Possible scenarios and responses by the newspaper company include:

- Company accepts readers' positioning and accepts blame, expresses shame at having treated its readers badly and apologizes to the readers. The company then has the duty to back down from the introduction of charges.
- Company accepts readers' positioning however rather than expressing shame and accepting blame, the company states it has mismanaged that particular situation and admits a "lesser type of wrongdoing by expressing embarrassment rather than shame" (Parrott, 2003: 34). Such positioning would impose the duty on the company to back down from introducing charges for content but without the weight of the former positioning.
- Company rejects readers' positioning and expresses anger at readers for making false accusations and denies wrongdoing. This is essentially a counter-attack with a counter-emotion; anger is met with counter-anger and the company asserts the right to charge for content.
- Company rejects readers' positioning as being greedy and positions as being proud that the company has managed to offer the free service for as long as it has; anger is countered with pride. Parrott (2003) would argue that the expression of pride contradicts the picture of the moral order implicit in the readers' positioning of the company as greedy. With such a positioning effort the company paints the picture of having been overly-generous for too long and that it now has the right to charge readers for content.
- Company rejects readers' positioning as being greedy but joins readers in their anger by positioning a third party as being blameworthy. The company then has a duty to identify those at fault, e.g. maybe advertisers have withdrawn support or the government has mismanaged the economy.
- Company rejects readers' positioning as being greedy by reinterpreting anger at charges being introduced as not actually being about people being angry but being resistant to change, perhaps more irritated than angry. Parrott (2003) writes how the positioning of irritation rather than anger "construes the situation as one of personal idiosyncrasy rather than of objective wrongdoing" (p. 36). In such positioning the company would assert the right to charge for content.

It is clear that in conveying a different interpretation of events the company is able to position more favorably than the way that was implicit in the readers' positioning. Parrott's (2003) work on positioning and the role of emotions shows how communication practitioners could increase the rhetorical effectiveness of their positioning efforts. Such efforts carry with them significant ethical implications and raise questions about power in positioning strategy. This will be explored later in this chapter.

Social norms and cultural rules are not always fully known in positioning encounters and the moral order needs to be established in dynamic time, as was evident in the newspaper example. This can be seen when a new organization enters a market, a new activist group appears on the scene, or perhaps when a program is being introduced into a new country or culture. By examining such encounters using positioning theory, we can consider how the moral order is established, what factors enable or constrain actions by involved parties, and what rights and duties are claimed and asserted.

Many public relations situations can come about through debates regarding rights and duties. A mining company might have legally acquired the right to mine an area but the local community might assert that the company does not have the right to mine. A health department can state that people have a duty to be immunized against whooping cough disease but a group of people might assert that they do not have such a duty. A debate centered on rights and duties was evident in an analysis of the campaign to enshrine no smoking in eating establishments in Colorado state law (Stokes and Rubin, 2010). The researchers used "rhetorical criticism" (p. 32) to analyze the language used in 500 documents retrieved from the Tobacco Archive and 300 documents made available through the GASP organization, in order to explore "the dominant themes and ways that each group's interests were served by discourse" (p. 32). The analysis of the documents side by side revealed "patterns of Phillip Morris thrusts apperceived and then thwarted by an activist parry" (Stokes and Rubin, 2010: 34).

In the campaign, each side was reported as having attempted to form symmetrical relationships with three key publics that supported their particular arguments, but having maintained an adversarial relationship with each other. Each strategy showed "the organizations working to respond to what each public might find important" but evincing "a clear effort to not change goals or behaviors in light of their adversary's position" (p. 35). Both sides developed messages that tried to align with the core values of Colorado residents. According to Stokes and Rubin (2010), Phillip Morris drove personal liberty and autonomy themes and GASP drove home citizens' rights to breathe clean air, emphasizing that they didn't object to smokers but did object to the smoke.

Both sides worked with their internal audiences to prepare them to defend against arguments from the opponent, essentially against the efforts of the other side to reposition them. The dispute's focus was firmly on rights and duties of various parties to the conflict: the right to smoke, the right not to inhale secondary smoke, the right to eat in a smoke-free environment, the right of eating establishment owners to run their businesses, the duties of employers to provide safe workplaces, the duty of smokers to not inflict their smoke on others and so on. It centered on the exercise of power, and which side could wield sufficient power to position their arguments, influence and potential consequences of legislators' decisions.

Positioning and legitimacy

Gregory and White (2008) identified that organizations have a key role to play at the societal level. Gregory (2013) says that,

> it is at this level that organisations strive to obtain and maintain their legitimacy or "license to operate" by seeking the approval of society as a whole for their operations (what they do) and activities (how they do what they do). At this level, organisations attempt to determine their purpose and place in the world and whether their endeavours will gain support.
>
> (Gregory, 2013: 83–4)

According to Slocum-Bradley (2008), "'legitimacy' is often treated as something that people, institutions, organizations or regimes 'have' or do not 'have'" and that it is a concept that is used by people to achieve social tasks (p. 209). Drawing on Slocum-Bradley's work, the legitimization/de-legitimization of parties in public relations episodes can occur through the attribution/withholding of rights and duties in a specific context:

> Actors also can be legitimized when positioned as having properly fulfilled the duties attributed to them. In the same vein, actors are de-legitimized when positioned as having failed to fulfill duties attributed to them.
>
> (Slocum-Bradley, 2008: 210)

For example, when an activist group positions farmers who allow miners onto their land as "selling out" and says they should lock out mining company representatives, the group is attributing to the farmers the duty to lock out the miners. The group can be seen to be attempting to de-legitimize both the action of allowing miners onto farms as well as the farmers who have allowed this to happen. Another example would be when health department spokespeople position parents who are seeking homeopathic immunization as placing their children at risk. The parents are being accused of not fulfilling their duty to their children and society. The department is thus de-legitimizing the action of getting homeopathic immunization as well as the parents who have taken such action. The department states that the parents should be using conventional medical immunization, and in doing so is attributing to parents the duty of seeking conventional medical immunization.

Attributing actors with the right or duty to act in such a way legitimizes actions in public relations episodes. An organization that is the victim of an attack on its reputation has the right to defend itself. Thus, insofar as the organization's action, e.g. issuing a strongly worded statement pointing out the errors in fact, is defined as a speech act (assertive) of "setting the record straight", then the organization's actions would have been legitimized. These examples highlight the importance of meaning construction in the processes of legitimization and de-legitimization in positioning contexts.

Positioning theory and power

A discussion of the power to position oneself or others, to exercise power to resist being positioned or to examine power relations between those in positioning situations could fill a tome in its own right. What power? Whose power? Positioning of others can be done with or without their consent and it is evident that social power is salient in many positioning encounters (Moghaddam, Harré and Lee, 2008: 10). As stated by Heath, Motion and Leitch (2010), "whether by dialogue or monologue, meaning is created and influences society as it defines power resources that are enacted at individual, organizational and societal levels" (p. 190). As positions are discursively constructed, the social construction of meaning can be seen to be central to the discussion of power and positioning:

> The rationale for power arises from meaning by which individuals, organizations, and societies variously and collectively manage relationships and risks. At its best, public relations creates community power resources that empower individual and organizational efficiency, not frustrate it.
>
> (Heath, Motion and Leitch, 2010: 192)

Power resources can be defined as social constructions, for example: interpretations of fact, evaluation, policy, and systems/relationships; as ultimate terms, they form the basis of identification and define the nature and quality of relationships (Heath, Motion and Leitch, 2010; Smudde and Courtright, 2010). In strategic intentional positioning, an organization implements the position that it is taking (or assigning to another) in the best way possible to achieve the desired outcome. In this way, practitioners seek on behalf of employers and clients to define through discursive positioning such things as situations, entities, value premises and social norms, even ways of thinking and acting. In this way practitioners and organizations attempt to wield power (Heath, Motion and Leitch, 2010). This is not necessarily a good or bad thing but it must be recognized for what it is. As Heath, Motion and Leitch (2010) state, "the strategic use of power and the end to which it is used determine whether it is positive or negative" (p. 195).

An example of what most people would consider a negative use of power would be in situations of unilateral positioning or "malignant or malevolent positioning" (Harré and Moghaddam, 2003: 6). This is when someone, a group of people, or an entity is somehow unable to effectively challenge, or indeed challenge at all, the positioning that another has assigned to them. Harré and Moghaddam, (2003: 6) call this "immoral" positioning. Sabat (2003) writes how initial malignant positioning can serve as the basis for subsequent storylines that resonate with, and reinforce, the original positioning. This makes it increasingly difficult for those being malevolently positioned to resist such efforts. Waymer's (2013) discussion of "non-voluntary publics" in public relations is a case in point where positioning theory's application might be one way of exposing public relations strategies that are seeking to develop relationships with those who would rather keep at a distance. This is "especially if these publics have a history of being manipulated, lied to, and/or taken advantage of, by the organization that is trying to foster a mutually beneficial relationship with them" (Waymer, 2013: 11).

The power differential between organizations and their publics has been at the crux of considerations of power and public relations for many years. Although some argue that dialogic or symmetrical two-way communication can address such differentials (e.g. Waymer and Ni, 2009), there are many circumstances where this does not work as "power derives from the ability to name and claim a sense of reality that is adopted and enacted by others" (Heath, Motion and Leitch, 2010: 197). In positioning episodes, the dynamic interplay of an organization seeking to position itself and others, while others try to reposition themselves or others, is essentially a power play. Organizations, audiences, publics and the local moral order in these situations play a role in the social construction of meanings as positions are being enacted in various contexts. At times such roles are collaborative and at other times they are competitive. Viewed from a discourse perspective, it can be seen that these are the situations in which power occurs within organizations and among constituents (Heath, Motion and Leitch, 2010). The work of Smudde and Courtright (2010) is helpful in teasing out this concept further. In public relations, power can be seen as something that is exercised through relationships, as there is no power inherent in something called public relations (Smudde and Courtright, 2010). However, in a positioning context, there may be no actual relationship with another entity as commonly understood.

An organization could be seeking to position a competitor organization in a particular way but, as there may be no lines of communication between the two organizations, the relationship is more abstract. Two project home building companies may relate to one another through a market, or in another example, a range of political organizations may relate through an electoral system. There are still "relations" between such entities, but not necessarily "relationships" involving dialogue of any type. The idea of relationship management as a central tenet to public relations does not hold up in these kinds of strategic positioning contexts. So in a positioning context, power can be exercised through such relations but there will be instances when an entity will never seek out communication of any sort with the organization it is trying to position (or resist being positioned by). Smudde and Courtright state:

> We believe power is a community-based phenomenon that people confer on each other through their relationships with one another based on hierarchical positions they hold, the rhetorical manifestation and recognition of relationships and positions through communicative acts, and the social implications these dimensions have on individual and, especially communal views of the system of relationships that exist and evolve between people.
>
> (Smudde and Courtright, 2010: 177)

Such a view is helpful for conceptualizing how power operates in public relations positioning, especially when viewing it from an organizational perspective. This is where critical scholarship can assist in gaining a more comprehensive view of the way positioning can work to wield power or to deny power to some groups in society, as such scholarship attempts to "unveil the hidden powers that alienate and marginalize portions of society" (Heath, 2009: 15). This next section will provide an overview of issues to be considered in public relations positioning through the three dimensions of power suggested by Smudde and Courtright: hierarchical, rhetorical and social (2010).

The hierarchical dimension of power in public relations positioning

In organizations there are hierarchies of power based on rank and position within the organization that relate to abilities to control people and their actions, to exercise authority, and also to dominate or oppress. Such power is at the center of political dynamics within an organization and, in the positioning context, relates to the organizational structure. For practitioners, the question of whether they are situated within the hierarchy and whether they can influence and inform decision-making is paramount (Grunig, 1992). Does a senior practitioner inform the decisions made about how positioning strategy is to be developed and implemented? Or does the decision on the positioning strategy simply get relayed to the practitioner for implementation?

It is suggested that organizations will value public relations management more if practitioners operate with greater levels of business acumen and in roles where they provide strategic counsel to senior managers (Arthur W. Page Society, 2007, cited in Smudde and Courtright, 2010; Lukaszewski, 2010). One way of operating more strategically within an organization is for practitioners to apply the positioning approach to public relations situations. By doing so practitioners can demonstrate an understanding of strategy by way of scenario planning, recognizing patterns as they emerge in dynamic environments, advising on the management of issues and applying action to address challenges. These are all part of Lukaszewski's (2010) vision for professional communicators.

The rhetorical dimension of power in public relations positioning

When public relations practitioners use language, symbols, knowledge, and discourse to create or influence the construction of meaning, this is where power and rhetoric intersect. According to Smudde and Courtright (2010) the rhetorical dimension of power can be associated with manipulative motives and negative associations such as "deception, lying, or even spin" or "on positive or neutral grounds…[and] is best associated with persuasion, results and influence" (p. 179). They declare that "at the intersection of rhetoric and power is choice" (p. 179) and, although they draw on the work of Heath, who argued that rhetoric was ethical in that it enabled people to engage in public or private dialogue, and that power intersected other choices (2000), Smudde and Courtright do not make it clear what is meant by choice. Organizations have a choice in whether they engage in public relations management activities; they have a choice in the nature of strategies and tactics employed; they have a choice in who they appoint to manage such activities; the practitioners engaged have a choice in the options presented to management, and so on.

The use of rhetoric by practitioners, which Mayhew (1997: 267) defines as "the means of creating and activating influence" by employing "systems of linguistic and visual meaning to evoke solidary attachments", aims to have targeted publics and audiences construct the meaning that the organization would like them to construct (James, 2009). The use of rhetoric and the construction of "zones of meaning" (Berger and Luckmann, 1966: 55; Heath, 2001: 45) through positioning, and techniques such as priming and framing (Hallahan, 1999), aims to make it as easy as possible for targeted publics and audiences to co-create the meaning intended by the organization. Although such techniques are all part of positioning techniques, it is the social force of speech-acts that is central to positioning theory. This is because by using speech-acts such as assertions, expressives, commitments and so on, practitioners draw on the power of words and images to change (or at times maintain) the way an aspect of the world is socially constructed.

The social dimension of power in public relations positioning

This third dimension concerns the relationships people have with one another, both within societies and organizations, and it can be seen that it articulates with the hierarchical and rhetorical dimensions. Smudde and Courtright (2010: 180) state that ethical considerations are inherent in this social dimension, specifically that "people accept and abide by rules of individual and collective good thinking and behavior". This can be seen to relate to positioning theory's concept of the local moral order and relates to public relations in the frequent situations where there is social conflict over positions taken and assigned:

> The final goal of applying positioning theory in disputes, according to Harré and Slocum (2003), is to identify who does and does not possess positioning power, the basis on which the power is allocated, and the role of differences in positioning power in the conflict (e.g. in making certain story lines more dominant). Dispute resolution is proposed to occur with new story lines that remake the local moral order and create a discursive space for a new norm to allow both parties to satisfy their long-term goals. Perhaps a key insight of positioning theory is that a new position will be viable to the extent it is embedded in a mutually acceptable story line.
>
> (Louis, 2008: 30)

The practitioner applying the Framework for Intentional Positioning in Public Relations will interpret the local moral order and use this interpretation to analyze the rights and duties associated with various positioning options that could be open to an organization. Once this analysis is undertaken, the practitioner can identify what storylines are open to the organization, given the position it is taking. Does the organization have the right to use the storyline? Does the organization have the social power to promulgate the storyline to support the positioning? Is there a mutually acceptable storyline? Drawing on the work of Meadows (2009) it can be understood that any position taken, or assigned to another, is in turn symbolically linked to the constructed social order and thus, from a positioning theoretical stance, enables the entity exercising the positioning power the affordances associated with that position.

Positioning, power and public relations

Public relations management is about wielding power, however defined. When public relations is viewed as the strategic creation and management of shared meanings by participants in unfolding situations, in order to forward the mission of the organization, it could not be otherwise. For instance when a company determines a position to be enacted on an issue, ideally it wants publics and audiences to come to a point where they support the position. This may involve the organization using communication methods to expand the repertoire of meanings available for a particular public or audience. One example seen in countries across the world including Australia, Canada, China, Russia and USA (World Coal Association, 2013) is the contested practice of what is known as coal seam gas (CSG) or coalbed methane extraction. When one thinks back a few years these terms were not heard outside specialist industrial circles but there is little doubt now that "the CSG issue is fundamentally a political issue" (Jaques and Galloway, 2012: 43).

With the quest for affordable energy, companies began a mission to extract gas from the coal seams below relatively small areas of privately owned land in countries across the world. From a positioning theoretical perspective it can be seen that the repertoire of meanings for those landowners was viewed by companies and government regulators as needing to be expanded. Subsequently, information was prepared to educate, inform and in some cases to persuade. Publics who were concerned about coal seam gas extraction formed and, in time, began to again expand the repertoire of available meanings for landowners, pointing out problems such as environmental and health impacts. The positions taken were essentially polar opposites and both sides of the issue sought to secure understanding, support and endorsement of their positions from third parties such as scientists, government regulators, individual politicians, celebrities and so on.

Taking Smudde and Courtright's (2010) three types of power it is evident that in such cases all parties are exercising hierarchical, social and rhetorical power. The mix of what types of power are being exercised may differ depending on a number of factors. These include the nature of formal and informal connections to government officials, politicians, media owners, individual journalists and so on. Many seasoned practitioners have seen unofficial channels being used, such as old school connections, family and friend connections, favors owing, religious affiliations and club membership favoritism. The mix of power types may differ over time. As different stages of the situation are reached more emphasis may be placed by either side on mobilizing social power or augmenting the use of rhetorical power; the 2010 film *Gasland* is a case in point. Coal seam gas proponents have found it difficult to surmount the power in the imagery of a household water tap emitting sufficient gas to create a flame. It seems that the lifelong political connections of project proponents and investors did not have as much power as the positioning enactment tactic of filming the lighting of a water tap.

Attempts to strategically construct a version of social reality through strategic positioning for the purposes of achieving an organization's mission, whatever that mission may be, is an attempt to wield power. Public relations activities, whatever their aims, are strategic acts that can be seen as attempts "to exert power and control over the organizational environment" (Holtzhausen, 2002: 255). Public relations practitioners wield power by way of working for organizations or causes that are intrinsically partisan and that exert social forces, whether negatively or positively, on the citizenry of wherever they are implemented. As Demetrious (2013) states, "public relations manufactures discourse to control and manipulate the meaning making process" (p. 28) and, as such, "the analysis of the social apparatus of public relations and its effects…needs greater attention" (p. 31). The means with which to undertake such an exercise may include the application of positioning theory to analyze specific public relations episodes and the wider "social apparatus". With its focus on rights, duties and obligations the theory has the capacity to move public relations research and practice into new areas, and to provide stronger links to the communication disciplines and other areas of scholarly inquiry.

Summary

This chapter expanded upon the concept of rights and duties that is at the center of positioning theory. It highlighted how rights and duties relate to the idea of the local moral order and the way power has been wielded in public relations episodes. The fact that definitions of public relations remain fluid was raised as an issue in terms of discussing power and positioning, as the way power can be conceptualized depends on one's definition of public relations. The relation of the ideas in positioning theory including rights and duties and the concept of the local moral order was explored through the work of Bourdieu, especially the concepts of "habitus" and "field". It is clear that this provides a fertile area for further research. Such research is only just beginning to emerge in the wider areas in which positioning theory is being applied.

Positioning power was explored through the three types of power in public relations as proposed by Smudde and Courtright (2010), namely hierarchical, rhetorical and social power. The example of positioning efforts by both those who are pro- and anti- extraction of gas from coal seams was given as a way of explicating how the forces between different types of power are exerted by different interest groups. These ideas are explored further in the next chapter through the Framework for Intentional Positioning in Public Relations.

References

Berger, B. (1999) The Halcion affair: public relations and the construction of ideological world view. *Journal of Public Relations Research*, 11(3): 185–203.

Berger, P. and Luckmann, T. (1966) *The Social Construction of Reality: A treatise in the sociology of knowledge.* London: Penguin.

Bourdieu, P. (1984) *Distinction: A social critique of the judgment of taste.* Cambridge, MA: Harvard University Press.

Bourdieu, P. (1990) *The Logic of Practice*. Stanford: Stanford University Press.

Bourdieu, P. (1991) *Language and Symbolic Power*. Cambridge: Polity Press.

Bourdieu, P. (1993a) *The Field of Cultural Production*. New York: Columbia University Press.

Bourdieu, P. (1993b) Haute couture and haute culture. In P. Bourdieu (ed.) *Sociology in Question*. London: Sage, pp. 132–9.

Chen, N. and Culbertson, H. M. (2003) Public relations in mainland China: an adolescent with growing pains. *The Global Public Relations Handbook*, 23–45.

Curtin, P. A. and Gaither, T. K. (2007) *International Public Relations: Negotiating culture, identity, and power*. New York: Sage.

Demetrious, K. (2013) *Public Relations, Activism, and Social Change: Speaking up*. New York: Routledge.

Galloway, C. J. (2013) Deliver us from definitions: a fresh way of looking at public relations. *Public Relations Inquiry*, 2(2): 147–59.

Gilpin, D., and Murphy, P. (2006) Reframing crisis management through complexity. *Public Relations Theory II*, 329–44.

Gregory, A. (2013) Corporate reputation and the discipline of communication management. In C. Carroll (ed.) *The Handbook of Communication and Corporate Reputation*, (Volume 49 of Handbooks in communication and media). Chichester, UK: John Wiley and Sons, pp. 81–93.

Gregory, A., and White, J. (2008) Introducing the Chartered Institute of Public Relations initiative. In B. van Ruler, A. Verčič and D. Verčič, (eds) *Public Relations Metrics: Research and evaluation*. Thousand Oaks, CA: Sage, pp. 307–17.

Grunig, L. A. (1992) Strategic public relations constituencies on a global scale. *Public Relations Review*, 18, 127–36.

Grunig, J. (2006) Furnishing the edifice: ongoing research on public relations as a strategic management function. *Journal of Public Relations Research*, 18(2): 151–76.

Hallahan, K. (1999) Seven models of framing: implications for public relations. *Journal of Public Relations Research*, 11(3): 205–42.

Hallahan, K., Holtzhausen, D., van Ruler, B., Verčič, D., and Sriramesh, K. (2007) Defining strategic communication. *International Journal of Strategic Communication*, 1(1): 3–35.

Harré, R. (2012) Positioning theory: moral dimensions of social-cultural psychology. In J. Valsiner (ed.) *The Oxford Handbook of Culture and Psychology*. New York: Oxford University, pp. 191–206.

Harré, R. and Moghaddam, F. (2003) Introduction: the self and others in traditional psychology and in positioning theory. In R. Harré and F. Moghaddam (eds) *The self and Others: Positioning individuals and groups in personal, political and cultural contexts*. London: Praeger, pp. 1–11.

Harré, R. and Slocum, N. (2003) Disputes as complex social events: on the uses of positioning theory. In R. Harré and F. Moghaddam (eds) *The self and Others: Positioning individuals and groups in personal, political and cultural contexts*. London: Praeger, pp. 123–36.

Heath, R. (2000) A rhetorical perspective on the values of public relations: crossroads and pathways towards concurrence. *Journal of Public Relations Research*. 12(1): 69–91.

Heath, R. (2001) A rhetorical enactment rationale for public relations: the good organization communicating well. In R. Heath (ed.) *The Sage Handbook of Public Relations*. Thousand Oaks, CA: Sage, pp. 441–4.

Heath, R. (2009) Introduction. In R. Heath, E. Toth and D. Waymer (eds) *Rhetorical and Critical Approaches to Public Relations II*. New York: Routledge, pp. 1–12.
Heath, R., Motion, J. and Leitch, S. (2010) Power and public relations: paradoxes and programmatic thoughts. In R. Heath (ed.) *The Sage Handbook of Public Relations*. Thousand Oaks, CA: Sage, pp. 191–204.
Holtzhausen, D. (2002) Towards a postmodern research agenda for public relations. *Public Relations Review*, 28, 251–64.
Ihlen, O. (2005) The power of social capital: adapting Bourdieu to the study of public relations. *Public Relations Review*, 31(4): 492–6.
James, M. (2009) Getting to the heart of public relations: the concept of strategic intent. *Asia Pacific Public Relations Journal*, 10, 109–122.
Jaques, T. (2008) A case study approach to issue and crisis management: schadenfreude or an opportunity to learn? *Journal of Communication Management*, 12, 192–203.
Jaques, T. (2009) Issue and crisis management: quicksand in the definitional landscape. *Public Relations Review*, 35(3): 280–6.
Jaques, T. and Galloway, C. (2012) Coal seam gas in Australia: can activists be effective from the margins? *Asia Pacific Public Relations Journal*, 13(2): 35–44.
King, C. (2010) Emergent communication strategies. *International Journal of Strategic Communication*, 4(1): 19–38.
L'Etang, J. (2006) Public relations and propaganda: conceptual issues, methodological problems, and public relations discourse. In J. L'Etang and M. Pieczka (eds) *Public Relations: Critical debates and contemporary practice*. Mahwah, NJ: Lawrence Erlbaum, pp. 23–40.
Louis, W. (2008) Intergroup positioning and power. In F. Moghaddam, R. Harré, and N. Lee, (eds) *Global Conflict Resolution through Positioning Analysis*. New York: Springer, pp. 21–40.
Lukaszewski, J. E. (2010) *Why Should the Boss Listen to You: The seven disciplines of the trusted strategic advisor* (Vol. 13). San Francisco: John Wiley and Sons.
McDonald, L. (2008) Identity crisis: the changing functions of public relations. Paper presented to *15th BledCom: Public Relations and Marketing: A relationship for re-examination?* Retrieved from www.bledcom.com/uploads/papers08/Identity_crisis.pdf
Mayhew, L. (1997) *The New Public: Professional communication and the means of public influence*. Cambridge: Cambridge University Press.
Meadows, B. (2009) Capital negotiation and identity practices: investigating symbolic capital from the "ground up", *Critical Discourse Studies*, 6(1): 15–30. doi: 10.1080/17405900802560025
Moghaddam, F., Hanley, E. and Harré, R. (2003) Sustaining intergroup harmony: an analysis of the Kissinger papers through positioning theory. In R. Harré and F. Moghaddam (eds) *The self and Others: Positioning individuals and groups in personal, political and cultural contexts*. London: Praeger, pp. 123–36.
Moghaddam, F. and Harré, R. (2010) Words, conflicts and political processes. In F. Moghaddam and R. Harré (eds) *Words of Conflict, Words of War: How the language we use in political processes sparks fighting*. Santa Barbara, CA.: Praeger.
Moghaddam, F., Harré, R. and Lee, N. (2008) Positioning and conflict: an introduction. In F. Moghaddam, R. Harré, and N. Lee, (eds) *Global Conflict Resolution through Positioning Analysis*. New York: Springer, pp. 3–20.
Moghaddam, F. and Kavulich, K. (2008) Nuclear positioning and supererogatory duties. In F. Moghaddam, R. Harré, and N. Lee, (eds) *Global Conflict Resolution through Positioning Analysis*. New York: Springer, pp. 247–60.

Moloney, K. (2006) *Rethinking Public Relations* (2nd edn). London: Routledge.

Parmentier, M., Fischer, E. and Reuber, A. (2013) Positioning person brands in established organizational fields. *Academy of Marketing Science*, 41(3): 373–87.

Parrott, W. (2003) Positioning and the emotions. In R. Harré and F. Moghaddam (eds) *The self and Others: Positioning individuals and groups in personal, political and cultural contexts*. London: Praeger, pp. 29–43.

Pieczka, M. (2002) Public relations expertise deconstructed. *Media, Culture and Society*, 24, 301–23.

Roper, J. (2005) Organisational identities, identification and positioning: learning from political fields. *Public Relations Review*, 31(1): 139–48.

Rothbart, D. and Bartlett, T. (2008) Rwandan radio broadcasts and Hutu/Tutsi positioning. In F. Moghaddam, R. Harré, and N. Lee, (eds) *Global Conflict Resolution through Positioning Analysis*. New York: Springer, pp. 227–46.

Sabat, S. (2003) Malignant positioning and the predicament of people with Alzheimer's disease. In R. Harré and F. Moghaddam (eds) *The self and Others: Positioning individuals and groups in personal, political and cultural contexts*. London: Praeger, pp. 83–98.

Slocum-Bradley, N. (2008) Discursive production of conflict in Rwanda. In F. Moghaddam, R. Harré and N. Lee (eds) *Global Conflict Resolution through Positioning Analysis*. New York: Springer, pp. 207–26.

Smith, J. (2008) *Normative Theory and Business Ethics*. Lanham, MD: Rowman and Littlefield.

Smudde, P. M. and Courtright, J. L. (2010) Public relations and power. In R. Heath (ed.) *The Sage Handbook of Public Relations*. Thousand Oaks, CA: Sage, pp. 177–89.

Stokes, A. and Rubin, D. (2010) Activism and the limits of symmetry: the public relations battle between Colorado GASP and Philip Morris. *Journal of Public Relations Research*, 22(1): 26–48.

Toth, E. (2009) Pluralistic Studies of Public Relations. In R. Heath, E. Toth and D. Waymer (eds) *Rhetorical and Critical Approaches to Public Relations II*. New York: Routledge, p. 48–60.

Waymer, D. (2013) Democracy and government public relations: expanding the scope of "relationship" in public relations research. *Public Relations Review*, 39(4), 320–31. http://dx.doi.org/10.1016/j.pubrev.2013.07.015

Waymer, D. and Ni, L. (2009) Connecting organizations and their employee publics: the rhetorical analysis of employee–organization relations (EOR). In R. Heath, E. Toth and D. Waymer (eds) *Rhetorical and Critical Approaches to Public Relations II*. New York: Routledge, pp. 216–32.

Weaver, C., Motion, J. and Roper, J. (2006) From propaganda to discourse (and back again): truth, power and the public interest, and public relations. In J. L'Etang and M. Pieczka (eds) *Public Relations: Critical debates and contemporary practice*. Mahwah, NJ: Lawrence Erlbaum, pp. 7–22.

World Coal Association (2013) Coal seam methane. Retrieved 12 June 2013 from www.worldcoal.org/coal/coal-seam-methane/coal-bed-methane/

3 A framework for intentional positioning in public relations

In the absence of a specific organizing framework for positioning in public relations, between 2009 and 2011, a provisional conceptual framework for intentional positioning in public relations was developed (James, 2011a). This task was undertaken because having a conceptual framework is potentially useful (Smyth, 2004) as: a) a tool to scaffold research, or, b) as a tool for program planning. A framework can assist researchers to make meaning of subsequent findings and can guide practitioners to consider strategic aspects of positioning programs. It was intended to be a starting point for reflection about positioning in a public relations context. Application of the framework was intended to assist in developing awareness and understanding of the positioning situation under scrutiny.

A specific framework was needed as positioning theorists "have treated talk in interaction as key to the process whereby positioning is accomplished" (Wilkinson and Kitzinger, 2003: 158). However, research (James, 2011a) indicated that in a public relations context, "talk in interaction" was not "key". The framework's development centered on adding a strategic communication dimension. The focus of strategic communication is on

> how an organization communicates across organizational endeavors. The emphasis is on the strategic application of communication and how an organization functions as a social actor to advance its mission. The purposeful nature of strategic communication is critical... strategic communication focuses on how the organization itself presents and promotes itself through the intentional activities of its leaders, employees, and communication practitioners. Of course, this does not exclude their use of relationship building or networks in the strategic process.
>
> (Hallahan, Holtzhausen, van Ruler, Verčič and Sriramesh, 2007: 7)

As such, the framework adds three specific domains to the positioning triangle originally put forward by van Langenhove and Harré in 1999 to accommodate the strategic communication that is central to public relations (Moloney, 2006). The provisional status of the framework was intentional, a way of positioning it as something innovative but not yet complete. It could be argued from a positioning theoretical perspective that at this time I did not have the right to position the framework as anything other than provisional. The work underpinning the framework's development was substantive but not all encompassing. Attempts to position it as something else, e.g. some kind of solution to all of the theoretical problems encountered in public relations, would have been seen as absurd.

In public relations, positioning efforts or responses to the positioning efforts of others are intentional in nature, and are undertaken to achieve some kind of outcome. Hence I added the "positioning goal domain". The idea in public relations that positioning is intentional and goal-directed led to the examination of the nature of positioning as reported by high-level practitioners. There were clearly different types of positioning happening in practice and these formed the basis of the "positioning type domain". The four types of intentional positioning were identified and discussed by van Langenhove and Harré (1999: 23–8) but placing these within the framework adds the strategic context of public relations practice. In this domain we can identify that organizations can deliberately position themselves, can deliberately position others, can be forced into positioning themselves and can be forced into positioning others. Evidence of these four types of positioning can be seen in accounts of practice from across the world.

In the provisional conceptual framework a third domain was identified, that of positioning purpose. However, having worked since 2009 at testing the framework using primarily qualitative research, as both a tool to guide positioning analysis in strategic communication or public relations contexts, and as an heuristic to guide the design of positioning programs for organizations (e.g. James, 2010, 2011a, 2012), something wasn't working consistently in this domain but it was proving hard to pin down. During 2013, when I started on a program of testing the rigor of the framework from a qualitative and quantitative coding perspective with research assistants, Dr Maulina Pia Wulandari and Ms Deborah Wise, this was one area where we kept seeing an issue. It was the synergistic alignment of attending stimulating academic conferences in mid-2013 (e.g. ICA in London, IAMCR in Dublin, Barcelona PR Meeting), spending my spare time combing through copious data and coding sheets, and immersing myself in my analytic and writing work whilst overlooking the Mediterranean Sea that helped me resolve this problematic domain. It was not about positioning purpose. It was, in line with the strategic context of public relations work, about undertaking strategic pre-positioning through the attribution of characteristics to the self or others prior to the actual positioning activity. This aligned to the concept of pre-positioning that has emerged in positioning theory in recent years and is now regarded as "the first phase" of a "positioning act" (Moghaddam and Harré, 2010: 9). The third domain of the positioning framework is now known as the "strategic pre-positioning domain".

This leads straight into the first vertex of the positioning triangle domain. The framework works in two ways, firstly to guide positioning program development and, secondly, to analyze positioning strategies that have happened in the past or that are unfolding in real time. In applying the framework as a diagnostic tool to analyze past practice, it is most helpful to first analyze storylines (which are part of the positioning triangle domain) and work through to identify the positioning goal of an organization. Such a goal may not be evident when first examining key messages of a campaign, but by working through the framework domain by domain, it becomes clear. For positioning analysis purposes the framework looks like Table 3.1.

In applying the framework as a guide to designing a communication program or campaign, it is most helpful to begin with the goal of the exercise and work through each domain until the process concludes with the positioning triangle domain (see Table 3.2). At this point, the position to be taken or assigned is determined, the way it will be enacted decided upon and the supporting storylines will be developed, most probably in the form of key messages that will weave through the various communication forms and channels. From here, scenario planning that works through the application of the proposed positioning strategy can be undertaken to identify areas that need to be adjusted before presentation and implementation.

A closer look at the framework

The positioning goal domain

This domain of the framework is that of intentional positioning being related to the desire to achieve a specific goal. From a program design perspective, if there were no clear goal, it would be pointless to expend resources on positioning. From a research perspective, determining the underlying positioning goal of past or current communication practice may be the very point of undertaking a positioning

Table 3.1 The framework for intentional positioning in public relations

<table>
<tr><td colspan="12">Positioning triangle domain</td></tr>
<tr><td colspan="4">Evidence of first positioning triangle vertex of position, i.e. entity's point of view of its own and stakeholders' actual and potential positions e.g. determine the desired position</td><td colspan="4">Evidence of second positioning triangle vertex of speech act/ action, i.e. language/ action used to achieve an specific consequence or outcome e.g. enact the desired position</td><td colspan="4">Evidence of the third positioning triangle vertex of storyline i.e. a storyline that the entity has chosen to promulgate through it public relations activities e.g. construct meaning through storylines about the position enacted</td></tr>
<tr><td colspan="12">Strategic pre-positioning domain</td></tr>
<tr><td colspan="12">Evidence of the attribution of qualities of character, intellect, or temperament, of the person/entity/organization in question.</td></tr>
<tr><td colspan="12">Positioning type domain</td></tr>
<tr><td colspan="3">Evidence of situations of deliberate self positioning</td><td colspan="3">Evidence of situations of forced self positioning</td><td colspan="3">Evidence of situations of deliberate positioning of others</td><td colspan="3">Evidence of situations of forced positioning of others</td></tr>
<tr><td colspan="12">Positioning goal domain</td></tr>
<tr><td colspan="12">Evidence of intended positioning related to a desire to achieve a specific goal</td></tr>
</table>

Table 3.2 Public relations positioning framework for positioning program design

Positioning goal domain			
Determine the specific goal to be achieved by intentional positioning			
Positioning type domain			
A situation of deliberate self positioning	A situation of forced self positioning	A situation of deliberate positioning of others	A situation of forced positioning of others
Strategic pre-positioning domain			
Identification and attribution of qualities of character, intellect, or temperament, of the person/entity/organization in question.			
Positioning triangle domain			
First positioning triangle vertex of *position*, i.e. entity's point of view of its own and stakeholders' actual and potential positions e.g. determine the desired position	Second positioning triangle vertex of *speech act/action*, i.e. language/action used to achieve an specific consequence or outcome e.g. enact the desired position	Evidence of the third positioning triangle vertex of *storyline* i.e. a storyline that the entity has chosen to promulgate through it public relations activities e.g. construct meaning through storylines about the position enacted	

analysis. The goal may not be immediately apparent however it is through the close analysis of the texts and context of the positioning episode that goals can be identified.

The positioning type domain

The four distinct types of intentional positioning (van Langenhove and Harré, 1999) were brought together as the second domain of the framework – namely:

- situations of deliberate self-positioning;
- situations of forced self-positioning;
- situations of deliberate positioning of others; and
- situations of forced positioning of others.

Within these four distinct forms of intentional positioning, the relevance of each form for public relations is detailed through an explanation and some examples:

Situations of deliberate self positioning: where an organization wishes to take a particular position for a specific reason

For example, where IBM's goal was to "assume a thought leadership position" in order to increase engagement with small- and medium-sized enterprises (Text 100, 2006); when a cancer prevention campaign was conducted to position breast self-examination as a desirable and normal activity amongst local women living in the Arab Emirates (Al Khaja and Creedon, 2010).

Situations of forced self-positioning: where forces outside an organization's immediate control necessitate the organization positions/repositions itself

For example, a positioning campaign by the Saudi Arabian government to restore the tarnished national image of Saudi Arabia in the post-9/11 era (Zhang and Benoit, 2004); where the US National Hockey League (NHL) ran a campaign that would "prod" fans to watch the sport in an effort to position/reposition the game as one worth watching again (Batchelor and Formentin, 2008: 160).

Situations of deliberate positioning of others: situations where an organization deliberately positions/repositions other entities for a specific reason

For example, where in Colorado the anti-smoking organization, GASP, and tobacco company, Phillip Morris, deliberately positioned each other's stance on changes to smoking laws as unacceptable (Stokes and Rubin, 2010).

Situations of forced positioning of others: situations where forces outside an organization's immediate control necessitate the organization position/reposition other entities

For example, when Hillary Clinton and Barack Obama had to position each other as being less worthy of standing for election to the US Presidency due to the nature of the political system in which such decisions are made (Harré and Rossetti, 2010).

This domain helps determine the communication strategy as it indicates whether the positioning campaign is being undertaken proactively or defensively. It can also shed light on the power relations operating in public relations episodes as it facilitates the examination of the organization's power to position itself and others, and also the positioning power being wielded by external entities. This could have implications for practitioners in terms of planning, resourcing and timing.

The strategic pre-positioning domain

The concept of pre-positioning has emerged in positioning theory in recent years and is now regarded as "the first phase" of a "positioning act" (Moghaddam and Harré, 2010: 9). Specifically:

> The first phase involves the attribution of qualities of character, intellect, or temperament, sometimes supported by biographical reports of past behavior of the person in question. In the second phase (positioning in the original sense of Davies and Harré, 1990), the person is assigned or refused a cluster of rights and duties to perform certain kinds of acts, thus constraining what someone, so positioned, can rightly do and say. Both phases presume the existence of a local moral order, a cluster of collectively located beliefs about what it is right and good to do and say,
>
> (Moghaddam and Harré, 2010: 9–10)

and:

> ...the discursive procedure by which a person is positioned as having (or not having) certain rights and duties is initiated and grounded or justified by an act of positioning as in phase 1 – that is, as competent/incompetent, trustworthy/untrustworthy, and so on with respect to performing the type of act in question...In phase 2, assignments to positions – that is, assignments of rights and duties to a person – depend on prior phase 1 evaluative descriptions of that person.
>
> (Moghaddam and Harré, 2010: 10)

This domain of the framework considers the intentional positioning aims to be achieved. The strategic pre-positioning domain draws on positioning theory as described above but also from public relations theory. Specifically, it draws from Berger's (1999) conceptualization of intentional representation and more critical definitions such as "public relations communication can be understood as the strategic attempt to control the agenda of public discussion and the terms in which discussion takes place" (Weaver, Motion and Roper, 2006: 17). This domain is central to the purposive construction of meaning with the strategic intention of an organization achieving its goals.

The positioning triangle domain – a more detailed look

The positioning triangle domain consists largely of the same positioning triangle that was first proposed by van Langenhove and Harré (1999). Harré and van Langenhove (1999: 10) put forward that positioning is underpinned by a mutually determining "positioning triangle" of position (of various actors), act-action (the social force of what is being said and done) and storylines (supporting narratives about things, events or people). They asserted that deliberate intention could be introduced at any of the three vertices of the triangle, and it was this point that was identified as having significant implications for positioning in public relations (James, 2011a). For example, in a public relations context the positioning triangle might look something like this:

- A government department health promotion program decides to adopt a certain position that young adults should not consume alcohol (this is the first vertex of the positioning triangle – position).
- The government department then declares its position by implementing a course of action such as launching a promotional campaign which asserts its aim to discourage alcohol consumption; it may also issue a statement arguing through speech acts, such as assertives, expressives (Searle, 1979) and so on, for a case for changes in legislation (this is the second vertex of the positioning triangle – speech act/action).
- The government department then develops and deliver particular narratives – key messages developed to be told through various channels over a period of

time to targeted publics and audiences (this is the third vertex of the positioning triangle – storylines).

It is the interplay of the three vertices that determines the positioning at any given time. The positioning strategy could potentially be changed at any of the three vertices and this would change the overall positioning. An extreme example for the purposes of demonstrating this interplay would be as follows:

- The government department decides to completely reverse its health promotion program position and now maintains that young adults should regularly consume alcohol (this is the first vertex of the positioning triangle – position).
- Such a change in position necessitates a change in the enactment vertex. The government department then declares its reversed position by implementing a course of action such as launching a promotional campaign designed to encourage alcohol consumption or issuing a statement arguing for a case for changes in legislation to allow this (this is the second vertex of the positioning triangle –speech act/action).
- Obviously, the government department cannot continue to promulgate the originally developed anti-alcohol storylines. It subsequently needs to develop and deliver particular narratives that encourage alcohol consumption by the targeted publics and audiences (this is the third vertex of the positioning triangle – storylines).

This is, as stated, an extreme example but does demonstrate that if one vertex of the positioning triangle changes, the other two vertices also need to change. In a less extreme example, we could look at what would happen to an organization if they were forced to reposition in some way by external forces. In this example, a local bar used to serve alcohol to patrons until 5am on weekends. It had positioned itself as the place to party all night but the bar was forced to change its position due to new legislation that had decreed that no alcohol could be served in such premises after 1am. This external force on the positioning triangle necessitated a change at the point where the positioning was being enacted, that is, the bar was no longer serving alcohol after 1am. It couldn't logically hold the position of being the place to party all night even had it wanted to. It no longer had a right to hold this position because the local moral order in the form of the local legislative authorities had decreed a change. As the speech act/action vertex of the positioning triangle had the bar serving alcohol only until 1am, the position vertex of the triangle changed to one where the bar's position was based on the concept of having fun responsibly.

Subsequently the narratives at the third vertex of the positioning triangle, storylines, also had to change. It would have made no sense to audiences to hear about partying all night when the bar closed at 1 am. As Harré (2006) states:

> The basic principle of analysis is that positions, as open sets of rights and duties, speech and other act categories and story lines are mutually

> determinative. Fixing one vertex of the positioning triangle fixes the other two. Successfully challenging any vertex redefines both of the others.
>
> (Harré, 2006: 230)

One can see that even at the storyline vertex of the positioning triangle, if a storyline was found to be based on untruths, this would necessitate changing not only the storyline but also the organization's actual position and its enactment.

Each vertex of the triangle can be said to mutually define the others – what Harré and van Langenhove (1999) call a "dynamic stability" (p.10). The first positioning triangle vertex is *position*, that is, the organization's point of view of its own and its stakeholders/publics' actual and potential positions. This desired positioning would be informed by research and stakeholder/public analysis informing the public relations activity's design and/or implementation.

The second positioning triangle vertex is *speech act/action*, that is, the organization's course of action chosen from among various possibilities. There is a clear link in this vertex with speech act theory and this is explored further in Chapter 5. Essentially, at this vertex of the triangle, the position is declared and enacted by what is said and/or done (the speech act/action). Speech acts are "intentional, meaningful acts performed with an expression or expressions…out loud, in writing, or 'in one's head'" and they are performed by "both speakers/writers and their audiences (when they understand the speakers/writers)" (Kearns, 1994: 50).

Speech act theory's fundamental tenet is that "all utterances state things but also do things", that is, that "all utterances have a meaning and a force" (Potter and Wetherell, 1987: 17). Austin (1962) referred to this force as the "illocutionary force" but in positioning theory this is primarily referred to as "social force" which

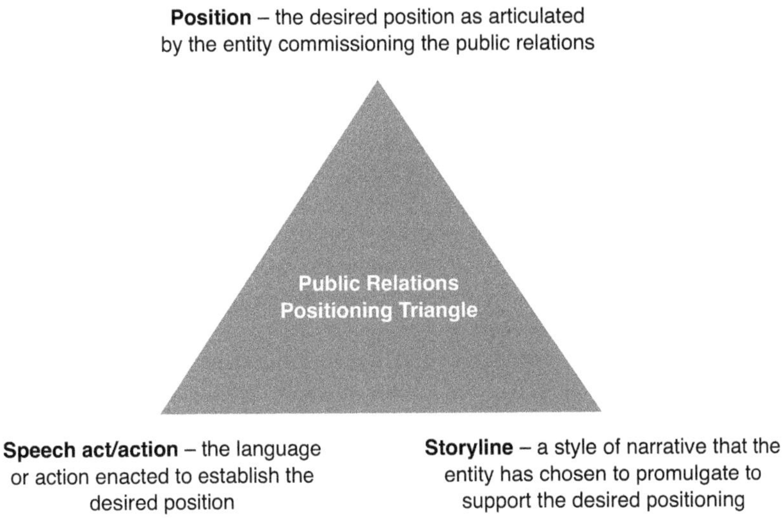

Figure 3.1 Public relations positioning triangle
Source: adapted from van Langenhove and Harré, 1999.

refers to "the context-dependent act that anyone performs by uttering a certain sentence" (Moghaddam, Hanley and Harré, 2003: 141). The most important part of this social force for public relations is the question of what is the point or purpose of what is being said, as Searle (1979: 2) explains:

> The point or purpose of an order can be specified by saying that it is an attempt to get the hearer to do something. The point or purpose of a description is that it is a representation (true or false, accurate or inaccurate) of how something is. The point or purpose of a promise is that it is an undertaking of an obligation by the speaker to do something.

My research has shown that in the context of public relations, what is being said (in speech, through actions and through texts of all types) has a point or purpose, which is to have target publics and audiences co-construct the meaning that practitioners intend for them. Speech acts/actions have the "power to shape certain aspects of the social world" (Harré and van Langenhove, 1999: 6) and are selected by communication practitioners for their abilities to achieve a desired goal or positioning, that is, speech act/actions have a force that is designed to cause a consequence – to inform, to persuade, to promise, to announce, and so on.

It should be noted that public relations practitioners may use or recommend the use of particular speech acts but these are not complete until someone interprets the act as having a social force. For example, an organizational spokesperson may apologise for some mishap that the company has caused. This is a speech act (expressive) that expresses being sorry. However if this apology is not heard, reported, accepted and so on, it has not been successful in exerting any social force. It is through successful, completed speech acts that positioning is enacted and storylines invoked (Slocum-Bradley, 2008).

The third positioning triangle vertex is *storyline*, that is, the storyline that the organization has chosen to promulgate through its communication activities. This is where the organization attempts to construct meaning through storylines about the position it has taken, the position it has been assigned or, the position it has assigned to another. However, the storylines available or invoked are in large part determined by the first two vertices. If, for example, the organization self-positions as being an environmentally responsible organization, the speech act/action would declare this positioning, essentially claiming the space where this meaning would be constructed, that is, a company asserts that it is an environmentally responsible company. This is the speech act.

The storylines available to the organization from these two vertices would be those relating to its positioning as environmentally responsible. To invoke other storylines would undermine the overall positioning strategy and the dynamic stability of the triangle would be disrupted. The storyline is not the narrative itself, which in public relations is often told through key messages delivered through various platforms in paid, earned and owned media. A storyline is essentially a style of narrative that contains firstly, a conventional flow of events and secondly, characters (van Langenhove and Harré, 1999). The communication practitioner plays a role in developing and delivering various narratives that: a) support the desired positioning and b) are consistent with the other two vertices of the positioning triangle, namely, the positioning vertex and the speech act/action vertex.

As narrative has the ability to reach out and connect with audiences, it is effective for engagement with internal and external stakeholders (Gill, 2009). A company that has declared itself to be environmentally responsible has only certain storylines open to it, that is, those that support the desired positioning. To pursue other storylines, e.g. narratives about the pursuit of maximum return to shareholders without due regard for environmental issues, would be incongruent with the positioning triangle and the desired positioning would not be achieved. This links back to the role of key messages in communication campaigns and the importance placed by practitioners on consistent messaging in supporting believability (Bruce and Tini, 2008; James, 2011b).

The issue of who delivers the storyline is also integral to how the overall storylines function in the sphere where meaning is co-constructed by the organization and intended and unintended audiences. It is the position of a particular character or actor in the chosen storyline that will "influence the rights of that actor to position others: an actor who is positioned as authoritative will have greater positioning rights than one who is not" (Slocum-Bradley, 2008: 107). It is clear that this relates to the social licence to operate of the organization that is commissioning the communication activity, but also to the perceived legitimacy of the spokespeople acting on behalf of the organization. The choice of the spokesperson in delivering key messages is regarded as a significant factor by public relations practitioners in message delivery success (James, 2011b). It can be seen that the positioning framework offers further insights as to why this is the case. It relates to the idea of symbolic capital (Bourdieu, 1991), that is, "the sociocultural prestige that lends to certain speakers an aura of authority in particular fields of discourse and before the relevant audience" (Rothbart and Bartlett, 2008: 233). Positioning theory has the potential to enhance understanding about how meaning is negotiated and what comprises some of what Berger (1999) called the "dynamic and comprehensive methods and processes of intentional representation in contested sites" that underpin public relations practice (p. 186).

A summary of the research that informed the development of the provisional conceptual framework for intentional positioning

In 2009, a provisional conceptual framework for intentional positioning in public relations based on applying positioning theory from the field of social psychology (Harré and van Langenhove, 1999) was developed. It was accepted for publication in late 2009 and appeared in the *Journal of Public Relations Research* in early 2011 (James, 2011a). In developing the framework it was applied to 57 Australian award-winning public relations communication campaigns from the period 1999–2008. All had won a Public Relations Institute of Australia Golden Target Award in their category – the highest award for public relations campaigns in the country.

The data to which the framework was applied was that generated by textual and thematic analysis of the award entry texts and the transcripts of interviews with a sample of 18 selected practitioners who had designed award-winning public relations campaigns during the period 2005–2009. The purpose was to identify the common aspects across the campaigns that contributed to successful positioning. This led to the framework's development and subsequent testing within the four domains. This was viewed as a first step to see whether it could be used to identify positioning efforts and techniques in public relations campaigns.

The application of the provisional positioning framework indicated that all campaigns in the study's sample had positioning elements within them. The judgments as to the categorization of positioning elements in the campaign award entries were based on the subjective textual analysis of the award entry texts and it was noted that this could be seen as a limitation of the study. It was acknowledged that another researcher may not have found evidence of ingratiation in the award entry texts and may have categorized these as positioning for some other purpose. It was evident however, that intentional positioning for some purpose had been undertaken and those positioning efforts has been specifically framed through enactment and storyline strategies.

The overall findings indicated that positioning happened at various stages of a campaign. The findings suggested that campaign research was undertaken to find out what was already in the minds of audiences and that the strategy then aimed through positioning efforts to retie the connections that already existed (Ries and Trout, 1981) in ways that better served the organization and that helped it to achieve its overall campaign goal. This tied in with the influence of ideas from the marketing positioning field in the development of Harré and van Langenhove's (1999) positioning theory. It also opened the door for further investigation of how the intended positioning meanings were co-constructed by both the organization that commissioned the public relations activity and the subjects of that activity, that is, target publics and audiences. Harré and van Langenhove (1999: 17) state, "it can be easily seen that the social force of an action and the position of the actor and interactors mutually determine one another". This was seen to further underpin the concept of fluidity of positioning and the construction of meaning within public relations campaigns as they unfolded.

Whenever positioning was occurring, several other forms of positioning were found to be occurring at the same time. It was clear that by positioning one's own organization, for instance, other organizations' positions might be altered or compromised in some way, necessitating a response such as a repositioning on their part (Harré and van Langenhove, 1999). This notion of fluidity was identified as one of the most important aspects of positioning theory for public relations. It helped to explain why campaign plans needed to be adjusted to accommodate changes in internal and external environments as the plan was implemented, exemplifying what Mintzberg (2007) calls emergent strategy.

King (2010) defined an emergent communication strategy as "a communicative construct derived from the interaction between reader/hearer response, situated context, and discursive patterns" (p. 20). James (2011a) reported that the work of

Mintzberg (2007) and King (2010) could be contextualized within a framework of positioning to assist in explaining why some campaigns were unsuccessful in spite of the best planning and design efforts: a failure to recognize and/or respond to emerging patterns in audience and stakeholder responses; a failure to accommodate the fluid nature of the positioning environment that publics inhabited (situated context), and a failure to pay due regard to the negotiation of meaning that was taking place (discursive patterns) as positioning and repositioning occurred. Further testing of the framework (James, 2012) has since strengthened this link between the concept of emergent strategy and public relations practice.

On the basis of the results and analysis of the initial development research projects (James, 2010, 2011a), it was concluded that, in a public relations context, the framework for positioning offered a more comprehensive approach to positioning than that found in marketing models. It also brought together elements identified by other public relations and strategic communication researchers into a single framework. It was clear that further testing and refinement was needed but this initial study's findings confirmed that positioning was a significant part of communication strategic practice. The positioning framework showed potential application in two areas. Firstly as an heuristic for analysis of public relations positioning activities and secondly, as a practical framework for designing positioning strategies in public relations programs and campaigns. The next sections report on work undertaken since these initial studies to demonstrate the framework's application in these two ways.

How positioning analysis using the framework can both "diagnose" and guide strategy

In the document, *Stopping the Australian Coal Export Boom: Funding proposal for the Australian anti-coal movement*, (Hepburn, Burton and Hardy, 2012), the anti-coal movement claimed the right to stall the development and expansion of one of Australia's key industries. The authors stated that their strategy was "to 'disrupt and delay' key projects and infrastructure while gradually eroding public and political support for the industry and continually building the power of the movement to win more" (p. 3). Their aim was to "delay the proposed increase in export capacity substantially (by several years)" (p. 3) and "to severely reduce the overall scale of the coal boom by some hundreds of millions of tonnes per annum from the proposed 800 Mtpa increase" (p. 3). But from a positioning perspective does this anti-coal group have the right to do this? Who has given the group this right or from where has such a right been claimed? Has this right been questioned or challenged?

The anti-coal group can be seen to have positioned themselves as a viable coalition of anti-coal groups/individuals standing between the current situation and environmental catastrophe. Their right to act to stall expansion of coal exports has been embedded in a positioning storyline about doing the right thing for the planet, e.g. "If the industry expands unchecked, it will . . . have devastating consequences for the global climate" (p. 4). It is evident through the application of positioning theory that if this group has self-positioned as doing the right thing for the planet they have, by default, positioned the coal industry as doing the wrong thing for the planet.

The coal industry is then on the defensive. However, the anti-coal group have also positioned themselves as having an uncertain future, e.g. "The Australian anti-coal movement is fragmented and underresourced" (p. 4). They therefore appealed, through their claimed right to the moral high ground, to people who wanted to do the right thing for the planet to come on board with their plan. There were two positioning triangles at play concurrently and these were:

Position: The coal industry is destroying the planet.	*Position:* The Australian anti-coal movement is fragmented and under resourced.
Enactment: Assertion of intent to disrupt and delay key projects and infrastructure while gradually eroding public and political support for the industry (speech act = assertive).	*Enactment:* Directed people who wanted to do the right thing for the planet to come on board with their plan (speech act = directive).
Storyline: "Change the story of coal from being the backbone of our economy, to being a destructive industry that destroys the landscape and communities, corrupts our democracy, and threatens the global climate" (p. 5).	*Storyline:* "We cannot win major ground in the fight against coal without building a substantially more powerful social movement than currently exists. Organizing and supporting communities to campaign effectively is the best way to leverage the investment of resources for maximum effect in building a powerful movement" (p. 11).

One of the strategies outlined is "Changing the story of coal" (p. 9). Having occupied the moral high ground position, this permits them to run with the storylines of "the negative environmental, social, health and economic impacts of the Australian coal industry" (p. 9). The document states:

> By changing the perception of the coal industry within key parts of the Australian community we can build new alliances, engage and mobilise new parts of the community, and gradually undermine the social license of the industry, thereby gradually removing political support.
>
> (Hepburn, Burton and Hardy, 2012: 9)

In one sense this document cements the anti-coal group's position but in another, it exposes some of the presumptions the group's self-positioning is built upon and these could be questioned by coal association public relations representatives. In a media statement responding to the release of the above document, one peak industry body stated:

> The Australian coal industry operates under two licences. The first is a tested regulatory licence that involves government at multiple levels and is monitored from day one of any project. The second is a social licence from the community, which we must invest in every day by addressing the impacts of the industry on local communities and the environment and making a positive social and economic contribution. We do not take either for granted. Many of the challenges we face have emerged as a result of our strong growth. We understand that mining communities have some legitimate concerns and we must work to address them.
>
> (Australian Coal Association, 2012)

In this response, the Australian Coal Association (ACA) states the two rights to operate it is claiming for the industry. The first right, the regulatory licence, is fairly straightforward in this context. Although contested by some, this right is regulatory and thus "sanctioned" by the state at present. Coal mining has a right to claim this position. With this right to mine comes the duties and obligations under the law, and the industry follows these. If it did not follow what was required under the laws and regulations there would be financial and other penalties imposed on companies and their operations. It could be argued that the ACA's position might have been strengthened if this was stated and proof points included (stronger enactment and storyline).

The second right, "a social licence from the community" is more nebulous in terms of the industry's positioning. With this social licence to operate, comes social and cultural obligations and duties (as with any position taken). The ACA's response infers that it recognises that this right must in some way be earned by the industry. The ACA's response, however indicates some uncertainty about whether it has a social licence to operate. This is expressed in the media release as stating that the ACA understands that "mining communities have some legitimate concerns and we must work to address them". It seems that the ACA is only tentatively claiming this socially constructed right. From a perspective of formulating positioning strategy for the ACA and the coal industry, why this would be the case needs further investigation.

Questions that could be asked include: Is the ACA uncertain of its position as having a social licence to operate? Is any uncertainty widespread or does it pertain to specific locales? What proof points does ACA have to make the claim of this right stronger? It is questionable whether the ACA could hold a stated position of having a social licence to operate when, in the same statement, the organization itself casts doubt on whether it is actually meeting the duties that are inherent in such a right in the Australian context. When this is viewed through the positioning triangle domain the "diagnosis" of why such positioning was not working for the organization becomes clear. The position itself, that is, that it has a social licence to operate, is not firm. The enactment of this weak position through the issuing of a statement in a media release may not have been wise, given the ACA had a weak position. The storyline that was given in support of the position was one that actually admitted that all community concerns regarding mining had not been addressed. The positioning triangle was not congruent in that each vertex was not aligned to the other.

If on further analysis it was found that the organization didn't have sufficient evidence of having a strong social licence to operate in support of its claim to such a position, this would indicate that the issue was probably not a communication issue. It was more likely to be problem with mining operations or issues related to past interactions with communities in mining areas. This in itself shows that a public relations positioning analysis could assist practitioners and management teams to tease out the communication issues from other issues.

However, if the organization did have proof points to show it could strongly claim this social right to operate mining, these should have been stated. In addition, credible third party endorsement of the proof points should have been sought and used, and practical examples should have been provided. In this way audiences see the position as being authentic, and efforts to maintain such a position are transparent. Such an approach could start to claim back some of the moral high ground for the coal mining industry.

A general way forward for the coal industry

Coal associations could argue the case on the same meaning-making terrain where the anti-coal movement has positioned itself, but this would be a proverbial case of a huge uphill battle to the moral high ground, which has been defined by the anti-coal group. Another option might be to shift onto more neutral meaning-making terrain and recast positions of both the coal mining industry and anti-coal groups. A recommended way forward is to map the trajectory of various scenarios as a desk exercise.

For example, one scenario would have the peak coal industry associations denouncing the claims about the coal industry and its global impact from the position it has been assigned by the anti-coal groups, that is, the position of being a global environment destroyer. Another scenario would have peak coal industry associations trying to re-position the anti-coal groups as something less than moral champions by challenging the underpinnings of their "doing good for the planet position" through a range of pre-positioning tactics. These could include finding holes in their scientific claims, highlighting various failings in the organizations or groups involved, or even attacking the credibility or integrity of individuals involved in such groups. It is not hard to visualize that such scenarios would in all probability track along a path that would backfire for the coal industry, and it could find itself positioned as a bully or worse.

Alternative scenarios would need to be workshopped with key personnel of industry associations as "inside" knowledge would not only inform scenario development but also the analysis of how any scenario could track. However, it would seem prudent that a public relations strategist would investigate a scenario where the coal industry could proactively self-position as an industry in transition, especially given its role in the world energy industry environment that is itself in transition (see Table 3.3).

This transition position brings with it a cluster of rights and duties such as striving to improve operations, environmental performance and community support. It also means having to share the stage with other energy players, including the renewable industry players, which some in the coal industry may find challenging. It should also be anticipated that some energy players would reject the coal industry's construction of the positioning meaning-making terrain, that is, the coal industry constructing a stage for the play out of several decades of transition instead of the "moral high ground" terrain that is the preferred stage of anti-coal groups.

Even in the face of such repositioning attempts, the coal industry could hold the transition position because the positioning analysis has indicated that it is one the industry has a right to hold. It can provide the proof points and other evidence to show that it can authentically claim the position. Such a strategy positions the coal industry as part of the energy solution for future decades of the twenty-first century, rather than the demon behind climate catastrophe which is the position in which the industry often finds itself. This exercise is not one attempting to "propagandize" the glories of the coal industry but is an exercise aiming to demonstrate that even the most controversial industries can utilize a positioning theoretical approach to firstly "diagnose" and analyze a public relations episode, and secondly, to devise a feasible and viable public relations positioning strategy.

Table 3.3 Positioning strategy for the coal industry

Framework domain	*Positioning strategy*
Positioning goal domain	To move toward having a comprehensive social licence to operate for the coal industry
Positioning type	Forced to proactively self-position the industry due to external criticism and active attempts to slow industry output.
Strategic pre-positioning	Self-attribute demonstrable characteristics such as: working to improve overall environmental outcomes, worker safety, and coal consumption efficiency; helping to bring cheap electricity to households; delivering economic benefits to mining communities.
Positioning triangle – *position vertex*	Position as an industry in transition, as a player in a world energy industry environment that is in transition.
Positioning triangle – *speech act vertex*	Assertions that the industry is one in transition to a cleaner future.
	Expressions of intent to work with communities to reach mutually beneficial outcomes.
	Commitments to work with communities to reach mutually beneficial outcomes.
	Directions to communities and individual coal companies as to how they participate in the transition process.
Positioning triangle – *storyline vertex*	Use a master plot (Tobias, 1993) such as a being on a "quest" (p. 59) to a better future to frame narratives and key messages to support the positioning.

How the positioning framework guided development of a public relations campaign

A large, regional local government council determined that it wanted to position "reduced consumption of energy" as a positive and desirable behavior for its residents. I was awarded a small, competitive environmental research grant to examine how the council's position could be translated into a strategic communication program using a positioning theoretical framework as a program design tool (James, 2011a, 2012). The council's management team was keen to ensure that beyond the communication team, staff members working in environmental programs and community outreach areas were involved in the campaign's design as it was felt this would increase feelings of ownership and commitment to the initiative.

The positioning framework was applied in a workshop that I conducted with 16 communication and environmental program employees to design the direction of a public relations plan for the council's desired positioning. The study concluded that the approach proved successful for both program design and staff engagement. In designing the positioning strategy, the framework domains were considered in a large group discussion involving all participants. The following summarises how the process unfolded.

Positioning goal domain

It was noted by the workshop group that if there was no clear goal, it would be pointless to expend council resources on a positioning campaign. The discussion led to a goal being articulated: to get local residents to understand the benefits of lowering their energy consumption.

Positioning type domain

The campaign for lowering energy consumption is an example of the council being proactive and "deliberately self-positioning" (James, 2011a: 105) on energy consumption.

Strategic pre-positioning domain

The group articulated that consumers who were likely to be motivated by building a campaign strategy around environmental issues were already acting to reduce resource consumption. The target audience for this new campaign comprised those who were not motivated by environmental factors. The group decided that it was best to position the target audience as having the attribute of "wanting to save money". This was decided upon as council research suggested that it could motivate a certain group of people to act. Energy saving was itself attributed the quality of being a way to save money. From this point the workshop turned from the strategic context to how such a program could be implemented. The final domain of the positioning framework, the positioning triangle domain, was applied to guide this work.

Position determined (first vertex of the triangle)

The group came to agreement that the position was that saving energy saved people money.

Position enacted (second vertex of the triangle)

The second pole of the positioning triangle is that the position must be declared or asserted in some way so it becomes known. Harré and van Langenhove (1999) suggest this takes place through speech acts/actions and this had been evident in public relations positioning studies to date (e.g. James, 2010, 2011a, 2012; Wise and James, 2013). Previously (James, 2010, 2012), I had applied five ways of using language in my research, namely Searle's "five general categories of illocutionary acts" (Searle 1979: viii) – assertives, directives, commissives, expressives, and declarations. This same process guided my conduct of this part of the workshop. I explained to participants how this enactment generally involved one or all of the following:

- Telling people how things are (assertives) – e.g. lowering resource consumption can save money and help save the environment.
- Getting people to do things (directives) – e.g. to support the council's campaign to lower household resource consumption through taking household action.
- Committing ourselves to doing things (commissives) – e.g. council would commit to assisting residents to lower resource consumption.
- Expressing feelings and attitudes (expressives) – e.g. council conveys the council's attitude that lowering resource consumption is desirable and can save residents money.
- Making declarations (declarations) – e.g. were there new or revised regulations that would support the council's position on lowering resource consumption?

The group was split into four smaller groups to consider categories one to four. We discussed the need for a fifth group to examine "declarations" but it was agreed to leave this as it mainly related to regulatory procedures at council level and that the need for changes to current regulations would only become apparent later in the program's implementation and monitoring stages. Workshopping the four categories shaped an implementation strategy in that it formed the basis of campaign actions and supporting messages through the development of storylines that supported the positioning.

Position supported through storylines (third vertex of the triangle)

I explained that in strategic positioning work, when there was a misalignment of words, actions and supporting storylines, public relations positioning could be seen to disintegrate. For example, the council couldn't be positioned as credible if it were to promote one way of lowering resource consumption whilst concurrently introducing regulations that made that very action hard for householders to achieve;

everything must align to the desired position. Ensuing discussion indicated this was understood and each group began the process of designing supporting storylines for their position and enactment ideas. These centred on the fact that as the council itself modelled good energy saving behaviour it had the right to talk about energy saving generally. They also focused on the point that if residents really wanted to save money, they had the duty to work on ways they could save energy, that is, saving energy makes sense and "cents"!

Outcome

It was clear that working through the first three domains of the positioning framework, that is, a) knowing what goal the client needed to achieve, b) what type of positioning was being done and c) what strategic pre-positioning characteristics were being attributed, clarified the direction for the positioning strategy's development. It was in the final positioning triangle domain that the development of implementation planning and tactics for the positioning commenced.

Workshop participants demonstrated through their discussions their understanding that all three poles of the positioning triangle needed to be addressed and aligned to enable the positioning to have any chance of success. What was notable was that once the desired position has been determined, it became evident to the participants that enacting the positioning had whole-of-organisation implications, not just those immediately related to the communication area. It was a revelation to some people present at the workshop that everything that an organization does could be viewed as conveying meaning and, that stakeholders and general audiences potentially interpret and make meaning from everything an organization does and says. The council was delighted with the outcomes of the workshop.

Summary

This chapter aimed to show the ways that a conceptual framework can work as a tool to scaffold research and analysis or as a tool for program planning. It presented the latest iteration of the Framework for Intentional Positioning in Public Relations and described its four domains: positioning goal, positioning type, strategic pre-positioning, and positioning triangle. It explained how and why the strategic pre-positioning domain had evolved from that presented in the provisional conceptual framework (James, 2010, 2011a). The evolution was based on ongoing testing of the framework and also on the developments in the wider positioning theory research area that has identified there are two phases involved in overall positioning efforts. The first phase is now described as pre-positioning, which involves the attributing of characteristics to self or others as a precursor to the second phase of positioning. This second phase, in which rights and duties that are operating according to the local moral order are either taken up or assigned, aligns with the "original" positioning theory presented by Harré and van Langenhove (1999) and is the truly innovative aspect in public relations positioning.

Also in this chapter, an overview was provided of the research (James, 2011a) that informed the development of the Framework for Intentional Positioning in Public Relations. The Framework was devised after examining dozens of award-winning public relations campaigns that had been successful in their positioning efforts. Each was shown to have demonstrated a clear goal, a certain type of positioning, a clear purpose and coherence in all three vertices of the positioning triangle, that is: the positions taken or assigned, their enactment strategies and their storylines in the form of key messages.

As research has shown that the Framework can be used to both analyze public relations episodes and past programs, and to also guide public relations program design, an example of both was provided in this chapter. The options open to a coal association that was being forced to self-position were presented following a positioning analysis of material that was available in the public domain (media release and organizational report). In the second example, an overview of the way the Framework guided the initial development of a campaign to encourage people to save energy was provided.

The testing of the Framework's rigor continues and more detailed application of the positioning framework is covered in Chapters 8 and 9. My hope is that other researchers and practitioners will be interested in testing the Framework in their own situations and contributing to both constructive critiques and iterative development of the Framework in coming years.

References

Al Khaja, M. A. and Creedon, P. (2010) Evaluating the effectiveness of the first breast cancer awareness campaign in the United Arab Emirates: lessons learned and next steps. *Public Relations Review*, 36(4): 386–8.

Austin, J. (1962) *How to Do Things with Words*. Clarendon: Oxford University Press.

Australian Coal Association (2012) *Broad Support for Coal Industry Welcomed*. Media release 7 March 2012. Retrieved from http://docs.noodls.com/viewDoc.asp?filename=76941/EXT/5DDE2104C05E1A7A975D6459AE29BC25EBF27CCB_D583184CA494C5A9EF83152698B667A9E6F7351E.PDF

Batchelor, B. and Formentin, M. (2008) Re-branding the NHL: building the league through the "My NHL" integrated marketing campaign. *Public Relations Review*, 34(2): 156–60.

Berger, B. (1999) The halcion affair: public relations and the construction of ideological world view. *Journal of Public Relations Research*, 11(3): 185–203.

Bourdieu, P. (1991) *Language and Symbolic Power*. Cambridge: Polity Press.

Bruce, T. and Tini, T. (2008) Unique crisis response strategies in sports public relations: rugby league and the case for diversion. *Public Relations Review*, 34, 108–15.

Davies, B. and Harré, R. (1990) Positioning: the discursive production of selves. *Journal for the Theory of Social Behavior*, 20(1): 43–63.

Gill, R. (2009) Building employee engagement and reputation through storytelling. In T. Flew (ed.) *Communication, Creativity and Global Citizenship: Refereed proceedings of the Australian and New Zealand Communication Association Conference 2009*, Brisbane. Retrieved October 31, 2009, from www.proceedings.anzca09.org

Hallahan, K., Holtzhausen, D., van Ruler, B., Verčič, D. and Sriramesh, K. (2007) Defining strategic communication. *International Journal of Strategic Communication*, 1(1): 3–35.

Harré, R. (2006) Positioning theory. In V. Jupp (ed.) *The Sage Dictionary of Social Research Methods*. Sage, pp. 229–30. Retrieved from http://srmo.sagepub.com/view/the-sage-dictionary-of-social-research-methods/SAGE.xml

Harré, R. and Rossetti, M. (2010) The right to stand and the right to rule. *Words of Conflict, Words of War: How the language we use in political processes sparks fighting*, 111–23.

Harré, R. and van Langenhove, L. (1999) *Positioning Theory: Moral contexts of intentional action*. Oxford: Blackwell.

Hepburn, J., Burton, B. and Hardy, S. (2011) *Stopping the Australian Coal Export Boom: Funding proposal for the Australian anti-coal movement*. Retrieved from www.abc.net.au/mediawatch/transcripts/1206_greenpeace.pdf

James, M. (2010) The use of intentional positioning techniques in government agencies' communication campaigns. In D. Verčič, and K. Sriramesh (eds) *Government Communication: Proceedings of the 17th International Public Relations Research Symposium BledCom*, pp. 140–7. Bled, Slovenia, Ljubljana: Pristop. Retrieved from www.bledcom.si/uploads/ppt2010/bledcom 2010 proceedings hi.pdf

James, M. (2011a) A provisional conceptual framework for intentional positioning in public relations. *Journal of Public Relations Research*, 23(1): 93–111. http://dx.doi.org/10.1080/1062726X.2010.505120

James, M. (2011b) Ready, aim, fire: the perceived role of key messages in public relations campaigns, *PRism*. 8(1).

James, M., (2012) Autoethnography: The story of applying a conceptual framework for intentional positioning to public relations practice. *Public Relations Review*, 38(4): 555–64. http://dx.doi.org/10.1016/j.pubrev.2012.05.004

Kearns, J. (1994) Meaning, structure and speech acts. In S. Tsohatzidis (ed.) *Foundations of speech act theory: philosophical and linguistic perspectives*. New York: Routledge, pp. 50–79.

King, C. (2010) Emergent communication strategies. *International Journal of Strategic Communication*, 4(1): 19–38.

Mintzberg, H. (2007) *Tracking Strategies: Toward a general theory*. Oxford: Oxford University Press.

Moghaddam, F., Hanley, E. and Harré, R. (2003) Sustaining intergroup harmony: an analysis of the Kissinger papers through positioning theory. In R. Harré and F. Moghaddam (eds) *The self and Others: Positioning individuals and groups in personal, political and cultural contexts*. London: Praeger, pp. 123–36.

Moghaddam, F. and Harré, R. (2010) Words, conflicts and political processes. In F. Moghaddam and R. Harré (eds) *Words of Conflict, Words of War: How the language we use in political processes sparks fighting*. Santa Barbara, CA: Praeger.

Moloney, K. (2006) *Rethinking Public Relations* (2nd edn). London: Routledge.

Potter, J. and Wetherell, M. (1987) *Discourse and Social Psychology: Beyond attitudes and behaviour*. London: Sage.

Ries, A. and Trout, J. (1981) *Positioning: The battle for your mind*. New York: McGraw-Hill.

Rothbart, D. and Bartlett, T. (2008) Rwandan radio broadcasts and Hutu/Tutsi positioning. In F. Moghaddam, R. Harré and N. Lee (eds) *Global Conflict Resolution through Positioning Analysis*. New York: Springer, pp. 227–46.

Searle, J. (1979) *Expression and Meaning: Studies in the theory of speech acts*. Cambridge: Cambridge University Press.

Slocum-Bradley, N. (2008) Discursive production of conflict in Rwanda. In F. Moghaddam, R. Harré, and N. Lee, (eds) *Global Conflict Resolution through Positioning Analysis*. New York: Springer, pp. 207–26.

Smyth, R. (2004) Exploring the usefulness of a conceptual framework as a research tool: a researcher's reflections. *Issues in Educational Research*, 14(2): 167–80.
Stokes, A. and Rubin, D. (2010) Activism and the limits of symmetry: the public relations battle between Colorado GASP and Philip Morris. *Journal of Public Relations Research*, 22(1): 26–48.
Text 100 (2006) IBM small to medium enterprise campaign: shifting industry perceptions. PRIA Golden Target Award entry – winner. Retrieved February 14, 2009 from www.lib.uts.edu.au/gta/?page=show&id=606
van Langenhove, L. and Harré, R. (1999) Introducing positioning theory. In R. Harré and L. van Langenhove (eds) *Positioning Theory: Moral contexts of intentional action*. Oxford: Blackwell, pp. 14–31.
Weaver, C. K. and Motion, J. (2002) Sabotage and subterfuge: public relations, democracy and genetic engineering in New Zealand. *Media, Culture & Society*, 24(3): 325–43.
Weaver, C., Motion, J. and Roper, J. (2006). From propaganda to discourse (and back again): truth, power and the public interest, and public relations. In J. L'Etang and M. Pieczka (eds) *Public Relations: Critical debates and contemporary practice*. Mahwah, NJ: Lawrence Erlbaum, pp. 7–22.
Wilkinson, S. and Kitzinger, C. (2003) Constructing identities: a feminist conversation analytic approach to positioning in action. In In R. Harré and F. Moghaddam (eds) *The self and Others: Positioning individuals and groups in personal, political and cultural contexts*. London: Praeger, pp. 157–180.
Wise, D. and James, M. (2013) Positioning a price on carbon: applying a proposed hybrid method of positioning discourse analysis for public relations. *Public Relations Inquiry*, 2(3): 327–53.
Zhang, J. and Benoit, W. (2004) Arab image: message strategies of Saudi Arabia's image restoration campaign after 9/11. *Public Relations Review*, 30(2): 161–7.

Part II

The positioning triangle and public relations

4 Determining the position in public relations

The first vertex of the positioning triangle

What makes a viable position in public relations? Determining a position for an organization or one of its services, programs or products depends greatly on the environment in which one is working. Positioning the immunization of babies as a positive thing to do when the audience is comprised of a new mum and dad, eager to do everything right for their child, could be seen as a fairly straightforward environment. However, determining a position in a more turbulent and complex environment can be challenging.

In the twenty-first century, complex and turbulent operational environments abound. They provide organizations with multiple publics and stakeholders, often holding diametrically opposed views on issues pertaining to the organization. Organizations at all levels partake in positioning activities and Wilkinson and Kitzinger (2003: 173) have shown that positioning is often done in pursuit of a goal such as "building a complaint" (e.g. about planned land-use activity such as housing development or mining), "deflecting responsibility" (e.g. positioning international currency issues as the problem with a country's economy rather than national fiscal policy), or, "launching a telling" for a specific purpose (e.g. exoneration from blame; launching a new product or service).

In terms of determining a position or positions for an organization to take up or assign to others, the broad consideration and application of two public relations theoretical approaches are suggested: co-orientation theory as proposed by Broom (1977) and contingency theory as proposed by Cancel, Cameron, Sallot and Mitrook (1997). Cancel *et al.* (1997) concluded that how one practices public relations "depends on assessment of a number of factors, ranging from antecedent conditions to current pressures and opportunities" (p. 33). They suggested 87 factors that affect the stance of an organization.

To reiterate the discussion in Chapter 1, "position" is sometimes used interchangeably with the word "stance" but when viewed through the lens of positioning theory, the words mean quite different things. Stance is most often discussed in the context of contingency theory and has been defined as:

> the general way in which management in an organization approaches conflict. Stances range from accommodative, a willingness to make concessions, to advocacy, a willingness to persuade others to your position.
>
> (Coombs, 2010: 484)

and:

> has been operationalized as the position an organization takes in decision making, which is supposed to determine which strategy to employ.
>
> (Pang, Jin and Cameron, 2010: 25)

A public relations position can be therefore seen as a discursively constructed point of intentional representation from where possibilities for action are established, or in some cases denied, in terms of the local moral order/s wherein the public relations activity is taking place for the purposes of achieving an intended outcome. Public relations positioning is defined as the actions taken to achieve the public relations position.

Positions in all contexts "are rarely defined in isolation" and are instead "defined relative to other positions in some complimentary or reciprocal fashion" (Parrott, 2003: 31). If an organization is positioning as "engaged with the community" it must have a community to engage with; if an activist group is going to act it needs to have a position against a project or practice it finds unacceptable. Parrott (2003) points out that positioning has its origins in strategic activities such as military generals positioning their forces in battle, or marketers positioning their products to draw business away from competitors; and that discursive positioning retains these same strategic connotations. Analyses of positioning typically depict actors as trying to establish for themselves a favorable position where positive attributes are sought, such as honesty or integrity and sometimes superiority to an opponent (Davies and Harré, 1990; Parrott, 2003). Research to date (James, 2010, 2011, 2012; Wise and James, 2013) has shown this to be the case in much public relations practice.

Strategic positioning, being the actions taken to achieve a desired position in a contested environment, is most often a sequence of moves (Parrott, 2003). In a positioning approach, all parties to the public relations episode are conceptualized as active participants. They are co-constructors of the meanings being made and of the positions being taken up or rejected. Practitioners, in conceptualizing practice in this dynamic way need to anticipate what are the possible and probable outcomes of enacting a position on behalf of an organization.

It is clear that public relations episodes are not just about "meaning". All aspects of social life "are constituted by two mutually influential parts": a) a material part consisting "of actions (physical activities) and objects (material realities)"; and, b) meaning consisting "of acts (the significance given to physical activities), symbols (the significance given to physical activities) and concepts" (Slocum-Bradley, 2007: 636). Public relations episodes are social constructs and they are given meaning through discourse that is enacted by various actors for various purposes. The things that public relations episodes are about, (that is, organizations, programs, products, services, people, ideologies, ideas and so on) are actors in a narrative that provides a context within which public relations positioning occurs. It is within the third vertex of the positioning triangle, storylines, that publics and audiences are offered "interpretive potentials" (Neff,

2008: 92), that is, opportunities to make sense of actions and events that comprise the public relations episode.

Positioning approaches

From the organization's perspective public relations can manage publics in two ways: buffering or bridging (Grunig, 2009). Buffering is described as creating "enough impressions in the publics' minds to allow the organization to buffer itself from its environment so that the organization can act without being interrupted by publics" (Kim and Ni, 2010: 49). Communication efforts are described as most often "tactical and technical messaging efforts" to influence how publics interpret the organization. In a positioning context, this is where an organization takes a position, or positions another entity, and takes the attitude that if it just keeps the key messages (storylines) coming out, somehow this will translate into publics accepting that position. This could be seen as taking quite a functional approach in which one takes a position that is not necessarily negotiable. Such a plan is likely to be couched in deliberate strategic planning language.

With a bridging approach to public relations, we see public relations trying to bridge gaps of interest, and positioning on problems between an organization and its environment by communicating interactively and proactively. It has more of a focus on trying to balance interests between parties. It is said to focus on enhancing the nature and quality of relationships with publics "rather than a set of messaging activities designed to buffer the organization from them" (Grunig, 2009: 9). The evidence suggests that either approach can work, depending on the context (James, 2011a).

How a position is determined is possibly where the hardest work lies for the public relations strategist. It is not difficult to come up with a position as such. Any organization can decide it would like to position itself or one of its products, personnel or services anyway it likes. However, whether that position is actually viable is another matter. This is where the skills of the public relations practitioner come to the fore. Practitioners could find themselves in several situations when it comes to positioning. Taking the initiative, they could suggest that an organization positions itself, or one of its offerings, in a particular way as part of a strategic public relations proposal. The practitioner may also identify that the organization is being positioned negatively by another entity and that this requires action. Alternatively, practitioners could find themselves directed by a CEO or Managing Director to come up with a strategic positioning strategy to support a new business direction. Either way the position has to be determined and should be one that is viable; this is the challenge. An unviable position is one that will not hold against a sustained attempt to destabilize it. In an ideal world, such positions would never be taken but it is evident that situations calling for a public relations response are sometimes less than ideal.

Examples of unviable positions are:

- A company positioning a project as safe for surrounding communities even though the management team knows the science supporting such a claim is uncertain. Even if the company's position on safety isn't exposed for many years, once the position is shown to be based on greed, exploitation of workers and the flouting of scientific evidence, the position will crumble in spite of competent efforts being undertaken at the second and third vertices of the positioning triangle. This inevitably will be expensive and damaging for the company.

- A community organization taking a position that it is of paramount importance to help abused children but then fails to do thorough checks on the backgrounds of its volunteers or paid employees who are working with such children. If it is discovered that one of these people has a criminal history involving child abuse, the credibility of the organization could be shattered. A discredited organization will not be seen by its publics and donors as having the right to position in this way and could even collapse completely.

So the challenge for public relations is to determine a viable position for an organization or indeed, to deter an organization from attempting to secure an unviable position. It should be noted that determining a viable position will not mean that an organization is protected from attempts to destabilize its position, or to reposition it completely. However evidence (James, 2010, 2011a) suggests it will be able to maintain the determined position if all three poles of the positioning triangle domain are in alignment and the organization has the right to position according to the local moral order in which it is operating. However, this does not mean that the position taken or assigned by an organization will remain static throughout any episode. It will mean that if the position itself is altered, the other two vertices of the positioning triangle will also need to change, that is, enactment and storylines.

Examples of unviable positions show that even the best enactment strategies and campaign tactics will not hold up if the position taken is not underpinned by demonstrable proof points and/or if the organization does not have the right within the local moral order to occupy or seek a particular position. This may be hard for some organizational management teams to accept; perhaps they know of situations where organizations have literally spun their way into favorable positions. Creating and implementing a public relations program where an unviable position is enacted and supported can be seen as another incarnation of spin. In an age of media technologies that potentially enable every citizen to be a reporter and publisher, it will become increasingly difficult for organizations to maintain unviable positions.

The Framework for Intentional Positioning in Public Relations has the potential to address this situation. This is because it aims to provide the scaffold or guide to assist practitioners to meet the challenge of demonstrating to senior management why positions taken need to be viable within the local moral order. It can also guide the development and implementation of viable positioning strategies for the organization. The Framework, when used to determine a position, is approached from considering the positioning goal domain, the positioning type domain, the strategic pre-positioning domain and then the positioning triangle domain – in that order.

Table 4.1 The application of the Framework in position determination

Framework domain	*Questions to consider*	*What needs to be known?*
Positioning goal	What can realistically be achieved through the positioning exercise? What is the desired outcome? How will it be measured? What would successful positioning look like?	Nature of communication environment; identity of entities impacted by intended positioning efforts; anticipated responses from those entities; nature of relationships with those entities (current, past and anticipated future); positions held by others on this and related areas?
Positioning type	Is this a situation of intentional self-positioning for the organization? Is the organization being forced in some way to position itself? Is it intentionally positioning another entity? Is it being forced to position another entity?	Parties to the public relations positioning hold what degree and what type of power? How could such power be potentially exercised in the positioning acts? What timeframes are impacting on positioning strategy (i.e. a crisis demanding a quick response or a planned program launch)?
Pre-positioning	What attributes are claimed or assigned? What can the organization potentially claim in terms of rights to position in certain ways?	What are the expectations of publics, audiences and stakeholders in terms of the local moral orders in which they operate? E.g. can the organization self-attribute qualities such as "exemplary", "best", "cheapest", "trusted"? Can it attribute qualities to other entities? What rights does the local moral order assign to the organization and other entities involved? With what duties are such rights associated?
Positioning triangle		
– Position/s	What positions are available given the local moral order? Are the positions to be taken up by the organization or assigned to another entity? Or both?	How could each position possibly play out? What scenarios need to be modeled for each position suggested? What further information is needed? Who needs to be involved in this decision-making and scenario planning? Managers? Consumers? Audience members? Internal/External stakeholders? Others?
– Enactment	What speech acts/actions would bring this positioning to life?	What social force would various speech acts/actions exert in shaping social reality – perceptions and/or behavior? What do intended audiences know about previous meaning-making results? What resources are available to the organization to enact the positioning in terms of social and symbolic capital? Budgets? Personnel? How do suggested speech acts/actions play out in the scenario planning?
– Supporting storyline	What storylines are available given the position/s taken? Which ones are closed off to the positioned entities? What are the proof points for the chosen positioning? What narratives could be used in support? What key messages should audiences co-construct as a result of these efforts?	What can and cannot be said by the various parties in terms of the positions taken and assigned? What is the current understanding of intended audiences in relation to the topic of the positioning? How should the interpretive offerings in the storylines be constructed to best coalesce with the various audiences' zones of meaning? How do suggested storylines operate in the scenario planning?

What position does an organization take or assign?

Although it is possible to pluck a position to be taken out of thin air, positioning theory indicates a position that is not attuned to the local moral order will not be viable. This means that communities and wider society will not see that the organization has the right to position in a certain way. If it does take a particular position, the organization will be required to undertake certain duties. For example, wanting to position as being "clean and green" comes with the duty of carrying out behaviors that are congruent with being clean and green. What such behaviors are will be determined in large part by the regulatory environments of particular locales but also by what is determined to be appropriate by communities of interest, which may not necessarily be geographically local. An example of non-geographically local public pressure can be seen when pressure is placed on multinational companies that operate in developing countries to stop the exploitation of children as cheap labor. Such publics will demand that a multinational company take a position of protecting the rights of children in all operational environments, even if local laws do not champion children's rights.

It is easy to imagine the uproar if a multinational company takes such a position (first vertex of the positioning triangle), proclaims it publicly (second vertex of the positioning triangle: position enacted) and weaves the storyline of supporting ethical work practices into its corporate documents and advertising (third vertex of the positioning triangle: position supported), only to be exposed as continuing to exploit child workers. Yes, the company may have had the right to take such a position but with such a position came the duty to avoid using child labor in all operations. To come back from such a de-positioning in the public eye, what Henriksen (2008) refers to as liquidation of a position, would require an intensive project to rebuild the right, as seen by interested publics, to take the position of supporting ethical work practices once again. Such a program would be one involving operational and policy changes, staff training and facility monitoring. Alongside this it could be envisaged that a program of supporting opportunities for children to live and learn in healthy and happy environments in the locales in which the company operated would be needed. An ongoing campaign to inform publics and wider audiences of its activities and its commitment to the position would also be required.

We see circumstances such as this across many sectors, not just in large multinational companies. With increasing access to information through the media, organizational websites and online media activities of interested communities and individuals, people can make the linkages between information sets more readily than ever before. This means it is likely to be discovered if, for instance, a government that on one hand says it is taking the position to support better educational outcomes for schools is found to be on the other hand slashing the budget for subsidized travel to school for poorer families.

When determining a position, the similarities to determining stance within a contingency theoretical perspective (Cancel *et al.*, 1997; Pang, Yin and Cameron, 2010) come into play. The "87 variables [that] have been identified that can change a stance" (Coombs, 2010: 484) could also be applied to determining a position. This is certainly an area that would benefit from future research.

However, unlike stance, there is firstly the point that a position isn't just something that is taken up by an organization, e.g. it is also something that can be assigned to other entities. One cannot assign a stance to another party, one can only guess or undertake research to determine what stance has been taken, or would be likely to be taken on the continuum of accommodation to advocacy. Secondly, positioning brings into play the rights and duties within the local moral order of particular positions and these can be seen to be what discursively determines what can logically be said and done by parties in the public relations episode.

The "position" itself

I have defined a public relations position as: a discursively constructed point of intentional representation from where possibilities for action are established, or in some cases denied, in terms of the local moral order/s wherein the public relations activity is taking place, for the purposes of achieving an intended outcome.

A public relations position can be seen as having two aspects, which aligns with the idea of two phases of positioning: pre-positioning and positioning. The first aspect is that of the social, psychological and moral characteristics that are attributed in a public relations episode to one's own organization/client (or its offerings) or to some other entity, that is, the strategic pre-positioning domain of the Framework. The second aspect relates to rights and duties. To position someone or an organization, e.g. as "generous" is "referred to as *an act of positioning*" (Slocum-Bradley, 2007: 638). According to Slocum-Bradley (2007), acts of positioning can be accountive or performative:

> In accountive positioning, the positioning is achieved through the accounts one gives of events, or narratives. In performative positioning, one positions oneself and others through the (discursive) acts one performs. For example, in issuing the compliment, "Well done!", I accountively position my interlocutor as a competent essay-writer, and I performatively position myself as a competent judge thereof.
>
> (Slocum-Bradley, 2007: 638)

So determining a position is not just determining a stance-point on a type of accommodation–advocacy continuum such as in a contingency theoretical approach (Cancel *et al.*, 1997), although such an approach can assist in determining positioning strategy. A practitioner must consider the accounts that might be given about a particular position as well as the discursive acts one might perform in relation to the position. The position itself is multi-faceted and both opens and closes down possibilities for both accounts and actions.

Effective public relations positioning therefore is when what is said about the position (the account) and what is done in relation to the position (the discursive act/performance) is aligned or congruent. To position an organization as one that respects people's privacy, such as happened in the public relations project I managed for the Australian Bureau of Statistics Census Program, the material produced to promote participation in the national census explained (storyline) the commitment (the speech act) of the Bureau to protect privacy (the position). This was the accountive positioning. The performative positioning was enacted through acts such as having selective screening of census workers for criminal history, the provision of privacy envelopes to households, the ability to complete census forms securely online, the destruction of paper forms after processing and so on. Such positioning constructs a discursive space where actors can take action in a given context; in this case the census worker can deliver a form to a home and householders can complete the form with a high degree of confidence. One can see that actions would be pursued or avoided depending on the context of the actors' positions. Outside of census time, the discursive space does not exist and people wouldn't be inclined to fill out long forms.

A relationship exists between discourse and practice in that "through discourse, discursive space is created that actors may choose to assume and from which certain actions are socially facilitated" (Slocum-Bradley, 2007: 651). This is the space wherein strategic public relations positioning takes place and practitioners need to ascertain what positions are available for their organizations and for others who are intended to be part of the public relations episode. If an organization's senior management team decides upon a position and informs the public relations manager to 'make it happen', the practitioner's first role will be to determine whether such a position is viable or achievable in the current environment, or in the environment that could conceivably exist at a certain time in the future. Hopefully, if the practitioner is part of the dominant coalition, she or he will be part of the determination process of the position. This would also involve work to ascertain which positions are viable, with such an exercise being undertaken using environmental scanning, a situational analysis and a positioning analysis.

The positioning analysis is discussed in Chapter 7 and will provide the insights to determine which positions are available for the organization and how others are currently positioned. The storylines being used by others about the issue at hand will often indicate what positions are taken and how they are being enacted. They help indicate how others are making sense of issues, and this knowledge helps practitioners develop available positions for their organization or client.

Positions are not "set and forget"

Although practice itself is often reported in case studies and textbooks as quite linear and orderly, those working in the industry report quite the opposite (e.g. James, 2012; Lane, 2007; Stokes and Rubin, 2010). Although it would be seen as optimal to be able to provide the formula for determining the position for an organization, this is not possible as it is not a static concept. Interestingly, Tirado and Gálvez (2007) see a position as existing in a relationship that is established between an "I" and "another" in an audience. This rings true when positioning is seen as intentional representation in a contested space and is most often constructed relative to other positions assigned or taken by others. Tirado and Gálvez (2007) state positioning is not at all static, "it is negotiated, and it changes and is adapted to the opinions of the others. In short, it moves and transforms within the interaction" (n.p. par 27), and this links with the concept of emergent strategy.

The concept of "emergent strategy" has entered the public relations and strategic communication fields (e.g. Gilpin and Murphy, 2006; Hallahan *et al.*, 2007; James, 2012; King, 2010; Macnamara and Zerfass, 2012) and has been shown to relate to notions of complexity and complex systems, that is, a system that "is never in the state of perfect, ongoing stability" (Gilpin and Murphy, 2006: 379). Applying Mintzberg's discussion of emergent strategy to public relations, King (2010) defines an emergent communication strategy as "a communicative construct derived from the interaction between reader/hearer response, situated context, and discursive patterns" (p. 20). The work of Mintzberg (2007) and King (2010) can be contextualized for public relations within a framework of positioning to assist in explaining why some campaigns are unsuccessful in spite of the best planning and design efforts. There may well have been a failure to recognize and/or respond to emerging patterns in audience and stakeholder responses; a failure to accommodate the fluid nature of the positioning environment that our publics inhabit (situated context); and/or a failure to pay due regard to the negotiation of meaning that is taking place (discursive patterns) as positioning and repositioning occurs.

Since Mintzberg's (1978) identification of emergent strategy there has been much written in management and strategy literature about what this means in terms of how organizations could or should operate, and how such a concept could be operationalized (Mirabeau and Maguire, 2013). Emergent strategy can be said to center on the idea of pattern recognition in the course of undertaking everyday work. Mirabeau and Maguire (2013) write how an autonomous emergent strategy can be harnessed by the organization so that it becomes the realized strategy, and is then integrated into the planned strategy. This resonates with both my own experiences of senior level practice and the way practitioners reported their practice to me in my research (James, 2011c). Clients or employing organizations have a plan with objectives they want to achieve. This might be something like positioning a local charity as worthy of people's donations. The planned strategy might be to undertake the regular annual door knock appeal and work would get underway to implement the plan. Then by chance, some celebrity comes to town and indicates to the practitioner that she has great regard for the type of work being undertaken by the charity and wants to help promote the donation drive.

The practitioner recognizes the potential in this and sees the pattern emerging of increased media attention and resulting coverage and so on, and decides to harness the celebrity's offer as part of the campaign. This is emergent strategy becoming realized strategy. If the exercise is successful and the celebrity is willing, the practitioner may weigh up including the celebrity's involvement in the following year's fundraiser. This would then become part of the planned strategy for the following year. The skill of practitioners lies in firstly recognizing the opportunity in the emerging pattern of behaviors happening around them and secondly integrating it into the planned communication strategy. There is also skill in recognizing when an emerging situation may not be opportune for the current strategy and in being able to argue the case for not changing course. This is a fairly simple explanation of working with the idea of complexity and emergent strategy. Although integrating an opportunity might seem to make things more "complicated", being open to what is referred to as "complexity absorption" can increase an organization's ability to adapt in changing and turbulent environments (Ashmos *et al.*, 2000, cited in Gilpin and Murphy, 2006: 384).

This is how positioning strategy unfolds in a public relations context. Practitioners are monitoring the discursive space/operational environment for indications and patterns that suggest whether positions are being supported or challenged. However, there is much a practitioner can do prior to going "live" with a positioning strategy and this is where scenario planning can be a very valuable exercise. Grunig (2013) states that although management scholars have used scenario planning for some time, the practice remains underutilized in public relations. He advocates public relations managers using such a practice to show other managers what publics might do in given situations, and what situations or issues managers' decisions may create. Gilpin and Murphy (2006) draw on the 2001 work of Daft and Weick and describe scenario planning as part of a practical approach for applying the complexity-based paradigm for public relations within the concept of "enacting organizations" (p. 386). These are organizations that "assume the world to be indeterminate, yet actively engage with it rather than passively reacting to occurrences" and have managers playing "an active part in the entire interpretation cycle, from awareness to sensemaking to learning and back again" (Gilpin and Murphy, 2006: 386). Scenario planning "offers the advantage of practice in reasoning processes without producing, as its final output, a set of procedures to which the organization is expected to adhere" and can be seen as "a means of mental exploration" (Gilpin and Murphy, 2008: 169).

Gilpin and Murphy's (2008) work on complexity absorption in organizations facing crisis management situations is readily adaptable to strategic positioning contexts. Complexity absorption can mean giving up "exactitude and certainty" for "increased flexibility and adaptiveness" (Gilpin and Murphy, 2008: 173). One can see that in an organizational environment aiming for complexity reduction, the idea of determining a single position and working to maintain that position at all costs would be appealing. Complexity reduction, according to Gilpin and Murphy (2008), is a traditional management approach that places a high value on stability, certainty, order and predictability. It aligns with the concept of buffering (Grunig, 2009; Kim and Ni, 2010), where organizations do not want the added complexity of engaging with publics if they can somehow avoid it.

However, no matter how ordered and linear public relations practice can seem when reported in case studies and award entries, today's practice is known to be complex and often undertaken in a non-linear way. The training of public relations practitioners to recognize patterns in evolving environments and to be able to improvise, moving emergent strategy into realized strategy, may be critical for effectively managing positioning. This is because practitioners need to be able to "read" the environment while a) determining the position to be taken, or assigned to another, and working through possible and probable scenarios, and b) while enacting and supporting the position, that is, during the implementation and monitoring stage.

They need to be able to recognize when the organization's position is being discursively constructed by intended audiences in the way they intended or whether there is neither engagement with nor resistance to the organization's efforts. The practitioner needs to be able to diagnose situations where efforts are being made by other parties to destabilize the desired position, and to determine whether any aspect of the positioning strategy needs to be changed.

This doesn't mean that the organization's original position necessarily needs to be changed, although that may be a possibility. It may be the case that the position taken is very sound in terms of the organization's right to hold or take it. The practitioner may need to further enact the position or further support through additional or stronger storylines. The storylines need to integrate the proof points that demonstrate the organization's right to position in the way it has. However, in the scenario planning, such resistance may have been anticipated, especially if some of the organization's proof points demonstrating its right to take the position were not as strong as they could have been. In this case, a different position may have been canvassed with one of the scenario planners determining it to be one where there would be less contest about the right to claim it. If such had happened, this may be the time when it is adopted by the organization (the first vertex of the positioning triangle). This would necessitate a change in the speech act/actions taken (the second vertex of the positioning triangle) and the storylines (the third vertex of the triangle). A key tenet of positioning theory is that all three vertices of the positioning triangle must remain in a "dynamic stability" (Harré and van Langenhove, 1999: 10), that is, in order for positioning to hold there can be no incongruence in the three vertices.

Resistance to a position taken or assigned by an organization can occur at any one of the three positioning triangle vertices. The position itself may need to be changed if the resistance is on the basis of rights and duties seen to be operating in a particular moral order. Audiences or publics may declare that the right to the position does not exist, or is not sufficiently established (Wise and James, 2013) or, they may resist on the basis that the duties that are seen to be part of the position, according to the local moral order, are not being undertaken to a sufficient extent, or at all. This is when positioning becomes even more complex, as depending on the local moral order, the same position could be simultaneously co-constructed as intended in one instance and be resisted in another instance.

Thorough scenario planning can anticipate when these circumstances could arise but it could be argued that one cannot be prepared for every single contingency. Maguire and Hardy (2013) suggest on the basis of their studies on the discursive construction of risk, that instead of trying to control risk,

> very different social ordering, perhaps called "sensing", might also be important insomuch as actors rely on practices such as intuiting, in which they use experience and tacit knowledge to process weak signals to conclude that something is wrong (Weick and Sutcliffe, 2011) – for instance, they actively look for unusual situations and listen for strange sounds.
>
> (Maguire and Hardy, 2013: 250)

This concept of "sensing" aligns with those of emergent strategy and complexity absorption in public relations. In a positioning monitoring sense, practitioners are actively scanning the environment for "unusual situations and strange sounds", that is, patterns emerging in media reportage, stakeholder engagement and so forth that would indicate the degree to which the positioning strategy is holding.

Crystallizing positions in public relations

Rather than positions simply being determined, set, and forgotten about, positions can be seen as being continuously negotiated in particular public relations episodes. This is because they are enacted (second vertex of the positioning triangle) by both the initiator of the episode and other entities that are involved in the episode. However, it can be said that there are times when positions undergo a process of "crystallization" which can be said to be "a process that finishes processes of change or negotiation for the time being" (Henriksen, 2008: 54). An example of this would be in a political campaign where candidates have been undertaking public relations positioning efforts to become elected into office. Once the election takes place and a candidate has won, they are effectively positioned as the winner, taking up the role of office until the next election is immanent. The position therefore has "crystallized" into a role for a period of time. Henriksen (2008: 52) states that roles differ from positions in that "roles are given by a structure that reaches beyond the particular interaction, whereas positions are continuously negotiated in the particular here and now social interaction". The political situation of achieving office following a public relations positioning campaign is such an example.

However, in a public relations sense, it seems that a position itself can crystallize rather than changing into a role as Henriksen (2008) describes. An example would be when, following a natural disaster, a local governor decides that an after dark curfew is needed to maintain safety of life and property. A public relations campaign works to position a certain behavior as both necessary and mandatory. The positioning would be enacted through regulations and announcements. Speech acts, namely declaratives and assertives respectively (Searle, 1979) would be used. The storyline would be crafted as one focused on protecting life and property, and would include information about penalties for breaches. Such a position would be crystallized in the sense that is would be non-negotiable for the period that the regulations remained in force. It would be the position itself that would be crystallized for a time, not a role.

This idea of crystallization can be seen in current public relations practice when a firm positioning goal is set for a public relations activity. Organizations want their desired position to be achieved, to "crystallize". This is seen as a wanted outcome as it relates to goal achievement but also to issues around resource deployment. A fixed, achieved position appears to be one where less effort can be exerted and fewer resources applied. A position in constant flux is a "hungry beast" in terms of public relations resources and energy. Further understanding of this phenomenon would be gained by pursuing a line of research inquiry in this area.

Another example would be when a mutually agreeable position is negotiated between parties that had been previously at odds over a mining project. One would imagine that such a position might be formalized in some way for a period of time. Henriksen's (2008: 54) idea of "fixed enactments" in a social interaction comes to the fore here. In our mining example, an agreement or memorandum of understanding would be an example of a fixed enactment "which forces the turn of events into specific trajectories across the social interaction". In this situation time and effort is saved as the need to repeatedly negotiate rights and duties related to disparate positions is removed while the position is crystallized:

> By manifesting power through the crystallisation, the negotiation of perspectives ceases, allowing the current understanding or relation to be formalized and gain structural legitimation. …By formalising the agreement through crystallisation, the structural integration provides the partners involved with power to enact the agreed solution by reference to the agreement.
>
> (Henriksen, 2008: 54)

We can see how this relates to public relations efforts in positioning when disputation and negotiation regarding positions end through such crystallization. Of course this does not always mean that all parties are happy with the outcome, as was seen in the GASP anti-smoking campaign against Phillip Morris that resulted in the trend toward more smoke-free statutes going forward (Stokes and Rubin, 2010).

Some positioning efforts in public relations do not crystallize at all, such as in the case of efforts to position western military action in Afghanistan in a positive light. One can see in Dimitriu's (2012) analysis of strategic communication during the mission in Afghanistan, although he did not examine positioning as such, the importance of narrative and storylines, and their framing, to public relations and strategic communication:

> Terrorist organizations and insurgencies are not bound by the guidelines of ethical reporting and can send out their reports on the airwaves based on half-truths and untruths. In order to gain sympathy and support among their supporters and to widen the split with the government they continually try to broadcast western actions in injustice frames. That is, whether or not by exploiting the media, both government activities and activities of the coalition troops are deliberately framed by placing them in a context that will delegitimize them. The result is to put the West in a dilemma – a choice between speed and accuracy of reporting. If western troops first conduct an extensive investigation before presenting our version, it is questionable whether this is at all effective, since the incidents have occurred several days earlier and have already been widely exploited by the opponent. By the time the investigation is rounded off and presented it no longer has much news value. On the other hand, if the report is rapidly produced and contains untruths this can destroy western credibility.
>
> (Dimitriu, 2012: 204–5)

Examining Dimitriu's work through a positioning theoretical lens, the centrality of storylines to attempt to positively position western military efforts is evident. Dimitriu (2012: 197) describes how the realization that "the actual outcome of tactical operations is less important than what the local population thinks of it" is gaining currency in military thinking. Whilst not advocating that the positioning theoretical lens could or should replace all other analytical approaches, in cases like this it is clear that it could deepen the analysis of and shed further light on flaws in current strategic communication practice and inform future direction. The issue of the local moral order, the right to position one's own organization or activities and those of others, and the responsibilities that accompany such positioning is central. As the position itself dictates the right to use certain storylines and restricts the use of others, Western interests could better hone the positioning strategic planning and implementation. It seems evident that the insurgents are in many instances gaining the upper hand in the positioning war.

Dimitriu diagnoses a key issue for Western military "stratcoms" (2012: 192) centeres on having multiple target audiences with efforts "aimed at undermining and delegitimizing the opponent, gaining support and legitimacy from the local population, from the electorate at home, the international public and all other (relevant) target groups" (p. 192). He writes of the importance that none of the messages designed for these target audiences conflict with each other:

> The heart of a Stratcom strategy is a single, carefully constructed strategic narrative based on existing ideas and values…a strategic narrative needs to be communicated throughout the whole apparatus down to the lowest levels as everyone needs to "live the story" for a strategic narrative to be effective… Stratcom is not only a matter of deliberate exercises in communication and crafting a master narrative, but also about the wittingly and unwittingly sent messages throughout an entire state or alliance – everything communicated, not only by words but also by deeds.
>
> (Dimitriu, 2012: 197)

A strategic public relations positioning theoretical perspective aligns with the first three assertions. It takes into account the perceptions of all possible relevant target groups; aims at undermining and delegitimizing the opponent; gaining support and legitimacy from diverse target groups; and, ensures that messages do not conflict with each other. It is from this point that the approaches begin to diverge. Does the organization, in this case the military coalition, need a master narrative? Or does it need to determine a "master position" that is viable, that it has a right to take up, from the views of the various local moral orders within which it communicates?

Positioning theory would argue the latter and here lies the huge public relations challenge. Such an exercise is further complicated by what Dimitriu (2012: 206) calls a paradox in that "as a result of the new media there is an increased cultural awareness and deeper differentiation between these groups, yet at the same time there is a single, global listening audience". It may be that the only "master" position that the military would be seen by the various local moral orders to have a right to, and the abstract concept of the local moral order of a "global listening audience", may be incongruent with the political agenda of the various coalition partners. A public relations positioning analysis may in fact further indicate the operational issues and challenges that have plagued the initiative since its inception over a decade ago. There may be no such viable master position as the military task at hand is in itself unviable and the goals unclear.

A small study conducted with an environmental organization confirmed the inherent problems of developing a coherent public relations positioning strategy when the goal and mission of an organization was unclear (James, 2012). However, if there was such a position for the Western forces in Afghanistan, the strategic prepositioning, the positioning itself, and the subsequent narrative/storylines this enabled them to use, would not actually be a "master narrative". The ensuing speech acts/actions and storylines would need to be congruent with the "master position" but could be enacted and communicated through word and deed in different ways. This would still mean the positioning triangle would need to maintain its "dynamic stability" (Harré and van Langenhove, 1999: 10) if the position had any hope of crystallizing.

In other situations, positions crystallize in ways in which the initiator of the effort did not want it to. Such as in the case of Dominique Strauss-Kahn, whose post-trial publicity, defined as "media relations efforts to find a middle ground between a judicial ruling and public acceptance", was analyzed by Xifra (2012: 477). From the context of Xifra's study, it was clear that Dominique Strauss-Kahn was attempting to position himself in the minds of the French people as a suitable Socialist Party candidate for the presidency of France. This was after he had been charged with the sexual assault of a hotel maid. Charges were eventually dropped due to issues related to the credibility of the victim. Dominique Strauss-Kahn did admit to an inappropriate sexual encounter with the maid but denied the assault. Xifra's study indicated that in spite of the image repair strategies adopted by Dominique Strauss-Kahn, surveys of French people indicated that their opinion of his public image remained unchanged or worsened. Applying positioning theory, it can be seen that he failed to position himself as he wanted to, with the majority of French people crystallized in their position that he was an unsuitable political candidate.

Liquidating positions in public relations

If positions can be crystallized, according to Henriksen (2008), they can be liquidated, and this is highly relevant to public relations practice. In the above example, it can be seen that Dominique Strauss-Kahn had identified the fixed, crystallized position held by the French people. He was seeking to reposition himself in their eyes, liquidating the fixed negative position they held. Liquidation seeks to:

> unsettle the current discourses by questioning the commonly accepted meanings of what goes on. A reason for doing so could be to either change

> current practice, or to position oneself within that practice…By liquidating a fixed perspective, the enactors are allowed to look for new approaches to a given problem or situation, rather than having to stick to the fixed approach.
>
> (Henriksen, 2008: 55)

In adapting Henriksen's work for a public relations context, it is interesting to explore what happens when a party wants to challenge a long-held position of another in order to advance its own mission. We can see what has happened across much of the Western world in regards to same-sex marriage, with many political and other leaders stating their positions on this controversial issue, either in support or otherwise of legislative changes to permit such marriages to proceed. The position held by many people that marriage was a union between a man and a woman was "crystallized" in religious texts and in legislation. Those in support of changing this fixed position began to unsettle the current discourses by questioning the commonly accepted meanings of marriage in order to change the current practices and legislation, and to permit same sex couples to marry. By liquidating the fixed position on marriage, those in favor of changes looked for new approaches to both community attitudes and legislation. From their perspective, the time had come for the fixed position on marriage to change.

This process aligns to Henriksen's description of liquidation and provides a further context for consideration in determining positions to be taken or assigned. This is by questioning whether there are fixed, or crystallized, positions that need to be liquidated as part of the positioning strategy. It is worth noting that Henriksen's (2008) work discusses the process of liquidating roles, which he states can be viewed as consisting "of a series of positions" (p. 57), so that the positions tied up in the roles can be addressed singly instead of as a cluster. This is beyond the scope of this current work but does set the stage for further consideration of if and how public relations positioning contributes to the construction of roles within organizations and wider society.

What is interesting in public relations positioning is that often the entity that is being positioned by another is not present at the moment of the positioning act being initiated. Especially with written or recorded texts, communication takes place through time and space and is not immediate, as it would be in a conversation or live debate situation. Bazerman (2012) writes about this phenomenon in a general sense, suggesting that if the initiator of the communicative act comes to mind "they appear as acts of imagination based on limited clues obtained from prior texts or interactions, rather than as embodied presences" (p. 227). The exchanges in the social media space are interesting as they could be seen to operate along a continuum of immediacy and distance in time and space. For example, a post on social media sites such as Twitter or Facebook could be responded to within seconds or at some other time, minutes, hours or days later. Bazerman's (2012) general insights again shed light on this within a public relations context. This is because so much of the communication effort used in public relations positioning acts is written-text based and this has limitations. These include the abilities of practitioners to express what it is that is desired to be said, and, the abilities of audiences to interpret what is offered to them.

This again ties in with the strategic importance of practitioners working to construct zones of meaning and tying what meanings they would like audiences to construct to that which they already know. It highlights the need for practitioners to think visually as well as textually in terms of enactment and storylines. With social media offering so much potential to drive audience traffic to what has been termed "engagement media" (Edelman, 2010), the opportunities to enact and support an organization's positioning effort have never been greater. Engagement media is a combination of new, social, and owned media that allows companies and brands to engage directly with stakeholders to deliver content and build relationships (Edelman, 2010). One can see this is not just for large corporations or government agencies but also for small businesses or activist groups. Organization-branded and owned video channels on platforms such as YouTube or Vimeo, photo channels on sites such as Instagram, Flickr and Pinterest, blogs, websites, Facebook pages and so on offer more channels than ever before to enact and support positions.

The desired public relations position thus needs to be determined, constructed and expressed within such a zone so that intended audiences have an increased chance of creating the intended meaning. Once a shared meaning has begun to be co-constructed, it can be seen that it would be possible to build on that meaning, introducing new incremental information to help deepen understanding of the position being taken or assigned. Bazerman (2012) suggests that it is not only the words that are used that facilitate such understanding but that it also rests in the selection and use of domains of communication and genres of communication. It is evident that this is part of the repertoire of public relations and strategic communication skills. This idea of domains and genres of communication is explored further in the next chapter, Chapter 5.

Summary

This chapter provided a detailed description of factors to be considered in determining a position to be taken up or assigned to another. A public relations position was defined as a discursively constructed point of intentional representation from where possibilities for action are established, or in some cases denied, in terms of the local moral order/s wherein the public relations activity is taking place for the purposes of achieving an intended outcome. Public relations positioning was defined as the actions taken to achieve the public relations position.

The Framework for Intentional Positioning in Public Relations has been shown to have the potential to guide the determination of a viable position. This is because it aims to provide a scaffold or guide. This can be used to assist practitioners to meet both the challenge of demonstrating to senior management why positions taken need to be viable within the local moral order and, of guiding the development and implementation of viable positioning strategies for the organization.

Effective public relations positioning therefore is when what is said about the position (the account) and what is done in relation to the position (the discursive act/performance) is aligned or congruent. This is determined primarily by the system of rights and duties associated with positions according to the local moral order within which the positioning is taking place. It was noted that the position itself might need to be changed if resistance to positioning efforts is encountered on the basis of the efforts being seen as unacceptable within a particular moral order. Such an environment can be viewed as complex. As such, conceptualizing public relations practice within ideas of emergent strategy, complexity absorption and risk management was considered to reflect the realities of dynamic positioning practice.

The idea of crystallizing and liquidating positions was introduced as a way of encapsulating the way much public relations practice is conceptualized. A fixed, achieved position can be seen to have crystallized and is related to goal achievement, but also to issues around resource deployment. A crystallized position appears to be one where less effort needs to be exerted and fewer resources need to be applied. A position in constant flux can be a "hungry beast" in terms of public relations resources and energy. Organizations however, also seek to liquidate positions by attempting to unsettle the current discourses in order to either change current practice, or to position themselves within that practice.

The chapter aimed to demonstrate that practitioners can work through position planning, issues anticipation, the mapping of probable challenges to an organization's position, and plot any anticipated counter strike's chances of success. This will provide sound evidence for them to discuss a positioning strategy with the organization's decision-makers. If practitioners can engage anticipated opponents to a position to try and find a more amenable one, a position acceptable to both parties may be found.

References

Bazerman, C. (2012) Genre as social action. In J. Gee and M. Handford (eds) *The Routledge Handbook of Discourse Analysis*. London: Routledge, pp. 226–38.

Broom, G. (1977) Coorientational measurement of public issues, *Public Relations Review*, 3, 110–119.

Cancel, A., Cameron, G., Sallot, L. and Mitrook, M. (1997) It depends: a contingency theory of accommodation in public relations, *Journal of Public Relations Research*, 9(1): 31–63. http://dx.doi.org/10.1207/s1532754xjprr0901_02

Coombs, W.T. (2010) Crisis communication: a developing field. In R. Heath (ed.) *The Sage Handbook of Public Relations*. Thousand Oaks, CA: Sage, pp. 477–88.

Davies, B. and Harré, R. (1990) Positioning: the discursive production of selves. *Journal for the Theory of Social Behaviour*, 20(1): 43–63.

Dimitriu, G. R. (2012) Winning the story war: strategic communication and the conflict in Afghanistan. *Public Relations Review,* 38(2): 195–207.

Edelman, R. (2010) The third way: public Engagement. *The Digital Reset: Communication in an era of engagement*. New York: Edelman, pp. 2–3. Retrieved from www.newmediaacademicsummit.com/documents/NMAS_whitepaper_2010.pdf

Gilpin, D. and Murphy, P. (2006) Reframing crisis management through complexity. *Public Relations Theory II*, pp. 329–44.

Gilpin, D. and Murphy, P. (2008) Reframing crisis management through complexity. In C. H. Botan and B. Hazelton (eds) *Public Relations Theory II*. Marwah, NJ: Lawrence Erlbaum, pp. 375–92.

Grunig, J. (2009) Paradigms of global public relations in an age of digitalisation. *PRism,* 6(2) http://praxis.massey.ac.nz/prism_on-line_journ.html

Grunig, J. (2013) Furnishing the edifice: ongoing research on public relations as a strategic management function. In S. Krishnamurthy, A. Zerfass and J. Kim (eds) *Public Relations and Communication Management: Current trends and emerging topics*. New York: Routledge, pp. 1–26.

Hallahan, K., Holtzhausen, D., van Ruler, B., Verčič, D. and Sriramesh, K. (2007) Defining strategic communication. *International Journal of Strategic Communication*, 1(1): 3–35.

Harré, R. and van Langenhove, L. (1999) *Positioning Theory: Moral contexts of intentional action*. Oxford: Blackwell.

Henriksen. T. (2008) Liquidating roles and crystallising positions. In F. Moghaddam, R. Harré and N. Lee (eds) *Global Conflict Resolution through Positioning Analysis*. New York: Springer, pp. 41–64.

James, M. (2010) The use of intentional positioning techniques in government agencies' communication campaigns. In D. Verčič, and K. Sriramesh (eds) *Government Communication: Proceedings of the 17th International Public Relations Research Symposium BledCom*. Bled, Slovenia, Ljubljana: Pristop, pp. 140–7. Retrieved from www.bledcom.si/uploads/ppt2010/bledcom 2010 proceedings hi.pdf

James, M. (2011a) A provisional conceptual framework for intentional positioning in public relations. *Journal of Public Relations Research,* 23(1): 93–111. http://dx.doi.org/10.1080/1062726X.2010.505120

James, M. (2011b) Ready, aim, fire: the perceived role of key messages in public relations campaigns, *PRism*. 8(1).

James, M. (2011c) *The Strategic Construction of Intended Meaning in Australian Public Relations Campaigns through yhe use of Key Messaging and Positioning Techniques*. Thesis submitted for the award of Doctor of Philosophy, University of Newcastle. http://nova.newcastle.edu.au/vital/access/manager/Repository/uon:7594?queryType=vitalDismax&query=%22james%2C+Melanie%22

James, M. (2012) Autoethnography: the story of applying a conceptual framework for intentional positioning to public relations practice. *Public Relations Review,* 38(4): 555–64. http://dx.doi.org/10.1016/j.pubrev.2012.05.004

Kim, J. and Ni, L. (2010) Seeing the forest through the trees: the behavioural, strategic management paradigm in public relations and its future. In R. Heath (ed.) *The Sage Handbook of Public Relations*. Thousand Oaks, CA: Sage, pp. 35–57.

King, C. (2010) Emergent communication strategies, *International Journal of Strategic Communication*, 4(1): 19–38. doi: 10.1080/15531180903415814

Lane, A. (2007) Empowering publics: the potential and challenge for public relations practitioners in creative approaches to two-way symmetric public relations. *Australian Journal of Communication*, 34(1): 71–86.

Macnamara, J. and Zerfass, A. (2012) Social media communication in organisations: the challenges of balancing openness, strategy and management, *International Journal of Strategic Communication*, 6(4): 287–308.

Maguire, S. and Hardy, C. (2013) Organizing processes and the consturction of risk: a discursive approach. *Academy of Management Journal*, 56(1): 231–55.

Mintzberg, H. (1978). *Patterns in Strategy Formation*. Management science, 24(9), 934–48.
Mintzberg, H. (2007) *Tracking Strategies: Toward a general theory*. Oxford: Oxford University Press.
Mirabeau, L. and Maguire, S. (2013) From autonomous strategic behavior to emergent strategy. *Strategic Management Journal*, doi: 10.1002/smj.2149
Neff, B. (2008) Speech act theory: an approach to public relations leadership. In T. Hansen-Horn and B. Neff (eds) *Public Relations: From theory to practice*. Boston, MA: Pearson, pp. 89–103.
Pang, A., Jin, Y., and Cameron, G. (2010) Strategic management of communication: insights from the contingency theory of strategic conflict management. In R. Heath (ed.) *The Sage Handbook of Public Relations*. Thousand Oaks, CA: Sage, pp. 17–34.
Parrott, W. (2003) Positioning and the emotions. In R. Harré and F. Moghaddam (eds) *The self and Others: Positioning individuals and groups in personal, political and cultural contexts*. London: Praeger, pp. 29–43.
Searle, J. (1979) *Expression and Meaning: Studies in the theory of speech acts*. Cambridge: Cambridge.
Slocum-Bradley, N. (2007) Constructing and de-constructing the ACP Group: actors, strategies and consequences for development, *Geopolitics*, 12(4): 635–55. doi:10.1080/14650040701546095
Stokes, A. and Rubin, D. (2010) Activism and the limits of symmetry: the public relations battle between Colorado GASP and Philip Morris. *Journal of Public Relations Research*, 22(1): 26–48.
Tirado, F. and Gálvez, A. (2007) Positioning theory and discourse analysis: some tools for social interaction analysis. *Forum Qualitative Sozialforschung/Forum: Qualitative Social Research*, 8(2). Retrieved from www.qualitative research.net/index.php/fqs/article/view/248/547
Wilkinson, S. and Kitzinger, C. (2003) Constructing identities: a feminist conversation analytic approach to positioning in action. In R. Harré and F. Moghaddam (eds) *The Self and Others: Positioning individuals and groups in personal, political and cultural contexts*. London: Praeger, pp. 157–80.
Wise, D. and James, M. (2013) Positioning a price on carbon: applying a proposed hybrid method of positioning discourse analysis for public relations. *Public Relations Inquiry*, 2(3): 327–53.
Xifra, J. (2012) Sex, lies, and post-trial publicity: the reputation repair strategies of Dominique Strauss-Kahn. *Public Relations Review*, 38(3): 477–83.

5 Enacting the position in public relations

The second vertex of the positioning triangle

It is evident that you can pick up a chess piece and position it on a different square on a chessboard. But how can you position something, or reposition something, that you can't touch? Something that exists only in the market place of ideas, that is, the contested environment where meanings are wrangled, constructed, deconstructed and reconstructed (Berger, 1999; Heath, 2001)? The answer lies in using a force that has nothing to do with physical touch and everything to do with the social force that can be exerted by words and texts in their widest sense. In his seminal work on speech act theory, Austin (1962) tells us that words do things. How? When statements are made, or certain actions are undertaken, (like holding up your hand in the stop sign) they can exert a force. As Slocum-Bradley (2007) states, "words, phrases and concepts do not have rigid meanings intrinsic to them, but rather people use them to *do* things" (p. 637). This is the major tenet of speech act theory with speech acts seen not as simply conveying information but being created for the purposes of action (Neff, 2008).

The Framework for Intentional Positioning in Public Relations, as described in Chapter 3, draws on speech act theory within the positioning triangle domain. It is at the second vertex of the positioning triangle, where the desired positioning is enacted, that speech act theory comes into play. The second vertex of the positioning triangle is when the desired position of the initiator of the communication activity is enacted through a speech act such as an assertion or a commitment. From a research perspective, the ability to identify speech acts enables the intention of the "speaker", in terms of what he or she wants the "listener" to do, to be determined (Revlin, 2013). In designing public relations tactics, a knowledge of speech act categories can assist in developing the positioning enactment plan.

In strategic public relations, practitioners work to influence or delimit possible interpretations of an organization's words and actions. With a handshake they may be attempting to enact certain positions, such as positioning the political leader as a diplomatic influencer, or a CEO as in control of a deal. Other players may be attempting to resist that positioning and indeed be trying to reposition by attempting to change the context of the action, positioning the political leader as a thug; or the CEO as riding roughshod over stakeholders. Further exploration of speech act theory and its role in explaining the enactment of positions is warranted.

This chapter will provide an overview of speech act theory, the related scholarship within the public relations field and its role in positioning theory. An account of how positioning has been enacted in practice is then provided, followed by a description of how speech act theory can provide guidance for positioning enactment strategies in public relations.

Speech act theory overview

It is sometimes seen as a theory of language but Searle, Kiefer and Bierwisch (1980) made the argument that speech act theory is an extension of the theory of meaning, and is thus a branch of the theory of communication. Public relations practitioners, although they may not have actively realized it, are working in the realm of this theory all the time. Harré and Moghaddam (2003) tell us "every socially significant action, intended movement, or speech must be interpreted as an act, a socially significant performance" (p. 6). They use the example of a handshake, as an intended action. It can mean congratulations, closing a deal or can be a greeting. This simple action, in a public relations context, can be designed by the practitioner as part of a larger set of performances, for example in a diplomatic meeting as part of a media event; or in a corporate communications situation when a deal is sealed. The action does something, it creates meaning. It is not just a handshake. When this action is shown in news footage, a news page photograph, an annual report, an organizational video, or an activist website, the meaning intended by the practitioner and the meaning constructed by audiences may be quite different.

The theory is based on the assumption that the basic unit of human communication is not a sentence or phrase but a speech act. A speech act can be defined as "an utterance noted and attended to" (Bazerman, 2012). A speech act is the performance of certain kinds of acts such as making statements, thanking people, asking questions, describing, congratulating and so on (Searle, Kiefer and Bierwisch, 1980). Speech acts exert a social force and work to shape the construction of social reality. Searle (1979), who built on the work of Austin (1962), suggested five ways of using language, or "five general categories of illocutionary acts" (Searle, 1979: viii):

1. we tell people how things are (assertives);
2. we try to get them to do things (directives);
3. we commit ourselves to doing things (commissives);
4. we express our feelings and attitudes (expressives); and,
5. we bring about changes in the world through our utterances (declaratives).

These five categories provide a meaningful method with which to analyze or design positioning enactment strategies. Since Searle's work, there have been other attempts to expand on the categories and these have had various levels of take up in the linguistic and related fields (e.g. Carr, Schrock and Dauterman, 2012; McKaughan, 2012; Nastri, Pena and Hancock, 2006), but each takes Searle's categories as a reference point. Positioning theorists in the main, and on the occasions where public relations scholars have addressed speech act theory, have primarily engaged with Searle's five categories.

In a public relations sense, a practitioner's work needs the audience to take up their offering and together co-construct the meaning and define the speech act. That is, if the act was intended to be some sort of commitment, did the audience decode it as such or as something else? The practitioner's job is to work to maximize the chances of the audience constructing the intended meaning and thus create the desired speech act that advances the organization's mission. This is an important aspect of the discursive practice of practitioners, especially as it pertains to the concept of positioning. In analyzing positioning strategy, the method involves looking at the categories of language used in given texts and identifying evidence of one or more of the five general categories of speech acts in the context of the discourse within which the text is situated (e.g. media release, corporate video). The particular speech acts can be classified under these five headings.

This approach is more than just looking for verbs in the text such as "announce" or "proclaim", which is the most common error people make with speech act theory, but looks at the illocutionary act in its entirety (Searle, 1979). An illocutionary act can be seen as the act of saying something, the literal meaning of what it is that is being said. In speech act theory, illocutionary acts are contrasted with perlocutionary acts, and this is where the theory becomes very interesting and relevant in the strategic communication sense. A perlocutionary act has to do with "those effects which our utterances have on hearers which go beyond the hearer's understanding of the utterance" (Searle, Kiefer and Bierwisch, 1980: vii), or, as stated by Dresner and Herring:

> A perlocutionary act is an action performed through an utterance that depends for its identity not only on the speaker's intentions but rather also on the effect of the utterance on its audience. Persuading, for example, is a perlocutionary act, to the extent that the speaker succeeds in actually persuading the addressee…
>
> (Dresner and Herring, 2010: 253)

So an illocutionary act such as stating something can be done for the purpose of achieving the perlocutionary effect of convincing or persuading. In terms of positioning analysis, one can ask questions such as, what perlocutionary effect was the practitioner seeking when using a certain phrase? In program design, we can look at what positioning effect we are seeking in our target audiences and design the words or actions accordingly. It should be noted that in much positioning theory academic literature, the term "social force" is used rather than illocutionary or perlocutionary force and this term refers to "the context-dependent act that anyone performs by uttering a certain sentence" (Moghaddam, Hanley and Harré, 2003: 141).

A speech act can perform several acts simultaneously with the intent of the speaker being a key distinguishable factor. According to Bach (1998) a speech act encompasses:

1 the act of saying something;
2 what is being done by what is being said (such as declaring, requesting, promising); and,
3 how one is trying to affect one's audience.

With much public relations practice centered on using language to achieve specific outcomes, the stated strategic goals and the authority of the organization, and its spokespeople appointed to perform the illocutionary act, become a key focus of research. This is where speech acts particularly relate to intentional positioning efforts. The speech act is more than the "propositional content" but also includes the concept of "illocutionary" (Searle, 1979: vii) or "social" (Moghaddam *et al.*, 2003: 141) force. The most important part of this force is what Searle calls the "illocutionary point" (1979: 3): what is the point or purpose of what is being said, as Searle (1979: 2) explains:

> The point or purpose of an order can be specified by saying that it is an attempt to get the hearer to do something. The point or purpose of a description is that it is a representation (true or false, accurate or inaccurate) of how something is. The point or purpose of a promise is that it is an undertaking of an obligation by the speaker to do something.

In general situations, most illocutionary acts are not intended to have specific social effects (Searle, 1979) but it can be argued that in the context of public relations, most *are* intended to have such effects, that is, to have target publics co-construct the meaning that public relations practitioners intend for them. Bach (1998, n.p.) states, "the perlocutionary act is a matter of trying to get the hearer to form some correlative attitude and in some cases to act in a certain way". The evidence in the research findings (James, 2010, 2011a), and in the examples later in this chapter, indicate this is what organizations were attempting in their public relations activities, and according to their evaluation statements, actually achieved.

Speech act theory in public relations scholarship

Speech act theory has only had intermittent attention from public relations scholars over the last four decades (e.g. Burkart, 2007, 2009; Ehling, 1975; James, 2010, 2011a; Neff, 1998, 2008; Pearson, 1989; Radford, 2012; Smudde and Courtright, 2012; Xifra and Girona, 2012). It has not gained traction as a mainstream theoretical approach to conceptualizing public relations practice or research, primarily having been explored in the context of dialogical and ethical contexts. Work to connect speech act theory and positioning theory in public relations has only appeared in recent years (James, 2010, 2011a; Wise and James, 2013) and this has moved more towards examining speech act theory in the context of purposive communication and strategic intent, in some ways linking back to Ehling's (1975) early work.

In 1975, Ehling drew on Searle's speech act theory to develop his argument that public relations management was embedded in the concept of purposeful behavior. In trying to move public relations theory away from transmission models of message communication, Ehling focused on the production of meaning for a purpose. He highlighted that the construction of purposeful meaning in a public relations context would not be achieved unless the intended audience members attended to the speech act produced. The meaning produced from the speech act is a result of "joint choice-making and mutual communication" (Ehling, 1975: 32) with "the important unit of analysis [being] the act of [meaning] *production*, not merely or solely the message produced" (Ehling, 1975: 22). In 2012, Smudde and Courtright expressed much the same idea in that communication is viewed as successful if

> the hearer identifies the attitude expressed in the way the speaker intends him or her to identify it. This is the very stuff of public relations as practitioners seek to inspire cooperation between their organizations and publics.
>
> (Smudde and Courtright, 2012: 894)

This idea that the speech act itself is only complete when the potential for interpretation has been somehow taken up by participants in a communication episode has remained a key theme in public relations scholarship on speech act theory. Smudde and Courtright (2012: 894) further address this stating that speech act theory gives us a way to explain how language and social conventions for language use combine during people's communicative actions, which are contingent upon their individual thoughts, feelings, and actions (even their intentions, goals, perceptions, and social and communication competencies).

This idea of speech act completion by audience members/dialogue participants present in the public relations literature aligns with general developments in the theory since Austin (1962) and Searle's (1970, 1979) work. That the speech act is not just the utterance but its success at creating a social fact, both in the recognition of its accomplishment and in terms of the content of the utterance (Bazerman, 2012), relates to the other theme that emerged in the public relations literature, namely, the application of Habermas' theory of communicative action. This theme focuses on the role of speech acts in establishing and maintaining "equal freedom among participants to initiate and maintain discourse" (Pearson, 1989: 73; Burkart, 2007, 2009). This idea is at the heart of linking this theoretical approach to dialogical/symmetrical ideas (Berger, 1999; Pearson, 1989). Pearson states:

> Freedom to initiate and maintain communication means equal opportunity to use communicatives – speech acts that involve saying, speaking, asking; freedom to challenge and explain means equal opportunity to use constatives – speech acts that involve asserting, describing, explaining; freedom from manipulation means equal opportunity to use representatives – speech acts that involve admitting, confessing, concealing, denying; equality vis-a-vis

> power means equal opportunity to use regulatives – speech acts that involve commanding, forbidding, allowing, warning.
>
> (Pearson, 1989: 75)

Such a taxonomy was suggested as being able to drive more ethical communication between an organization and its publics by according all communication spokespersons equal opportunity to use all four categories of speech acts (Pearson, 1989). Pearson saw coorientation theory as affording a way of testing hypotheses about the relationship between communicators' perceptions of the dialogical or ethical nature of communication and their perceptions about communication rules, within which the public relations episode was occurring. He saw communication rules as pivotal to ethical practice and one can relate this concept to that of the local moral order in operation at the site/s of the public relations episode. Practices involving the use of speech acts contrary to the local communication rules may have less chance of success, especially in terms of building consensus around issues or positioning an entity or its offerings in a particular way.

Similar themes emerge in Burkart's (2007, 2009) scholarship on Habermas and public relations. He highlights that speech act theory and speech acts are a central part of Habermas' examination of the human communication process that focuses on understanding as a fundamental democratic process. Burkart argues that the principles of Habermas' theory of communication can form the basis for examination of public relations and underpins the "consensus oriented public relations approach" (2009: 144). Like Pearson, (1986), Burkart (2007, 2009) presents Habermas' proposition of ideal speech situations where all parties participating in the discourse have the same access and ability to choose and use speech acts as forming an ethical basis for public relations.

Neff (2008), although linking ethical public relations and speech act theory, moves away from Habermas and discusses speech act theory in the context of the coordinated management of meaning (CMM). She suggests that it is the intent of a communication exchange that reveals the ethical dimensions:

> What the human brings to the dialogic situation in terms of intent is what creates the ethical potential. Intent is ingrained in the process through the idea of allowing completeness in speech enactments, responses to speech acts, and the element of time. All are factors of much import revealed only as the exchanges progress. Therefore, a dialogic approach is the means for allowing intent to be fully expressed when viewed within a speech act analysis, and these enactments bring the ethical dimension to full expression.
>
> (Neff, 2008: 97–98)

In public relations the speech act is placed at the intersection of culture, the self, the public relations episode, and the relationship component (Neff, 2008). It is this that shapes the "interpretative potential" (Neff, 2008: 92) of the speech act. Neff is critical of approaches to public relations practice that view publics as malleable and easily manipulated, where campaigns avoid interacting with publics for fear of losing control. She suggests a dialogic approach, where speech acts are sequenced with the intention of action, and are based on interactivity (Neff, 2008).

Neff (1998) described Searle's speech act category of expressives as particularly powerful in terms of there being no requirement for this category of act to be grounded in reality, i.e. it is expressing an attitude or opinion, and has the capacity to enable other speech acts to be enacted (2008: 95). She sees this category of speech act as being instrumental in providing an organizational leadership role for public relations professionals, as working with such speech acts gives the public relations role a particularly powerful impact on the communication process (Neff, 2008) and with this comes an ethical dimension which must consider all participants in the communication process, including the "'intent' of the participants" (Neff, 2008: 97). Speech act analysis within a positioning analysis of a public relations episode can potentially indicate the ethical dimensions as described by Neff (2008). A positioning analysis of a single text such as a media release, speech or brochure can highlight the author's intent in terms of the speech acts used in the positioning. However, it is only in analyzing the reception of such a text, the responses to that text, whether the positioning of the organization and others is accepted, or whether there are subsequent attempts to reposition parties within the episode, that the fuller picture emerges.

Neff (1998) suggests that speech act theory shapes much of the thinking behind the idea that it is language that shapes social reality and that it has helped shift ideas away from notions that communication is information. She advocates for conceptualizing organizations as only existing in language and that an organizational relationship "lives in communication" (2008: 90). According to Neff, we must acknowledge that organizational relationships can only be created through "languaging" and that "relationships thus are grounded in communication and derive empowerment from expression" (2008: 91). This is congruent with Smudde and Courtright's (2012) view that speech is a form of action or intentional behavior and that the "interaction between a speaker (e.g. an organization; corporate speaker) and a hearer (publics) draws its rhetorical energy from intentions and inferences, including inferences about unintentional attitudes expressed in symbolic actions" (p. 894).

It is further reflected by Radford (2012) in the assertion that "a knowledge claim is always an appearance of discourse, manifest as a speech act that is produced with respect to other claims. Taken together, a body of knowledge is constituted by the ways in which particular texts are put into relationships with other texts" (p. 53). It is evident that in public relations, organizations and their publics communicate through texts and use speech acts to shape constructions of reality that facilitate the achievement of the desired outcomes of parties involved in the episode. This reflects poststructuralist thinking in the idea that truth is a social construction and as such is contestable, and further, that discourse can be structured into speech acts (Xifra and Girona, 2012). This suggests that it is the process of identifying speech acts that gives the clue to the discourse being invoked in public relations positioning texts, and further, that in designing a positioning program to invoke a specific discourse, one uses certain categories of speech acts.

Speech act theory in positioning

Davies and Harré (1999) argue for the productive interrelationship between positioning and the illocutionary force of speech acts. They relate the poststructuralist paradigm to positioning in that it recognizes the way discourse is constituted through particular practices, such as speech acts, and also acknowledges the ability of people to exercise choice in relation to those practices. They posit that a speech action becomes a speech act, thus achieving its social force, only to the degree that it is taken up by those involved in the encounter. This is a key point in positioning enactment for public relations. The degree to which the interpretative potential is taken up as intended by the practitioner is a way of measuring the success of that particular effort. In the examples detailed below, this was seen as being the case, with the enacted positioning supported by carefully constructed storylines. Harré and van Langenhove (1999) define the difference between the two discursive acts, speech acts and storyline, as follows:

> Declarations consist of those speech-acts in which the speaker gives some sort of report on how things or events appear from the speaker's point of view. Point of view refers both to the speaker's locus in time and space as well as his or her reputation for reliability and other moral qualities, his or her "character" as Goffman called it. Narrations, on the other hand, consist of those communicative productions in which there is a storyline. People present themselves and others, as actors in a drama.
>
> (Harré and van Langenhove, 1999: 8)

However, there are instances when a speech act such as a declaration can also be a narration and the differences and similarities are not always straightforward (Harré and van Langenhove, 1999). In positioning analysis, it has been found that the same sentence can be used to perform several speech acts. Which speech act it is can depend on the storylines that people involved perceive to be in use (Davies and Harré, 1999). If, for example, a mining company sought to position a government regulator as supportive of a project, it will have asserted that this was the case. At the same time if that same company sought to position a community activist group as being unsupportive of the project, it would have asserted that this too was the case. A positioning analysis should be able to account for the positioning, aiming to examine the episode in order to show if and how both positions were taken up by the parties, namely the regulator and the activist group. It should show how various understandings of supportive and unsupportive positions were derived and crucially, in terms of examining the process of establishing the meaning of speech acts, examine which storyline the parties took themselves to be embedded within (Davies and Harré, 1999).

Another aspect of speech act theory that has application to positioning, and specifically to public relations positioning, is the notion of causation. According to Slocum-Bradley (2008), "whilst a speech act may 'incite' or 'encourage' (social force) a particular action, it can never 'cause' it" (p. 211). She states the analytical distinction that defines causation as being "a determinate relationship (under certain conditions) between two events" and that in positioning theory, "the relationship between two social forces is not causal but normative" with one social force making another appropriate in some circumstances (p. 211). Slocum-Bradley (2008) provides the following examples to demonstrate:

> if George compliments Hillary on her choice of clothing, it may be appropriate for her to reply with an expression of gratitude. However, one social force does not "cause" another: Hillary can choose to slap George instead. Someone "encouraged" to kill another person can refuse.
>
> (Slocum-Bradley, 2008: 211–12)

This means that an understanding of the normative context generated should not be taken as sanctioning certain actions or as a suggestion that alternative options were unavailable to actors in an episode. Slocum-Bradley (2007) suggests that "one option is to counter the meaning-system proposed – that is, the positionings and the resulting normative framework – with an alternative meaning system that provides alternatives for action" (p. 212). When examining public relations efforts through the lens of positioning theory, it is evident that this is what is occurring in much of the practice reported from around the world. The next section reports on accounts of practice that show how enacting the positions through speech acts aligned with the overall successful positioning efforts.

Using the second vertex of the positioning triangle in public relations analysis: positioning enactment

To demonstrate how positioning is enacted in public relations campaigns the Framework for Intentional Positioning in Public Relations was applied to past reports of award-winning government agency/public sector organizations' campaigns in Australia. All the campaigns in this snapshot of examples won a Public Relations Institute of Australia Golden Target Award in their categories, the highest award in Australia for public relations. The analysis was first undertaken to examine whether positioning in public relations was different to that seen in commercial marketing, as marketing as a rule is not generally associated with government-sponsored communication. It set out to investigate whether government agencies' and other public sector organizations' campaigns employed public relations positioning techniques, as defined by James (2011a), in their quest to achieve communication goals. These examples show that positioning undertaken by such government agencies and organizations is something quite different to that which is seen in marketing contexts. The data to which the Framework was applied was that generated by textual and thematic analysis of the award entry texts.

Positioning a move to a new government agency

The aim of this campaign was unambiguous – the campaign was called "Converting staff perceptions" (Department of Water, 2007) and its "overriding goal was to shift staff perceptions, building a positive, motivated and dedicated workforce which would ensure the new Department of Water was able to open to the public, ready for business as scheduled". This was taking place in an environment where "staff morale was very low", where there was "active resistance to the formation of the new agency" from the existing two agencies, and where it was acknowledged that staff were experiencing "change fatigue". Applying the Framework, it could be seen that an agreed position had been reached in that the new department was being formed and staff needed to not only move to the new department, they needed to feel positive and enthusiastic about the move.

The enactment of the positioning through speech acts was evident through the use of:

- assertives: the staff were told the way things were going to be, that is, that there was going to be a new Department of Water;
- directives: management tried to get the staff to do things, for example "use staff who were positive about the formation of the new department to influence and inspire those fatigued by constant change"; and,
- commissives: management committed to doing things, e.g. avoiding "at all costs, long-winded and poorly-defined statements of corporate values" instead, "setting out to give staff clear direction, to set concrete goals and to deliver on time, every time".

At the third vertex, storylines, supporting key messages and actions were consistent, clear and delivered through a variety of channels including emails, bulletins, personalized letters, newssheets and face-to-face presentations. The other channels were the use of staff "who were positive about the change process as 'brokers' to assist in building the new organization", brochures and leaflets about the new department, media relations tactics and advertorials.

This campaign exhibits characteristics of deliberate self-positioning. The positioning was undertaken with a specific strategic goal and, according to the award entry, the goal was met with the new department opening on schedule. Staff survey results, less than a year after the move, indicated that the staff were "among the most engaged and committed to their jobs in the country – placing the Department in the top 25 per cent of organizations in Australia".

Positioning a commencement time for tertiary study

This university recruitment campaign "Don't Let Another Year Go By" (Northern Territory University, 2003) stemmed from a need to fund expansion and amalgamation plans through midyear enrolments into its courses, which were traditionally lower than early year enrolments. Applying the Framework to the campaign it could be seen that there was a clear positioning of the middle of the year as a good time to start a course at university.

This position was enacted through with speech-acts including:

- assertives: told people how things were, that is, that time was passing them by and that it was time to act. These aimed to "impart a sense of urgency among potential students";
- directives: directed interested people to enroll in the courses.

The overall campaign message "Don't let another year go by" was "designed to play on a public feeling of 'it's already June...where has the year gone?'" This message was seen as particularly relevant to "mature-age professionals and parents of teenagers, who are more likely to believe that 'time is passing them by'". The campaign message within the storyline, was promulgated through letterbox deliveries, websites and media and advertising. It was supported by a comprehensive follow-through communication plan implemented through call centers, the university "info shop" and information days.

The campaign could be interpreted as deliberately self-positioning but it was also deliberately positioning others, that is, potential students, as perhaps being left behind for another year in order to invoke the urgency that was desired in the campaign. The positioning type could be seen as self-promotion primarily in an effort to "sell" courses in order to secure income for the university. The campaign had clear goals in driving enrolment inquiries and the targets set were exceeded, thus being reported as an excellent result.

Positioning a disease threat: state government level

This campaign aimed to help keep Equine Influenza (EI, or horse flu) out of the state of Victoria (Department of Primary Industries, 2008). It was evident that the disease threat was being positioned as serious, and one that warranted people behaving differently to usual practices. The agreed positioning, that EI was a serious threat, was evident through the descriptions of the possibility of the Spring Racing Carnival, especially the world-renowned Melbourne Cup, not proceeding and the subsequent financial loss to the state of some $630 million.

The agreed positioning was enacted through speech acts including:

- assertives: delivered by the Chief Veterinary Officer, who established and asserted the seriousness of the situation with EI;
- directives: which directed people to comply with biosecurity measures; and
- declarations: where it had been declared an offence to partake in certain activities and behaviors, e.g. transporting horses in proscribed areas.

The storylines supporting the assertives were delivered through information packs distributed to media and to people attending public meetings; those supporting directives were included in advertising materials and included lines such as "Horse flu. Take it seriously before it takes its toll"; and those supporting declarations included messages such as "Cross the line and you'll pay the fine" at border crossings on billboards, and so on. The type of positioning was forced self-positioning – the emergence of the disease threat in adjacent states had forced the state of Victoria to take action. The campaign goal was achieved with no cases of EI detected in the state and very high levels of awareness amongst surveyed audiences of the key campaign messages.

Positioning a new maternity unit – state government level

This campaign aimed "to establish Kaleeya Hospital's new unit as a credible and trusted facility in an extremely short time frame – in the face of significant operational challenges and enormous opposition from a 'Save Woodside' group" led by a high-profile ex-politician. The positioning triangle domain can be clearly seen in that the first vertex is the desired positioning as articulated in the challenge, that is, to position Kaleeya Hospital's new unit as a credible and trusted facility in an extremely short time frame. This desired position was enacted through:

- assertives: the politician announced that the old maternity unit would close and the new one would open;
- directives: issuing information and instructions about using the new facility to get local residents and staff to support the new unit;
- commissives: committing to providing a modern facility; and
- expressives: acknowledging feelings and attitudes about the old facility.

The storylines at the third vertex of the positioning triangle were developed to "stay positive" and were delivered through media campaigns, information materials, public meetings and tours, and "information circulated about the new unit was factual, clear and accurate across all materials" to "counter rumor and misinformation" (Mills Wilson Communication Consultants, 2006).

The positioning type was deliberate self-positioning. The positioning was undertaken within the context of the campaign goal that was "to secure support for the move and instill confidence in the new maternity unit". The outcome was unambiguously reported – "results were outstanding. The opposition campaign failed and the new maternity unit opened on April 3 with an established identity" (Mills Wilson Communication Consultants, 2006).

Positioning a consultation process

In the "Promising our Children a World Class Hospital" campaign (Socom, 2006), the Royal Children's Hospital (RCH) commissioned a local public relations agency to devise a public consultation process that would canvas the views of a wide range of stakeholders regarding the rebuilding of the hospital. As stated in the award entry, "its current location in inner-Melbourne parkland was ideal for sick children, but a vocal range of environmentalists and local residents wanted to move the hospital out of the park". It was clear that the hospital management itself wanted to rebuild on the same site but as it was "situated in a pocket of inner city parkland, the rebuilding was contentious" and that "the new RCH could be positioned as another 'land grab'" by those opposing the development. The RCH "had a history of bad blood with its neighbors" and one of the stated challenges was to negotiate a site for the RCH that "would not compromise its position as a world class hospital". The situation forced the hospital to take a path of action that saw it position the consultation process as genuinely seeking the best solution for sick children and the wider community.

This positioning was enacted through:

- assertives: the options for the rebuilding were presented along with the advantages and disadvantages of each;
- directives: stakeholders, both those within the identified publics of "environmentalists and local residents" and wider community members, were directed to take part in the consultation process; and,
- commissives: were used to highlight the commitment to the transparency of the process.

The third positioning vertex of storylines to support the position is clear in the six key messages listed in the award entry. These were promulgated through a range of channels including media, letterbox drops, direct mail, workshops, exhibitions and advertising.

The positioning was forced self-positioning because without the vocal opposition of the environmentalists and local residents such an exercise would not have been required. This occurred in the context of the strategic goal of determining "how the best children's hospital could be built in the best location with maximum community support". One of the reported results was that 84 percent of media reports "reflected positive aspects of the new hospital" and in the evaluation it was reported that the state government would rebuild the RCH on its existing site.

Positioning a power-restoration effort

Powerlink is a government-owned corporation that owns, develops and operates a high voltage electricity transmission network. Following a storm, the only working transformer supplying a small town was severely damaged and the inability to repair/replace it immediately "increased the potential for negativity and suspicion among stakeholders" as a similar incident had happened in recent history. It was identified that a strong public relations campaign (Powerlink, 2007) was needed "to cultivate and maintain mutual understanding with target publics". There was going to be a lengthy period of days or weeks without power and so the power-restoration effort was positioned by Powerlink in a way that demonstrated to stakeholders that all that could be done was being done, that it was being done as quickly as possible, and that it was a "highly complicated power restoration effort".

This positioning was enacted through:

- assertives: telling people about the situation, communicating "honest and accurate messages to instill realistic expectations";
- commissives: committing to providing practical support to reduce hardship; and
- expressives: expressing understanding about the hardship.

Supporting storylines were evident as "Powerlink and Ergon Energy worked closely from both an operational and communications perspective to identify solid key messages designed to inform and instill confidence in stakeholders". The media was used to promulgate key messages and individual briefings were held for ministers, the mayor and other key stakeholders. It is clear that this is forced self-positioning as a result of a major transformer outage. The overarching goal and all objectives were achieved or exceeded as the following evaluation statement shows: "negativity towards Powerlink and Ergon Energy was mitigated and importantly, organizational reputations were protected, and in fact strengthened".

Discussion of examples

Each of the campaigns had a clear strategic intent to persuade, educate, motivate and otherwise get target publics to co-construct meanings intended for them. The organizations, having determined what position they desired to achieve (the first vertex of the positioning triangle), undertook speech acts/actions to enact that position, most often through statements to target publics made through direct communication channels or the media. All enacted their positioning through the use of assertives, which aim to tell people how things are (Searle 1979, viii). However, in addition to using assertives, in other cases the positioning was also enacted through requests, orders or propositions to target publics, in what could be termed directives (Searle 1979). Several campaigns also showed evidence of using what Searle (1979) described as commissives – where organizations committed to do something; a few award entries illustrated elements that could be identified as expressives, where feelings and attitudes are expressed; and only one campaign could be shown to have used declaratives, which was an instance where laws were introduced to declare behavior illegal.

The communication campaigns of the government agencies and public sector organizations intended to position their idea, their offering or their service in a particular way in the minds of target publics and audiences. It is clear they employed a range of techniques to enact the intended positioning, primarily using assertives, that is, telling people or asserting the way things were or should be. The storylines that followed essentially played the role of supporting the position and its enactment. Positioning activities were employed to facilitate target publics and audiences constructing the meaning that the government agency/public sector organization intended for them. These are in the main not marketing communication campaigns but campaigns designed to construct an "interpretive potential" (Neff, 2008: 92). They each worked to persuade or influence identified target publics and audiences to view something a particular way or undertake a certain action, thus facilitating the achievement of specific organizational goals.

The next section will demonstrate how speech acts, used within the Framework, can enact a strategic positioning campaign.

Using the second vertex of the positioning triangle in program design

Speech acts do not convey information as such but work to change aspects of social reality. In public relations positioning, the successful speech act enacts the position, literally bringing the desired positioning to life. In developing speech acts for a public relations positioning program it is worth considering what Searle and Vanderveken (1985) suggest are the seven conditions of the "successful and non-defective" (p. 12) performance of speech acts. These are summarized below and adapted to a public relations context:

1 Has an *illocutionary point*: the illocution, that is the action performed by saying or writing something, has a point or purpose. Public relations efforts have to have a strategic intent otherwise it would be pointless to undertake any action (e.g. Heath 2001; James, 2009; Moloney, 2006). The speech act developed as part of the public relations positioning effort must have an action it aims to achieve, that is, it must have a point and purpose.
2 Has the correct degree of *illocutionary strength*: that is, that an order may have too much strength or force for a particular situation, whereas a request may be more appropriate and lead to a desired outcome. In public relations it is regular practice to conduct a situational analysis and such analysis, if it incorporated a positioning analysis, could give clues as to what illocutionary strength is required in the specific speech act/s. The local moral order within which the positioning efforts are being undertaken will determine what degree of strength parties have in terms of the right to make their illocutionary point. Over-stepping this socially determined right could result in targeted audiences and publics constructing different meanings from the interpretative potential of the speech act from those intended by the organization.
3 Uses the correct *mode of achievement* if needed: that is, some speech acts require a specific mode of achievement, e.g. for an order to be followed it needs to be issued by a person in authority; a witness in court doesn't just give an account, he or she testifies. In public relations, practitioners may need to recognize when conditions determine that a speech act is likely to be unsuccessful. This might mean pointing out to an enthusiastic spokesperson for your organization that she or he will not be recognized in the local milieu as having authority to make particular assertions or promises. It might mean using a more senior spokesperson or even liaising with higher authorities such as government bodies or law enforcement agencies to determine ways in which conditions could be made more appropriate for the communication effort. For

example, a CEO who is attending the scene of a crisis may be granted a higher degree of authority to speak within the local moral order than if she or he was filmed in the boardroom.

4 Uses appropriate *propositional content conditions*: that is, what is said is congruent with the conditions that one is operating within. For example, you cannot successfully apologize for acts for which you hold no responsibility; you cannot promise that an organization in which you have no role will undertake something. In public relations positioning this relates to the authority, both formal and informal, to communicate about a subject. An example would be when preparing a crisis response and determining for which acts your organization should apologize, and for considering which other authorities should be co-opted to comment on areas for which your organization has no authority (e.g. police operations; hospital situation).

5 Correctly presupposes the *preparatory conditions* are satisfactory: that is, for instance, someone to whom an apology is about to be issued is known to have viewed the situation as suitable for an apology; they recognized something as being wrong. In public relations this relates to being able to read and interpret the environment in which a communication effort is being considered.

6 Expresses the *sincerity condition*: that is, that the psychological state specified by the sincerity conditions of the propositional content aligns. According to Searle and Vanderveken,

> an insincere speech act is one where the speaker performs a speech act and thereby expresses a psychological state even though he does not have that state. Thus an insincere statement (a lie) is one where the speaker does not believe what he says…An insincere speech act is defective but not necessarily unsuccessful. A lie, for example, can be a successful assertion.
>
> (Searle and Vanderveken, 1985: 18)

It is evident that the degree of sincerity in any communication act undertaken within a public relations episode relates primarily to the ethical dimension of practice and perhaps, unfortunately, to the chances an organization has of being "caught out" in the lie.

7 Has the correct degree of *strength of the sincerity conditions*: that is, does the speech act express an appropriate degree of sincerity, e.g. it may not be appropriate to beseech when a simple request may suffice. In a public relations context one can see that to over-emphasize conditions when it is inappropriate to do so may backfire. This is especially in terms of levels of trust needed when such added emphasis may be needed, e.g. in times of crisis. If a blood bank was always imploring people to donate blood, when a desperate need actually existed, the speech act of imploring may not be successful as people have heard it too frequently in times of non-crisis.

According to Searle and Vanderveken (1985), context must also be considered in the performance of speech acts and this should be accounted for in the design of the public relations positioning effort. Searle and Vanderveken (1985) use the example of "I will come back in five minutes" (p. 27) as possibly being, depending on the context, a promise or a prediction. In a public relations context, the assertion of a company that their operations may cease in the near future could be interpreted by audiences as either a threat or as a prediction, again depending on context. Such an assertion may be met with dread by audiences who are employed by the company, whilst others such as environmental activists may see the assertion as a cause for jubilation if issues such as pollution were to cease.

Searle and Vanderveken (1985) also suggest four things to be considered in an evaluative context, based on the seven conditions listed above, and these also can be applied in public relations positioning planning efforts. Firstly, plan to ask at evaluation points to what degree did the organization succeed in achieving the illocutionary point? Secondly, were the propositional content conditions achieved? Thirdly, were the preparatory conditions correctly presupposed? Lastly, to what degree did the spokesperson express and possess the psychological state, that is, the sincerity conditions, and was the correct degree of strength evident in the sincerity conditions?

A practitioner can work to design speech acts that meet with all of the seven suggested conditions as a way to help ensure speech acts have the best chance of success in a public relations positioning effort. Such a list of condition definitions may also help practitioners defend their decision-making when putting forward recommendations regarding program elements such as content, spokespeople, timing, communication, environmental conditions and so on. Such things are often worked into practice at "gut-level" or instinct (James, 2011b) and practitioners may welcome a more rigorous way to structure and justify practices.

Summary

This chapter examined the concept of enacting public relations positioning efforts through the use of speech acts. An overview of speech act theory set the context and then a review of how speech act theory had been addressed in public relations academic literature was undertaken. What emerged from both the overview of the theory and the review of its application in public relations was the idea that a speech act was not complete until the intended audience members took up its proposition. From a public relations perspective it is suggested that a measure of success of a practitioner's efforts is when the meaning constructed by intended audience members, through the interpretive potential inherent in the speech acts used, aligns with that intended. The role of speech acts in progressing equal opportunity to partake in public discourse was also explored in the public relations literature.

A study of how positioning was enacted within Australian government-sponsored campaigns was presented to demonstrate how enactment, and speech acts in particular, were part of the overall positioning framework and the positioning triangle domain of that framework. Lastly an approach for incorporating speech act theory into the design of positioning enactment strategies was suggested for consideration. In the next chapter, the role of storylines in public relations positioning will be examined.

References

Austin, J. (1962) *How to Do Things with Words*. Clarendon: Oxford University Press.

Bach, K. (1998) Speech acts. In E. Carig (ed.) *Routledge Encyclopedia of Philosophy*. London: Routledge. Retrieved from www.rep.routledge.com.library.newcastle.edu.au/article/U043.

Bazerman, C. (2012) Genre as social action. In J. Gee and M. Handford (eds) *The Routledge Handbook of Discourse Analysis*. London: Routledge, pp. 226–38.

Berger, B. (1999) The Halcion affair: public relations and the construction of ideological world view. *Journal of Public Relations Research*, 11(3): 185–203.

Burkart. R. (2007) On Jurgen Habermas and public relations. *Public Relations Review*, 33, 249–54. doi:10.1016/j.pubrev.2007.05.002

Burkart, R. (2009) On Habermas: understanding and public relations. In O. Ihlen, B. van Ruler and M. Fredriksson (eds) *Public Relations and Social Theory: Key figures and concepts*. London: Routledge, pp. 141–64.

Carr, C., Schrock, D. and Dauterman, P. (2012) Speech acts within Facebook status messages. *Journal of Language and Social Psychology*, 31, 176–96. doi: 10.1177/0261927X12438535

Davies, B. and Harré, R. (1999) Positioning and personhood. In R. Harré and L. van Langenhove (eds) *Positioning Theory: Moral contexts of intentional action*. Oxford: Blackwell.

Department of Primary Industries (2008) Equine Influenza. PRIA Golden Target Award entry winner. Retrieved from www.lib.uts.edu.au/gta

Department of Water, Western Australia (2007) "Converting staff perceptions" PRIA Golden Target Award entry winner. Retrieved from www.lib.uts.edu.au/gta

Dresner, E. and Herring, S. (2010) Functions of the nonverbal in CMC: emoticons and illocutionary force. *Communication Theory*, 20, 249–68.

Ehling, W. (1975) PR administration, management science, and purposive systems. *Public Relations Review*, 1(2): 15–43.

Harré, R. and Moghaddam, F. (2003) Introduction: the self and others in traditional psychology and in positioning theory. In R. Harré and F. Moghaddam (eds) *The self and Others: Positioning individuals and groups in personal, political and cultural contexts*. London: Praeger, pp. 1–11.

Harré, R. and van Langenhove, L. (1999) *Positioning Theory: Moral contexts of intentional action*. Oxford: Blackwell.

Heath, R. (2001) A rhetorical enactment rationale for public relations: the good organisation communicating well. In R. Heath (ed.) *The Sage Handbook of Public Relations*. Thousand Oaks, CA: Sage, pp. 441–4.

James, M. (2009) Getting to the heart of public relations: the concept of strategic intent. *Asia Pacific Public Relations Journal*, 10, 109–22.

James, M. (2010) The use of intentional positioning techniques in government agencies' communication campaigns. In D. Verčič and K. Sriramesh (eds) *Government Communication: Proceedings of the 17th International Public Relations Research Symposium BledCom*. Bled, Slovenia, Ljubljana: Pristop, pp. 140–7. Retrieved from www.bledcom.si/uploads/ppt2010/bledcom 2010 proceedings hi.pdf

James, M. (2011a) A provisional conceptual framework for intentional positioning in public relations. *Journal of Public Relations Research,* 23(1): 93–111. http://dx.doi.org/10.1080/1062726X.2010.505120

James, M. (2011b) Ready, aim, fire: the perceived role of key messages in public relations campaigns, *PRism*, 8(1): 1–18.

McKaughan, D. (2012) Speech acts, attitudes, and scientific practice: can Searle handle 'Assuming for the sake of Hypothesis'? *Pragmatics & Cognition*, 20(1): 88–106. doi 10.1075/pc.20.1.04mck

Mills Wilson Communication Consultants (2006) Kaleeya Hospital Maternity Unit. PRIA Golden Target Award entry winner. Retrieved from www.lib.uts.edu.au/gta/show.php?id=592

Moghaddam, F., Hanley, E. and Harré, R. (2003) Sustaining intergroup harmony: an analysis of the Kissinger papers through positioning theory. In R. Harré and F. Moghaddam (eds) *The self and Others: Positioning individuals and groups in personal, political and cultural contexts*. London: Praeger, pp. 123–36.

Moloney, K. (2006) *Rethinking public relations* (2nd edn). London: Routledge.

Nastri, J., Pena, J. and Hancock, J. T. (2006) The construction of away messages: a speech act analysis. *Journal of Computer Mediated Communication*, 11, 1025–45.

Neff, B. (1998) Harmonizing global relations: a speech act theory analysis of PRForum. *Public Relations Review*, 24(3): 351–76.

Neff, B. (2008) Speech act theory: an approach to public relations leadership. In T. Hansen-Horn and B. Neff (Eeds) *Public relations: from theory to practice*. Boston, MA: Pearson, pp. 89–103.

Northern Territory University (2003) *Don't Let Another Year Go By*. PRIA Golden Target Award entry – winner. Retrieved from www.lib.uts.edu.au/gta

Pearson, R. (1989) Beyond ethical relativism in public relations: coorientation, rules, and the idea of communication symmetry. *Public Relations Research Annual*, 1(1–4): 67–86. doi:10.1207/s1532754xjprr0101-4_3

Powerlink (2007) *Returning Power to Collinsville*. PRIA Golden Target Award entry winner. Retrieved from www.lib.uts.edu.au/gta

Radford, G. (2012) Public relations in a postmodern world. *Public Relations Inquiry*, (1): 49–67. doi: 10.1177/2046147X1142214

Revlin, R. (2013) *Cognition: theory and practice*. New York: Worth.

Searle, J. (1970) *Speech Acts: An essay in the philosophy of language*, Cambridge: Cambridge University Press.

Searle, J. (1979) *Expression and Meaning: Studies in the theory of speech acts*. Cambridge: Cambridge University Press.

Searle, J., Kiefer, F. and Bierwisch, M. (1980) Introduction. In J. Searle, F. Kiefer and M. Bierwisch (eds) *Speech act theory and pragmatics*. Dordrecht, Holland: Reidel.

Searle, J. and Vanderveken, D. (1985) *Foundations of Illocutionary Logic*. Cambridge: Cambridge University Press.

Slocum-Bradley, N. (2007) Constructing and de-constructing the ACP Group: actors, strategies and consequences for development, *Geopolitics*, 12(4): 635–55. doi:10.1080/14650040701546095

Slocum-Bradley, N. (2008) Discursive production of conflict in Rwanda. In F. Moghaddam, R. Harré and N. Lee (eds) *Global Conflict Resolution through Positioning Analysis*. New York: Springer, pp. 207–26.

Smudde, P. M. and Courtright, J. L. (2012) In search of message design best practices: the Silver Anvil Award winners archive. *Public Relations Review,* 888–97.

Socom (2006) *A world-class hospital.* PRIA Golden Target Award entry winner. Retrieved from www.lib.uts.edu.au/gta

Wise, D. and James, M. (2013) Positioning a price on carbon: applying a proposed hybrid method of positioning discourse analysis for public relations. *Public Relations Inquiry*, 2(3): 327–53.

Xifra, J. and Girona, R. (2012) Frank Capra's Why We Fight and film documentary discourse in public relations. *Public Relations Review*, 38(1): 40–5.

6 Supporting the position in public relations

Storyline, the third vertex of the positioning triangle

Most public relations work, it could be argued, is directed at laying claim to a position, "that is, to certain rights and duties, which are then taken up as frames for a strip of life narrative" (Moghaddam and Harré, 2010: 21). Once a practitioner has identified the position to be taken or assigned, the rights and duties associated within the social context of that position, and, how the position will be enacted, he or she then turns to the supporting storylines. The promulgation of messages that aim to shape target audiences' construction of reality can be seen as central to much practice as reported by practitioners (James, 2011b; Smudde and Courtright, 2012a). Such messages are part of the narrative that is developed by an organization to help communicate its point of view, its interpretation of reality and its position at any given time; essentially "strategic self-storying", which Johansen (2012) defines as, "the intentional story told by organizational members in order to present and promote their organization" (p. 233). As Smith and Sparkes (2008) so elegantly put it, "we live in story-shaped worlds" (p. 295). Drawing on discourse, organizations construct the storylines and develop the narratives that will support their position.

The concept of the right to take or ascribe a position is a key differentiator that sets positioning theoretical approaches to public relations apart from traditional ones. Alongside the concept of rights within the local moral order comes the concept of duties and obligations. Within positioning theory, when an organization takes a position, or tries to position some other entity, access to certain storylines closes off. This means that an organization will not have the right to use some storylines if it takes a particular position, according to the local moral order. Take the situation of a corporately sponsored sporting team whose members are involved in a drunken brawl whilst partying at a nightclub. Such situations, and the subsequent publicity, can cause sponsors to review their decision to associate their brand with sporting organizations involved in off-field behavior that is unacceptable to their customers or to the community in general (Wilson, Stavros and Westberg, 2008). In attempting to manage the situation, the following day the team management takes the position that the team members are sorry for their actions. They enact that position publicly through speech acts including making an apology, committing team members to personally paying for damage at the nightclub and announcing that the sports association will fine the team members for bringing the sport into disrepute.

The storylines that are closed off for team members and management in such positioning include:

Hero storyline:	"We're so tough we can fight wherever and whenever we like", "We know the nightclubs are happy to have our team in their establishment no matter what we get up to as we're sports heroes".
Famous and rich storyline:	"We're so famous and rich we can do what we like".
Boys will be boys storyline:	"Oh well, a bit of alcohol and a bit of a rumble, that's what real men do".

Why would these be closed off? Because the local moral order, that is, what social norms determine to be the right thing to say and do in this situation would view such responses as unacceptable in terms of sponsorship, being role models to younger people and being brand advocates. In this context, there are some storylines that the organization will be obligated to develop and use, and yet others that the organization will have the right to develop and use, but may elect to not use them at particular times or at all.

The storylines available for team members and management in such positioning include:

Formal apology storyline:	"The club is sorry for the damage and the inconvenience and disruption caused", "On behalf of the players, the club unreservedly apologizes for the undesirable behavior", "We're instigating an investigation to ensure that those responsible will be held to account".
Responsibility storyline:	"Some players can't be held responsible for behavior"; "Drunk and didn't know what they were doing", "Club management will subsequently ban alcohol use for players during the sport season".
Health storyline:	"Several team members struggling with alcohol abuse/addiction issues"; "Club management will increase its support and ensure all medical treatment required for players is made available".

This means that for a public relations practitioner, having undertaken a positioning analysis, in addition to the normally prescribed SWOT (strengths, weaknesses, opportunities, threats) analysis, there will be clear indications on what messages can be used, should be used and importantly, should not be used. Tsetsura (2012: 5) observes "positioning within the process of discourse may limit the choices available as a conversation develops through joint actions of all participating in discourse because people try to make actions socially defined and appropriate". This is particularly pertinent when one is working in a cross-cultural or even global context. A positioning analysis will indicate what is acceptable according to the local moral order; what will work in one place may not work in another. Many practitioners know this instinctively after several years of practice but a positioning approach enables practitioners to articulate this knowledge. This in turn helps instruct emerging practitioners to learn about making judgments in the strategic public relations context. Importantly for many, it also helps break down what in many cases seems like tacit knowledge into articulable steps that could be quantified in terms of time taken to undertake them, and then billed to clients. At the storyline development stage, positioning work is strategic work, and the Framework for Intentional Positioning in Public Relations provides a systematic approach to such work.

What is a storyline?

The storylines are the clues to understanding positioning in an analytical sense and they inform the development of key messages in the context of communication program design. The storyline is not the narrative itself, which in public relations is often told through key messages delivered through various platforms in paid, earned and owned media. A storyline provides context for the speech acts/actions and positions. Each storyline is seen to be "expressible in a loose cluster of narrative conventions" (Harré and Moghaddam, 2003: 6). The storyline in the public relations narratives gives insight into the types of power being wielded and ascribed, and describes positions being taken or assigned. There are master storylines and dominant narratives operating constantly in societies and these operate on the presumption that each member ascribes to a common story (Ochs and Capps, 1996). For the purposes of public relations positioning, I have adapted the work of Fivush, Habermas, Waters and Zaman (2011) to define storylines as schematic representations that contain abstracted information about the cultural standards in operation within local moral orders that are used for positioning purposes.

Storylines are familiar to the various societies in which they operate and are temporal, implicitly or explicitly linking the past with the present and future (Slocum and van Langenhove, 2003). In public relations, storylines are used to link a series of actions. Storylines give certain actions meaning "and tie them together in a manner that gives them a particular sense or rational appearance", with them often including "an explanation as to why various goals and means for their realization are selected" (Slocum and van Langenhove, 2003: 226). Although Slocum and van Langenhove's (2003) work primarily focuses on international relations and regional conflict, how they conceptualize the operation of storylines is directly applicable for public relations. Positioning theory, with its triadic interaction of position, speech act/actions and storylines brings together a confluence of other narrative-related theories and approaches used in public relations such as framing, storytelling, stance and rhetorical studies.

In 2011, a *Forbes Magazine* article lamented that it was hard to find successful plots for "the business narrative necessary for strategic public relations" (Hanlon,

2011, n.p.). Hanlon suggested plots for organizations on which to build their narratives and these can be seen as storylines. The following were suggested:

- Plot #1: your lucky stars (story ingredients: rising company, stellar talent)
- Plot #2: return of the hero (story ingredients: formerly incredible company experiences declining sales, market share, and questionable management. Original entrepreneur returns, reclaims the company and moves toward even greater success)
- Plot #3: the "doing the right thing" thing (story ingredients: conscious capitalism wins out)
- Plot #4: flipping bad news. Or, making lemonade (story ingredients: turning negative into positive, or the Midas touch)
- Plot #5: passionate zealotry (story ingredient: actually love what you do)
- Plot #6: superior being (story ingredients: company with seemingly omniscient powers pervades the earthly realm with supernatural powers. Extraterrestrial powers are an advantage.
- Plot #7: us vs. them (story ingredients: two pitched rivals slug it out in public, to the merriment of all)
- Plot #8: I'm so bad, I made it good (story ingredient: dominant personality able to spin repeated successes)

Although somewhat humorous, the suggestions demonstrate the concept of storyline; those schematic representations that public relations practitioners use when using storytelling to support the intended positioning efforts. Hanlon (2011) tells us that his list is far from definitive, with others including "egregious greed", "revenge", "against all odds", "deliverance from evil" and more. He concludes that storylines must be chosen to show how choices were both faced and made, what positions the various actors have taken up and assigned, and how the outcomes are being/have been attained. The narratives developed from the storylines must then add in elements such as emotion, characterization and setting to appeal to particular audiences, to facilitate them constructing the practitioner's intended meaning from the story's messages. For example, we can see many stories initiated by public relations practitioners working in the realms of medical and pharmaceutical research based on the storyline of "the discovery". The discovery storyline is "routinely told through the eyes of its discoverers and culminates in the climactic 'aha' moment of nature unveiled" (Franklin, 1988: 92).

Audiences generally know this storyline and know what to expect in the narratives. Story mediators such as journalists and program producers can work with the public relations teams for the various "discoveries" to source the required ingredients for programs and stories such as interviews, laboratory shots, footage of microscopes being used, people suffering and recovering from the disease that the discovery will help, and so on. It is evident that pharmaceutical companies don't like it much when this kind of storyline is strayed from too far. Storylines that privilege profit or highlight social inequities in access to new medicines are not the ones invoked to support the companies' desired positions. These are more likely to be invoked by groups that are critical of their operations and wish to position the companies as greedy or not working for the social good. So it is that the storyline provides the scaffold for the key messages and narrative that is shared with audience members to support the desired positioning.

Ochs and Capps (1996) in their influential work on narrating the self suggest that individuals use narrative activity to make sense of situations. Whilst acknowledging there are many ways of discussing narrative form and storylines, Gergen's (2005) work is also most helpful in conceptualizing storylines for public relations contexts as he is working within the social constructionist epistemology that aligns with positioning theory. Gergen (2005) suggested that there are narrative forms, which in positioning theory are storylines, that are "frequently used, easily identified and are highly functional" constituting "a ready vocabulary for rendering cross-time intelligibility" (p. 103). He discusses attempts to identify a finite set of storylines but concludes that from a culturally based view, there is no compelling argument for not accepting that there can be infinite story forms. However, Gergen (2005) does attempt to generate "a way of appreciating existing forms" as in his view, "all plots can be converted to a linear form with respect to their evaluative shifts over time" (p. 104). This sees him isolating three rudimentary forms of narrative: the "stability narrative" where the trajectory remains essentially unchanged with respect to a goal or an outcome; the "progressive narrative" where events are linked together incrementally to move things forward; and, the "regressive narrative" where decrements "characterize the movement over the evaluative dimension over time...depicting a continued downward slide" (2005: 104).

Within these three overarching categories of storyline, it is evident that public relations practitioners can use specific storylines or combinations of storylines strategically. It is relatively straightforward to map often-used public relations storylines to the three categories. For example, the stability storyline is employed in periods post-crisis to help position organizations as able to provide services, products or leadership in spite of events leading up to the current time. Such a situation is described by Rice and Sommerville (2013) with ministerial special advisers playing a significant communications role as inter-departmental negotiators to maintain "a level of stability in Northern Ireland not seen for over 40 years" (p. 7). However, they also report on partisan politicians in whose interest it is to perpetuate deep community divisions to ensure their parties' longevity and re-election prospects. Storylines employed by such politicians are not invoking the stability storyline but are creating instability through "the cultivation of controversial attention seeking issues and antagonistic politics" (p. 8). In another example of the stability storyline in action, Canel (2012) described how a section of the Spanish media took a position on what should happen at the 2004 national election that was held only days after the Madrid bombing attack. The editorial proposed a "remedy" which would be a "coalition government [PP–PSOE] whose priority will be to clarify events and return the country back to normal" (Canel, 2012: 220).

An example of the progressive storyline, where events are linked together incrementally to move things forward, can be seen in Yang, Klyueva and Taylor's (2012) discussion on how China achieved specific positioning outcomes through its public diplomacy efforts during the 2011 Libyan crisis. China was reported as having accomplished its foreign policy goals through strategically using relationships with Russia and Libya. China used the state-owned "People's Daily newspaper to communicate its self-image and frame international understanding of its role in the world order" (Yang, Klyueva and Taylor, 2012: 655). In taking a position of non-intervention, China "capitalized on the momentum to build up its soft power by standing close to the international community to resolve the conflict in Libya" (p. 660). Another strong example of a progressive storyline is seen in campaign case study examining promotional efforts undertaken by the American National Hockey League (NHL) "to promote itself to both fervent and casual fans" (Batchelor and Formentin, 2008: 156). The campaign aimed to rebrand and promote hockey after a season was lost due to a dispute between the national body and players. For external audiences, a "series of advertisements and related promotional materials were designed to send a central, unified message" (Batchelor and Formentin, 2008: 158), that promised to deliver great hockey for fans and sponsors. The campaign effort was designed to "prod fans into watching" (Batchelor and Formentin, 2008: 158).

Characterizing a regressive storyline is not as straightforward. It is evident that not many organizations would want to position themselves as regressing or being on a downward spiral. However, it is clear that on some occasions there are entities that may aim to position others using a regressive storyline. This can be seen in a political public relations campaigns where political parties or individual candidates seek to position opponents as potentially moving the agenda backwards in terms of economic or social reform. This was evident in the storylines invoked by American presidential candidate in 2012, Mr. Mitt Romney, who according to the *New York Times*, invoked the storyline of economic management and used his strength as a businessman as an advantage in an election dominated by economic discussions. Mr. Romney tried to persuade voters that President Obama's policies had not worked and that "he should be elected to complete the nation's economic recovery" ("Assessing Romney's Chances", 2012).

A campaign that aimed to increase public awareness and to influence government policy about issues surrounding genetic engineering could also be seen to have invoked a regressive storyline (Henderson, 2005). A coalition was formed and it undertook a campaign against the introduction of commercial field trials of genetically modified products in New Zealand. Three key messages permeated the campaign and these were to ban all field trials and commercial releases of genetically engineered organisms into the environment, to keep GE-foods out of the country, and to restrict genetic engineering to contained laboratories. Henderson reported that the GE Free campaign was "relatively successful from a public relations perspective" (p. 133) in that relationships with key publics were established, and concerned parties were given "a voice" and were encouraged to participate in the debate. It was "partially successful in influencing government policy" with the voluntary moratorium on genetic engineering commercial field trials being extended, ensuring that there could be "continuing debate about the regulatory environment" and contestation of "the dominant discourses about genetic engineering" (p. 133). The campaign could be described as having striven to construct a position against genetic engineering and then used strategies to develop and promulgate messages which would support and strengthen the positioning that New Zealand should not progress its adoption of genetically engineered food. Berger's (1999) contextualization of public relations as a means of constructing a particular worldview can be seen as relevant in these cases.

What can storyline analysis show in public relations?

Public relations episodes, like most social episodes, do not unfold in a random manner. They follow established patterns through the storylines (Harré and Moghaddam, 2003). In public relations, storylines are tied to the actors (individuals or organizations, for example) in the episode, who act out the storylines in a given situation, effectively making the episode a conjunction of overlapping storylines of all parties involved (Henriksen, 2008). The storylines and the public relations episodes are "mutually constituting" (Henriksen, 2008: 51). This means that the storyline has a determining effect on the public relations episode but at the same time is itself constituted through the interaction or anticipated interaction. In public relations situations, because the storylines are linked to specific actors in the episodes, the same storylines can carry across contexts; storylines are not "structurally enforced discourses" linked to specific contexts (Henriken, 2008: 51). However, this is not to say that storylines will not need to change or differ depending on the context, as Henriksen explains:

> As a road going through several countries, one behavior, or set of rights and duties, may be applicable to one section of the road, but not to another. It may not be meaningful to attempt to enact rights and duties that were structurally legitimate in one context in a different part of the storyline.
>
> (Henriksen, 2008: 51).

From a researcher perspective, whether analyzing a past campaign to learn from mistakes or best practice, or examining practice or communication artifacts for academic purposes, a positioning approach to storyline analysis can indicate why things did or didn't work in the context of particular campaigns or programs. This was particularly evident when Wise and James (2013) examined the positioning strategies of the then Australian Prime Minister, Julia Gillard, when arguing for the introduction of a carbon price on major polluters in Australian industry. The analysis indicated that the communication campaign was basically sound: messages were well crafted and consistent throughout, speeches well written, events suitably formal and so on. One may have been left wondering where to go with the analysis if not for positioning theory. It was this that led us to identify the impact on Ms. Gillard's positioning of local political events prior to the 2010 national election in which she formed a government. It could be seen that Ms. Gillard did not have the right, according to the local moral order in Australia, to position the carbon tax in a positive way.

Some analysts have suggested that the decision to proceed with the introduction of a carbon tax was the root cause of her eventual removal from office by her own political party in 2013. Had a public relations positioning analysis been undertaken as part of the strategic planning of communications associated with the legislation's introduction, it would have been clear that the communication environment was somewhat hostile. It would have indicated that more work would have been needed to be undertaken in order to construct the right (according to the local moral order) to introduce and position the carbon price in a positive way. In the eyes of the majority of the Australian voters, Ms. Gillard had no right to introduce a carbon tax. From a positioning theoretical perspective, the voters were right.

The storylines were never going to work in this context as the central position taken was flawed (Wise and James, 2013). This is why the positioning triangle can be used as a diagnostic tool of sorts for practitioners and as an analytical tool for researchers. One can imagine being a senior consultant being brought in on such a situation as Gillard's communication team found themselves in and applying the positioning framework. The key problem of a fundamentally flawed position would have been diagnosed; the position would need to have been amended to something that the local moral order deemed Ms. Gillard had the right to take. Such a move would have closed off the storylines that had been used to date and other storylines would have opened up; ones that Ms. Gillard would have been accorded the right, according to the local moral order, to use. This relates to the central tenet of positioning theory, that the positioning triangle must maintain its "dynamic stability" (Harré and van Langenhove, 1999: 10), which Harré articulates as follows:

> The constituents of the three vertices [of the positioning triangle] mutually determine one another. If any one changes – for example, by a successful challenge to the distribution of rights and duties – then all three change. Change the distribution of rights and duties and the storyline that has been realized thus far may be transformed. At the same time, the meanings of what has been said and done by the actors are also transformed. The future relations between the actors and the subsequent form taken by the unfolding strip of life will be different after changes in any three components of the positioning triangle.
>
> (Harré, 2012: 196)

In public relations positioning, it is through the storylines that organizations can potentially work to close down or open up conversations with publics, stakeholders and audiences more generally. Storylines are thus intrinsically linked to establishing and maintaining relationships and can be oriented towards bridging or buffering (Kim and Ni, 2010) an organization and its publics. Through the use of certain storylines and not others, public relations practitioners can be said to be constructing positions for their clients/organizations through discourse. To be effective they instinctively, or learn how to, tap into the known discourses of targeted audiences and publics. As Louis (2008) states:

> The construction of these story lines is a project of actors positioning themselves and others. Once constructed, the storylines are spread through speech and other acts targeting media and political outlets as well as individual conversation partners. Actors' unequal access to media and political outlets; their unequal abilities to reach and sway audiences with coercion, bribes, or credibility: All these reflect unequal power to promote storylines which in turn frame interpretations of a conflict and direct behavioral responses. Cultural fit too is unequally distributed, and essential for the creation and survival of a story line. Ability to recognize and express the culturally meaningful patterns of a storyline, the values that are embraced by a culture versus rejected, and the historical experiences that make new analogies believable and relevant versus far-fetched: This not only motivates the actors intrinsically as they create their story lines but also extrinsically, as actors strategically shape the stories to be accepted and disseminated by other audiences.
>
> (Louis, 2008: 26–7)

This describes the way practitioners attempt to work in the zones of meaning within which their target audiences and publics operate. They are tying the storylines that support the positioning they are striving to achieve or maintain to what is already understood. This includes clear patterns that can be discerned by targeted audiences and publics in narratives, discourse and action (Slocum and van Langenhove, 2003). However, such practices should not be seen as deterministic as "story lines do not make people act in a given way; rather, people use discursive tools to create meaningful experiences. People are the makers and users of these tools; in this way, they are craft masters of their reality" (Slocum and van Langenhove, 2003: 231). This approach recognizes the discursive practices already at work within audience groups and recognizes that people, programs, services, products and organizations have already been positioned by the discourses at work in their environments. Public relations practitioners can introduce new aspects into these environments but moves may need to be incremental unless the practitioner can devise ways in which people can be moved, literally from one position to another. According to Harré and Slocum (2003) a key insight of positioning theory is that a new position will be viable only to the extent it is embedded in a mutually acceptable storyline. People learn about new discourses and learn to use new discourses throughout their lives. Public relations practice in many instances can be seen to be influencing this and persuades people to take up new or altered positions that have been discursively constructed.

Using positioning theory to analyze public relations can provide insight into the active way practitioners and publics construct their social realities. Slocum and van Langenhove (2003: 232) suggest that "future studies could usefully focus on how new storylines, positions and acts can be engendered in the context of practical situations in a way that bridges the present into a desired future". By calling attention to the social forces of speech acts within specific storylines, the function that is being served by the acts/actions being undertaken can come into focus. Whether an organization's desired goal was achieved can be questioned and questions can be posed as to how one could better achieve a similar goal in future.

Storylines and communication conventions

Individual public relations practitioners don't make the rules and conventions for human communication methods such as conversations (Davies and Harré, 1999), or indeed for any communication episodes. They work within such conventions. Anything that a public relations practitioner produces can be seen only to have meaning if it is taken up by audiences, intended or otherwise. Public relations storylines, like speech acts, are encodings that are offered up for their "interpretative potential" (Neff, 2008) and are promulgated through channels and within environments where this is most likely to happen in the way the practitioner would like it to happen.

By adapting the work of Davies and Harré (1999) this approach can be defined as one of the determining factors of a public relations episode in which certain speech acts/actions are structured to deliver a kind of social force. In public relations, practitioners are seeking to shape the meanings people are constructing about an issue or aspect of organizational operations. Such speech acts/actions are not just what is said but also what is done, the non-verbal aspects of what an organization, or in fact any entity, undertakes in the social spaces in which they operate. So we could see that a public relations positioning storyline can scaffold the narrative to be more encompassing than what is merely said or written.

From the perspective of the audience, storylines can be taken up or not, decoded in the way the issuing organization would prefer or not, acted upon or not, and so on. It can be said that storylines allow positions to emerge, rather than seeing them as "pre-givens" prior to the situation at hand (Henriksen, 2008). Previous research (James, 2011b) indicates that public relations practitioners in many cases anticipate that their messages may be challenged and work to structure messages to maximize the chances of them being decoded in the preferred way. However this same research also indicated that much organizational thinking remains transmission oriented and presumes, and even hopes for, a passivity in audiences.

Taking a positioning approach to storyline development and promulgation recognizes that the environment into which messages are sent and in which meanings are constructed is dynamic in nature. It has been shown that practitioners aim for consistency in their messaging tactics and that this approach correlates with successful campaigns (James, 2011a, 2011b). However this doesn't mean that such consistency equates with a static, "set and forget kind of approach". Consistency was shown to mean that various speakers for an organization's position put forward the same storylines at any given time, not that one storyline was chosen at the campaign design stage and this was adhered to throughout the campaign. It is clear that research must be undertaken to determine the available positions, that is, what positions the organization and those in its environment, have a right to occupy or maintain. Developing the storylines in accordance with the research findings is sensible from a public relations perspective. This approach could be viewed as being aligned with proactivity rather than reactivity to specific situations.

Storylines can be seen to invoke discourse, the "institutionalised use of language and language-like sign systems" (Davies and Harré, 1999: 34). Like in all other domains, in public relations we can see discourses institutionalized at disciplinary, political and cultural levels. Discourses also develop around topics, and public relations practitioners work to shape such developments. For example, the unfolding of the discursive struggle around storylines related to contentious energy issues in many countries is very evident. The storylines invoked by organizations against the extraction of gas from coal seams (either coal seam gas or coalbed methane) are those centered on shedding light on the practice of "fracking" and its potential damage to aquifers beneath the earth's surface. These are often illustrated by the imagery of setting fire to water taps. In contrast, we see coal seam gas project proponents promulgating storylines of securing energy for the future and doing this in clean ways. These are often accompanied by images of serene countryside to show how things are left relatively undisturbed by their operations. One imagines that most of us were oblivious to the details of coal seam gas a few years ago but that now we probably have an opinion on the industry.

Specific industry practices such as fracking were not part of our everyday speech. Those promoting or criticizing the industry have had to initially tie their respective storylines to things that were already understood by their intended audiences. I would argue that the gas industry has been struggling to find a way to counter the extremely strong storyline imagery of the burning gas coming out of a farmhouse water tap. The strength of this storyline is that it ties so strongly to what people know to be true; that a safe and secure water supply is vital for life. If something disrupts this it invokes fear. The fact that these messages within the safe water storyline were not about some abstract sub-surface aquifer, a topic that in people may not have understood, but a tap in their house was the key to supporting the position that coal seam gas was problematic. To this day the industry has not invoked a storyline that has been able to counter-position successfully. The attempts to tie into the need for future energy supply or to highlight lack of impact on beautiful country landscapes have in large part failed (Jaques and Galloway, 2012).

It is interesting to grapple with the concept of what storyline would need to be invoked for the coal seam gas industry to successfully position where it wants to be. I have had these conversations with people involved in projects and tried to explain that it is not just the storyline that counts; that it conceptually comes back to having the right to position in a particular way in terms of the local moral order. I argue that the industry's issue is that, in the minds of many people, until the industry has proof that their practices will not cause damage to water tables they will not be seen as having the right to position as being a safe and viable industry. The points that are offered in reply are those related to risk; all energy projects have elements of risk and people live with this risk all the time. These are difficult discussions as they relate to quite complex scientific knowledge but they also relate to people's perceptions.

As Jaques and Galloway (2012) have explored, in particular sites where coal seam gas proponents want to set up projects, there are often people who firmly believe that companies have no right do so. This is often in spite of companies having the legal right to undertake a project; according to the local moral order operating in a particular community, there is no right. For people on farming land, for instance, until the risk to subterranean water supplies can be demonstrably negated, they view companies as having no right to mine the gas. They view these companies as having the moral obligation to either prove there is no or minimal risk or to move out of their area.

This is where the positioning triangle comes into play. The best-crafted storyline in the world won't convince these people to accept coal seam gas projects in their area. They view the company's position as flawed and therefore see the company as having no right to enact such a position in the first place. From a positioning theoretical perspective, the position held by the companies will need to change or they will need to construct the right to position in the way they currently want to, that is, they will need to prove they will not harm the water table. They currently cannot provide such evidence for all intended sites and so I suggest that they are unable to construct a right in the eyes of key publics to mine gas. Such a view may not be popular with coal seam gas project proponents but it does however explain why just spinning a storyline that a company doesn't have a right to use doesn't work.

Examples as described by Jaques and Galloway (2012) demonstrate how discourses compete with each other, trying to create distinct versions of reality and in the case of coal seam gas, incompatible versions of reality. Of course, there are more than these two discourses at work in any of the sites where coal seam gas projects are being considered. There are multiple discourses operating in all aspects of people's lives and these are constantly intersecting. They articulate with other discourses and the life experiences and attributes that each person brings to public relations episodes (Moffitt, 1994). Moffitt (1994) has written on how people have multiple positions on singular issues depending on circumstances and may hold quite divergent public and private views. This, she argues, makes the task for public relations practitioners, in terms of message design, extremely challenging (Moffitt, 1999). It is probable that people simply do not want certain industries to operate near their homes and deliberately decode and re-encode storylines to suit their own intentions. This is part of the dynamism of communication environments.

From storyline to narratives and key messages

Smudde and Courtright (2012a), in their exploration of messaging in public relations state that narrative theory generally has been under-explored in a public relations context. "Messaging", or the development of key messages, is one of the main methods employed to convey an organization's story or another entity's story from its own point of view. Courtright and Smudde (2009: 66) proposed that "key messages" were a component of strategic communication plans, stating that key messages are comprised of "two basic things". The first thing is "a theme, thesis or slogan that is the single idea around which all communications revolve"; the second being "copy points that serve as the basic proof or substance for detailed arguments that support the theme/thesis/slogan". In a positioning theory context, the "first thing" could be conceptualized as the positioning triangle of position, speech acts/action and storyline, with the second focusing on the narratives that can be told as a result of invoking a specific storyline.

Key messages have been defined in a public relations context as the information that organizations want their target publics to know (Mahoney, 2008), and public relations practitioners work with an understanding that such messages have the power to do certain things (James, 2011b; Smudde and Courtright, 2012a, 2012b; Wilson, 2001). Moloney (2006) states that "attitudes and behaviors only change after many rounds of messaging" (p. 131) and according to Wilson (2001), messages "are useless if they are not delivering a specific message to a target public so that the public will act to help us meet our objectives and accomplish our organizations' missions" (p. 217). Key messages can "increase organizational valence in the public domain, to nudge their companies back into the good graces of their primary stakeholders, and to improve or maintain organizational reputation" (Pratt, 2004: 15). This purported power of messages to do things sits firmly in the theoretical camp of speech act theory as addressed in the previous chapter.

From this perspective, effective messages that reach "strategically important audiences" can be seen as a "critical function in public relations" (Hallahan, 1999: 463). Practitioners work to ensure that their messages are effective, and Lane (2007) states that practitioners "fine-tune organizational messages to achieve strategic objectives" (p.72). Key messages are often presented as planned talking points that, far from being "uttered off the cuff", are "planned carefully, presented strategically" and are underpinned by research (Pratt, 2004: 15). The analyses of individual campaigns in the academic literature suggest that practitioners subscribe to this way of thinking in terms of their messaging strategies (e.g. Al Khaja and Creedon, 2010; Batchelor and Formentin, 2008; Berger, 1999; Henderson, 2005; Jo, Shim and Jung, 2008; Stokes and Rubin, 2010; Tilson, 2006; Vardeman-Winter, 2010; Zhang and Benoit, 2004). Such thinking links the theoretical underpinnings for public relations practice as suggested by Berger (1999), in that public relations practices "occur in a place, the site, in which practices of representation (in the forms of message, images and symbols) meet an 'other'" (p. 189). The sites, according to Berger, include "locations, forums, channels and contexts wherein virtually every form of human interaction and communication is conducted" and are invariably "congested, with multiple messages and appearances that are contested, fluid, and changing, thereby complicating meaning and understanding" (p. 190).

Recognizing that the environment into which messages are sent is congested, public relations practitioners can be seen to prepare carefully crafted key messages as part of their campaigns, especially in media relations campaigns or crisis management situations (e.g. Coombs, 2007; Fortunato, 2000; Lundy and Broussard, 2007). There is ample evidence in the campaign literature that the environment in which messaging and counter-messaging is being undertaken by public relations practitioners is congested with other entities trying to promulgate their own messages. This is well articulated within a positioning theoretical context where organizations are seeking to position themselves and others, and intentionally or unintentionally repositioning others. Moloney (2006) suggests that public relations is "conducive to at least one public good" and that is "the sustained and intense scrutiny by third parties of public wrangling amongst PR voices" which "can produce more accurate fact and truth statements in public life" (p. 39). However, he goes on to point out that "while accurate fact and truth statements may or may not be delivered by PR messages, their accuracy and truth components will invariably only be demonstrated to third parties after competitive public challenges from other messages" (p. 39). James (2011b) found that practitioners expect to have their messages and overall positioning challenged and that they apply resources and effort to minimize or circumvent these challenges.

Smudde and Courtright (2012a) state that "narrative theories should inform public relations message design because practitioners always tell the organization's side of a story, with an understanding of other sides of the story" (p. 893). They provide an overview of various narratives, linguistic and discourse approaches that public relations practitioners could consider. However in the positioning storyline development context, Gergen's (2005) work can guide the translation of storylines into narratives and specific key messages, that will effectively operate within the positioning triangle domain of the Framework for Intentional Positioning in Public Relations. Gergen (2005) set out criteria which he stated were "central in constructing an intelligible narrative in significant segments of contemporary culture" (p. 100). These criteria were: "establishing a valued endpoint" (p. 100–1); "selecting relevant events" (p. 101); "systematic ordering" (p. 101–2); "stabilizing identity" (p. 102); "causal linking" (p. 102–3); and, "narrative demarking" (p. 103). Drawing extensively on Gergen's work (2005: 100–3), I will undertake an exploration in the next section of how each criterion can guide practitioners' development of positioning storylines and messages.

Establishing a valued endpoint

The narrative invoked by the storyline being used in the positioning effort must establish a goal, explain an event, reach or avoid a state of being, or, reach a significant outcome. The endpoint is "typically saturated with value, that is, understood to be desirable or undesirable" (Gergen, 2005: 100). The endpoint introduces subjective bias into the story (that is, what is seen as desirable by one party may be seen as undesirable by another). In a public relations context, the endpoint and its value are invariably determined by the organization commissioning the public relations activity. Burkart (2009: 155) states that such value judgments "are not provable in the classical scientific sense" but are "anchored in the appropriate context of social norms or result from moral rules or ethical principles". For successful positioning to occur one can see that the endpoint and its value should align with what targeted publics and audiences understand and value, that is, does the local moral order ascribe the right to the organization to tell such a story? If not, how could such a right be constructed? If this is not possible, perhaps this is where the organization is compelled to reconsider whether its desired position is tenable.

Selecting relevant events

The narrative must also support the "endpoint" by giving accounts of selected events that make it more or less probable, accessible, important or vivid. The endpoint is what dictates what kind of events can be included in the account, that is, what makes sense. Take as an example a practitioner working on website content to support an aged care facility's position as increasing its focus on quality of life for its residents. The practitioner would need to draw relevant events into the narrative account such as the passing of new regulations, an increase in staff numbers, or the opening of a new facility story elements that were relevant to the final outcome desired.

Systematic ordering

The ordering of events within public relations narratives needs to make sense in terms of importance, interest value, and recency. Gergen (2005) indicates that in a contemporary Western context a temporal sequence is the most widely used. It is "a convention which employs an internally coherent system of signs...in Mikhail Bakhtin's terms, we may view temporal accounts as *chronotopes*, that is, as literacy conventions governing space–time relationships" (p. 102). In public relations, randomly ordering events would be nonsensical in a media release and it is evident that in most situations a systematic approach to ordering events would aid understanding and strengthen the story.

Stabilizing identity

In addition to the above criteria, the narrative must be coherent in terms of the identities of the character (or the identity and nature of an object). Imagine a public relations narrative working in the context of an environmental warrior storyline. It would not make sense if the main character's story described a change to long-standing forestry processes for the better but then included instances where that same character undertook polluting actions. In exceptions to the criteria, Gergen (2005) points out that these usually occur when attempts are made to explain some type of change in identity. For example, our environmental warrior might have once been the manager of an environmentally unsustainable manufacturing plant and the narrative centers on his change of views regarding how the world could be if only companies acted differently.

Causal linking

This criterion includes the notion of giving an explanation, "typically achieved by selecting events that by common standards are causally linked" (Gergen, 2005: 102). In public relations, the key messages emerging from the narrative will be better formed when events within the narrative are related interdependently. If the key message read something like, "our company opened and then other companies opened" it would be very uninteresting. Most importantly it wouldn't support a position of a company's activities driving something noteworthy such as economic development. If the key message read, "our company opened and then other companies who supply our component parts opened", then that makes the causal link and drives forward the storyline.

Narrative demarking

This criterion relates to the signals employed in public relations genres to indicate when a narrative begins and ends. Public relations genres and their conventions are well described by Smudde and Courtright (2012b). They point out that public relations can be suboptimal when there are "miscues in using a genre" (Smudde and Courtright, 2012a: 896). Gergen's (2005) criteria of narrative demarking can be applied both to public relations message and story design as part of practice but can also guide research, with the criteria setting out what to look for in texts in terms of positioning storylines and their supporting narratives.

Publics, audiences and storyline development

From a positioning theoretical perspective, even if practitioners are aiming to tie the storylines they develop to what people already know, what "knowing" do they aim for? Even if practitioners are basing campaigns on thorough research, how do they know what is in the research findings to be "true"? The fact is that they don't know and probably can't know unless they undertook extensive ethnography such as undertaken by Moffitt (1994), whose method goes some way to shedding light on this phenomenon but would be unwieldy in practice. Vardeman-Winter, Tindall and Jiang (2013) have stated that practitioners' limited understanding of how multiple identities shape publics' communication behaviors is impacting negatively on current public relations research and practice due to "the dominance of the traditional paradigm of publics' identity as comprised of discrete demographics" (p. 284). An approach based on "intersectionality" (p. 284), which conceptualizes the social constructions of identity as being multiple, constructed through the intersecting aspects of not only demographics but of the simultaneous effects within social groups of how oppression and privilege operate (Vardeman-Winter *et al.*, 2013), is proposed as a way forward for practitioners and researchers.

A positioning approach helps to unpack the dimensions surrounding the concept of local moral order and the rights and duties associated with taking up or assigning positions. Such an approach may be a way to explore how "more honest relationships with publics" (Vardeman-Winter *et al.*, 2013: 297) could be formed. Positioning theory may help researchers and practitioners develop more realistic understandings of their power and roles as related to publics, especially as it pertains to intentionally positioning to help organizations or clients to reach their goals. The key seems to be to conceptualize public relations episodes as multifaceted, where practice aims to achieve outcomes in a progressive and dynamic manner.

This is essentially related to that fact that people have the capacity to exercise choice when it comes to engaging in discourse and discursive practices. Davies and Harré (1999) argue that it is in the provision of subject positions through the constitutive force of each discursive practice that this choice takes place. This is relevant for public relations, as practitioners need to recognize that such subject positions incorporate a type of conceptual repertoire and a "location". This location is where a person sits within "a structure of rights and duties" but also where they sit within the contested space where meanings are constituted (Berger, 1999). A subject position determines the vantage point from which the phenomenon in question is viewed. An understanding of current subject positions held by target audiences and publics is important for practitioners seeking to develop the storylines to support desired positions. This understanding provides the insights into what words, images, metaphors and concepts would be relevant to people operating within particular discourses and within particular discursively constructed sites of meaning making.

The audience for storylines is paramount as audience members are not fixed entities with predictable responses but are constantly constituted and reconstituted through the discursive practices in which they take part. This means that the audience is potentially always open and changing depending upon positions that are being made available through their own and through others' discursive practice. As Davies and Harré state:

> Stories are located within a number of discourses, and thus vary dramatically in terms of the language used, the concepts, issues and moral judgments made relevant, and the subject positions made available within them.
>
> (Davies and Harré 1999: 35)

This encapsulates the domain of the public relations practitioner: determining the right choices for storyline development. In such practice, an organization is acting from a particular position, but also brings with it the history of the positions it has taken previously. These include not only the past positions that the organization itself determines it has taken in the past, but also those that others determine it has taken in the past. This is another layer of meaning that helps shape the local moral order and thus the positions and storylines that are open to the organization at a given time. A storyline may need to acknowledge past positions in the process of talking about the current position. This assists in constructing the right, in the eyes of the local moral order, to take or assign the current positioning. When analyzing positioning efforts in a research context, such acknowledgement of past positions should be sought as part of the clues indicating how positions were constructed.

This is also interesting in terms of how an organization responds when being positioned by others. The practitioner should recognize that the organization is not inevitably caught in the position that a storyline constructed by another or others' discursive practices suggests. For example, a not-for-profit organization helping illegal substance abusers may reject the "drugs use = criminal" storyline, instead positioning their services and clients through the "health care/health client" storyline. All players in the situation, including the audiences, would jointly construct the storylines in such a public relations episode. An organization's past positions, and how these were enacted, will come into play and can be drawn on to self-position in a different way to that assigned by a competitor or other body. Such public relations episodes unfold following what one organization says and does, in effect positioning another organization.

Drawing on the work of Davies and Harré (1999) this can be called interactive positioning. In the same episode the organization will also be striving to position itself – reflexive positioning. One should note however that not all positioning is intentional, in that not all repercussions of taking or assigning certain positions can be predicted or mapped accurately. From a public relations perspective, as many probable impacts of taking or assigning positions as conceivable should be mapped in the scenario planning stage. This is important as part of the issues management aspect in order to help determine available positions for an organization and to help in the development of supporting storylines. This relates to Bakhtin's (1986) concept of "addressivity", which is the quality of an utterance being directed to someone, constructed from the very start with possible responses in mind. As Bakhtin (1986: 95) states, the addressee

> can be an immediate participant-interlocutor in an everyday dialogue, a differentiated collective of specialists in some particular area of cultural communication, a more or less differentiated public, ethnic group, contemporaries, like-minded people, opponents and enemies, a subordinate, a superior, someone who is lower, higher, familiar, foreign, and so forth.

Practitioners often formulate their messages within specific storylines with an audience or addressee in mind. As Bakhtin (1986) would describe, this is in response to anticipated addressees who, in the end, may or may not respond at some future time. Drawing heavily from Bakhtin (1986: 95–6), adapting addressivity to storyline and narrative design within public relations practice would see practitioners acting in accordance with the responses they anticipate. This anticipated response, in turn, exerts an active influence on the message design (e.g., foreseeing objections, making provisos, and so forth). In the design process practitioners take into account the apperceptive background of the addressees' perceptions of the message: the extent to which the addressee is familiar with the situation, whether they have special knowledge of the given cultural area of communication, their views and convictions, their prejudices (from the practitioner's/organization's viewpoint), their sympathies and antipathies – because all this will determine their active responsive understanding of the messages. These considerations also determine the choice of a genre by the practitioner for the organization's narrative and key messages, the "choice of compositional devices", and, finally, "the choice of language vehicles", that is, "the style" of the messages (p. 96).

Public relations practitioners know that the role of those for whom messages are constructed is significant and that practice involves the anticipation of encountering the addressees', responses (James, 2011b). It can be seen that practitioners actually test out positions and storylines through research and consultative processes that inform the development of engagement strategies. In consultative processes it can be seen that practitioners identify what parts of storylines are taken up and what positions are considered and occupied in each storyline. If options that are on an organization's proverbial drawing board are offered as hypothetical scenarios, then positions and storylines can be tested out. This can happen with "live" research participants but can also be worked through within an organization, essentially undertaking a situational analysis from the positioning theoretical perspective. What positions are available and what storylines could be invoked as a result of such positions being taken or assigned? A storyline in a public relations context generally relates to a particular topic. It is in the telling of the narrative that the storyline's force is made determinate for the targeted audiences. Practitioners designing storylines should align them with the local expressive repertoires that they presume are in use, and towards which the organization, in a given situation, orients itself. For example, the expressive repertoires in use by a construction company will vary if the audience is comprised of shareholders and investors as opposed to local residents potentially impacted by a proposed development.

On examination, public relations episodes invariably display storylines. Whether one is analyzing, a past campaign or consultative process, or observing such a campaign or process unfold, the parties to the episode can be seen to be living out narrative conventions (Harré, 2006). Harré's work suggests that in a strategic communication situation, analysis of the expressive conventions displayed in the various actors' performances would reveal the storyline being lived out in the public relations episode. From a campaign or program planning viewpoint, such narratives can be anticipated to a large degree as the position taken or assigned by an organization will have been informed by the overall goal to be achieved. Possible and probable scenarios can be formulated based on how those narrative conventions are likely to play out in the context of rights and duties associated with positions. This process of storyline analysis can inform decision-making associated with proceeding in particular ways within a communication program.

The understanding that individual audience members have of their own positioning, within their social reality, articulates the meaning that is constructed by them when they encounter and engage with an organization's intentional positioning effort. Those audience members' readings of the storyline may be quite different to what was intended. This could especially be the case if positioning campaign elements designed for one audience (e.g. shareholders) are encountered and engaged with by other audiences (e.g. community members or activist groups). This notion of fluidity of positions and of meaning-making is one of the most important aspects of positioning theory for public relations and may help explain why campaign plans need to be adjusted to accommodate changes in internal and external environments as the plan is implemented. It centers on the dynamic stability of the positioning triangle being maintained.

Summary

This chapter provided a detailed description of the concept of storylines and how they function within the positioning triangle domain of the Framework for

Intentional Positioning in Public Relations. Storylines were defined as schematic representations that contain abstracted information about the cultural standards in operation within local moral orders that are used for positioning purposes. Storylines are essentially comprised of the master narratives that operate in societies and of which the societal members have an understanding. The potential usefulness of using positioning theory to analyze public relations to provide insight into the active way practitioners and publics construct social reality was explored. By calling attention to the social forces of speech acts within specific storylines, the function that is being served by the acts/actions being undertaken can come into focus.

An overview of how storylines operated within narrative conventions was provided and this led into an examination of how such conventions structured an approach to storyline and message development in public relations positioning. Gergen's (2005) criteria for constructing an intelligible narrative in contemporary culture were adapted for a public relations context to guide message design. The role of audiences in conceptualizing narrative and message design in public relations was then considered and the concept of "addressivity" (Bakhtin, 1986) was introduced as a way of applying such considerations in message design and analysis. Through reinforcing the role of storylines as part of the positioning triangle domain and reiterating the importance of maintaining the dynamic stability of position, act/actions and storyline for successful positioning, it is hoped that this has impressed upon readers the interdependence of the three vertices of the triangle so they act as a unified positioning domain.

References

Al Khaja, M. A. W. and Creedon, P. (2010) Evaluating the effectiveness of the first breast cancer awareness campaign in the United Arab Emirates: lessons learned and next steps. *Public Relations Review*, 36(4): 386–8.

Bakhtin, M. (1986) The problem of speech genres. In M. Holquist (ed.) *Speech Genres and Other Late Essays*, (Translated by V. McGee). Austin, TX: University of Texas Press, pp. 60–102.

Batchelor, B. and Formentin, M. (2008) Re-branding the NHL: building the league through the "My NHL" integrated marketing campaign. *Public Relations Review*, 34(2): 156–60.

Berger, B. (1999) The Halcion affair: public relations and the construction of ideological world view. *Journal of Public Relations Research*, 11(3): 185–203.

Burkart, R. (2009) On Habermas: understanding and public relations. In O. Ihlen, B. van Ruler and M. Fredriksson (eds) *Public Relations and Social Theory: Key figures and concepts*. London: Routledge, pp. 141–64.

Canel, M. (2012) Communicating strategically in the face of terrorism: the Spanish government's response to the 2004 Madrid bombing attacks. *Public Relations Review*, 38(2): 214–22.

Coombs, T. (2007) *Ongoing Crisis Communication: Planning, managing, and responding* (2nd edn). Thousand Oaks, CA: Sage.

Courtright, J. L. and Smudde, P. M. (2009) Recall communications: discourse genres, symbolic charging, and message design. *International Journal of Strategic Communication*, 4(1): 58–74.

Davies, B. and Harré, R. (1999) Positioning and personhood. In R. Harré and L. Van Langenhove (eds) *Positioning Theory: Moral contexts of intentional action*. Oxford: Blackwell.

Fivush, R., Habermas, T., Waters, T. E. and Zaman, W. (2011) The making of autobiographical memory: intersections of culture, narratives and identity. *International Journal of Psychology,* 46(5): 321–45.

Fortunato, J. (2000) Public relations strategies for creating mass media content: a case study of the national basketball association. *Public Relations Review*, 26(4): 481–97.

Franklin, S. (1988) Life story: the gene as fetish object on TV. *Science as Culture*, 1(3): 92–100.

Gergen, K. (2005) Narrative, moral identity, and historical consciousness: a social constructionist account. In J. Straub (ed.) *Narration, Identity, and Historical Consciousness*. New York: Berghahn, pp. 99–119.

Hallahan, K. (1999) Seven models of framing: implications for public relations. *Journal of Public Relations Research*, 11(3): 205–42.

Hanlon, P. (2011) 8 master storylines for business storytellers, parts 1&2. *Forbes*. Retrieved from www.forbes.com/sites/patrickhanlon/2011/10/10/8-master-storylines-for-business storytellers-part-1/ and www.forbes.com/sites/patrickhanlon/2011/10/12/8-storylines-for-business-storytellerspart-2/

Harré, R. (2006) Positioning theory. In V. Jupp (ed.) *The Sage Dictionary of Social Research Methods*. Sage, pp. 229–30. Retrieved from http://srmo.sagepub.com/view/the-sage-dictionary-of-social-research-methods/SAGE.xml

Harré, R. (2012) Positioning theory: moral dimensions of social-cultural psychology. In J. Valsiner (ed.) *The Oxford Handbook of Culture and Psychology*. New York: Oxford University, pp. 191–206.

Harré, R. and Moghaddam, F. (2003) Introduction: the self and others in traditional psychology and in positioning theory. In R. Harré and F. Moghaddam (eds) *The self and Others: Positioning individuals and groups in personal, political and cultural contexts*. London: Praeger, pp. 1–11.

Harré, R. and Slocum, N. (2003) Disputes as complex social events: on the uses of positioning theory. In R. Harré and F. Moghaddam (eds) *The self and Others: Positioning individuals and groups in personal, political and cultural contexts*. London: Praeger, pp. 123–36.

Harré, R. and van Langenhove, L. (1999) *Positioning Theory: Moral contexts of intentional action*. Oxford: Blackwell.

Henderson, A. (2005) Activism in "paradise": identity management in a public relations campaign against genetic engineering. *Journal of Public Relations Research*, 17(2): 117–37.

Henriksen, T. (2008) Liquidating roles and crystallising positions. In F. Moghaddam, R. Harré and N. Lee (eds) *Global Conflict Resolution through Positioning Analysis*. New York: Springer, pp. 41–64.

James, M. (2011a) A provisional conceptual framework for intentional positioning in public relations. *Journal of Public Relations Research,* 23(1): 93–111. http://dx.doi.org/10.1080/1062726X.2010.505120

James, M. (2011b) Ready, aim, fire: key messages in public relations campaigns. *PRism*, 8(1): 1–18.

Jaques, T. and Galloway, C. (2012) Coal seam gas in Australia: can activists be effective from the margins? *Asia Pacific Public Relations Journal*, 13(2): 35–44.

Jo, S., Shim. S. and Jung, J. (2008) Propaganda or public relations campaign? International communication on the war against Iraq. *Public Relations Review*, 34, 63–5.

Johansen, T. (2012) The narrated organization: implications of a narrative corporate identity vocabulary for strategic self-storying. *International Journal of Strategic Communication*, 6(3): 232–45.
Kim, J. and Ni, L. (2010) Seeing the forest through the trees: the behavioural, strategic management paradigm in public relations and its future. In R. Heath (ed.) *The Sage Handbook of Public Relations*. Thousand Oaks, CA: Sage, pp. 35–57.
Lane, A. (2007) Empowering publics: the potential and challenge for public relations practitioners in creative approaches to two-way symmetric public relations. *Australian Journal of Communication*, 34(1): 71–86.
Louis, W. (2008) Intergroup positioning and power. In F. Moghaddam, R. Harréand N. Lee, (eds) *Global Conflict Resolution through Positioning Analysis*. New York: Springer, pp. 21–40.
Lundy, L. and Broussard, J. (2007) Public relations in the eye of the storm: lessons from professionals in the wake of Hurricanes Katrina and Rita. *Public Relations Review*, 33, 220–3.
Mahoney, J. (2008) *Public relations writing in Australia*. South Melbourne: Oxford.
Moffitt, M. (1994) Collapsing and integrating concepts of "public" and "image" into a new theory. *Public Relations Review*, 20, 159–70.
Moffitt, M. (1999) *Campaign Strategies and Message Design: A practitioner's guide from start to finish*. Westport, CT: Praeger.
Moghaddam, F. and Harré, R. (2010) Words, conflicts and political processes. In F. Moghaddam and R. Harré (eds) *Words of Conflict, Words of War: How the language we use in political processes sparks fighting*. Santa Barbara, CA: Praeger.
Moloney, K. (2006) *Rethinking Public Relations* (2nd edn). London: Routledge.
Neff, B. (2008) Speech act theory: an approach to public relations leadership. In T. Hansen-Horn and B. Neff (eds) *Public Relations: From theory to practice*. Boston, MA: Pearson, pp. 89–103.
New York Times (2012) Assessing Romney's chances. Retrieved March 21, 2013, from http://elections.nytimes.com/2012/candidates/mitt-romney
Ochs, E. and Capps, L. (1996) Narrating the self. *Annual Review of Anthropology*, 19–43.
Pratt, C. (2004) Crafting key messages and talking points: or grounding them in what research tells us. *Public Relations Quarterly*, (Fall), 15–20.
Rice, C. and Somerville, I. (2013) Power-sharing and political public relations: government–press relationships in Northern Ireland's developing democratic institutions. *Public Relations Review*, 39 (4): 293–302. http://dx.doi.org/10.1016/j.pubrev.2013.07.014
Slocum, N. and van Langenhove, L. (2003) Integration speak: introducing positioning theory in regional studies. In R. Harré and F. Moghaddam (eds) *The self and Others: Positioning individuals and groups in personal, political and cultural contexts*. London: Praeger, pp. 123–36.
Smith, B. and Sparkes, A. C. (2008) Narrative and its potential contribution to disability studies. *Disability & Society*, 23(1): 17–28.
Smudde, P. M. and Courtright, J. L. (2012a) In search of message design best practices: the Silver Anvil Award winners archive. *Public Relations Review*, 888–97.
Smudde, P. M., and Courtright, J. L. (2012b) *Inspiring Cooperation and Celebrating Organizations: Genres, message design, and strategies in public relations*. New York: Hampton.
Stokes, A. and Rubin, D. (2010) Activism and the limits of symmetry: the public relations battle between Colorado GASP and Philip Morris. *Journal of Public Relations Research*, 22(1): 26–48.

Tilson, D. (2006) Devotional-promotional communication and Santiago: a thousand-year public relations campaign for Saint James and Spain. In J. L'Etang and Pieczka, M. (eds) *Public Relations: Critical debates and contemporary practice*. Mahwah, NJ: Lawrence Erlbaum, pp. 167–86.

Tsetsura, K. (2012) A struggle for legitimacy: Russian women secure their professional identities in public relations in a hyper sexualized patriarchal workplace. *Public Relations Journal*, 6(1): 1–21.

Vardeman-Winter, J. (2010) Using the cultural studies approach to understand health decision-making among a teen public. *Public Relations Review*, 36(4): 383–5.

Vardeman-Winter, J., Tindall, N. and Jiang, H. (2013) Intersectionality and publics: how exploring publics' multiple identities questions basic public relations concepts. *Public Relations Inquiry,* 2, 279–304. doi:10.1177/2046147X13491564

Wilson, L. (2001) Extending strategic planning to communication tactics. In R. Heath (ed.) *The Sage Handbook of Public Relations*. Thousand Oaks, CA: Sage, pp. 215–22.

Wilson, B., Stavros, C. and Westberg, K. (2008) Player transgressions and the management of the sport sponsor relationship. *Public Relations Review*, 34(2): 99–107.

Wise, D. and James, M. (2013) Positioning a price on carbon: applying a proposed hybrid method of positioning discourse analysis for public relations. *Public Relations Inquiry*, 2(3): 327–53.

Yang, A., Klyueva, A., and Taylor, M. (2012) Beyond a dyadic approach to public diplomacy: understanding relationships in a multipolar world. *Public Relations Review*, 38(5): 652–64.

Zhang, J. and Benoit, W. (2004) Arab image: message strategies of Saudi Arabia's image restoration campaign after 9/11. *Public Relations Review*, 30(2): 161–7.

Part III

Applying positioning theory to public relations research and practice

7 Analyzing positioning strategies in public relations

Given the relatively recent application of positioning theory to public relations, it is too early to prescribe specific "must-use" methods for analyzing positioning in public relations contexts. Qualitative methods such as thematic analysis (James, 2010; Tsetsura, 2012), textual analysis (James, 2011), autoethnographic approaches (James, 2012) and positioning discourse analysis (Wise and James, 2013) have been used to date. However, being such a new approach in the field, the hope is that positioning theory will excite people and that future research will further explore methods for positioning analysis.

There is particular potential to explore positioning theory through practice-based research using methods such as action research (Rapoport, 1970) and practitioner-based inquiry (McIntyre, 2006; Lawrence and Murray, 2000), especially in terms of examining the subjective agency of the practitioner-as-researcher (Kerrigan, 2013).

Outside of a public relations context, methods of positioning analysis reported in the literature are primarily qualitative and include narrative analysis (Harré and Slocum, 2003), conversational analysis (e.g. Wilkinson and Kitzinger, 2003), discourse analysis (Niska and Vesala, 2013; Walton, Coyle and Lyons, 2003), and rhetorical analysis (Badran, 2010). Slocum-Bradley (2007) states that while many researchers are undertaking discourse analysis, "few do so in a systematic manner" (p. 636) and she recommended undertaking the analysis using the "positioning triad" to guide analysis and to avoid simply "producing a narrative about another narrative" (p. 636). Such an approach aligns with applying the Framework for Intentional Positioning in Public Relations, which was adapted from the work of Harré and van Langenhove (1999).

As well as some concern about discourse approaches, the other area of possible confusion in positioning analysis is around the analysis of storylines and the analysis of frames. According to positioning theorists (Harré and Moghaddam, 2003), storyline analysis is central in terms of analyzing the meaning of the positioning efforts. The concept of storyline is focused on the unfolding of the overarching master "plot" and the narrative conventions that open up within the positioning context. This contrasts with framing, which Hallahan (1999) defined as a technique that focuses attention on the elements within the story frame, effectively "delimiting the subject matter" (p. 207). He described the framing process as not just one of inclusion but also of exclusion and of adding emphases to specific elements. There is certainly a case for analyzing the framing of narratives within storylines however, it is the storyline that provides the most accessible way to begin a positioning analysis.

Public relations research applying positioning theory as an analytical tool: studies so far

Public relations positioning in government communication campaigns: James (2010)

This research reported on testing and development of the Framework for Intentional Positioning in Public Relations and applied the Framework to government agency/publicly-funded organizations' campaigns as a way of examining whether positioning in public relations was different to that seen in commercial marketing, as marketing as a rule is not generally associated with government communication (James, 2010). It set out to investigate whether government agencies' and other public sector organizations' communication campaigns in Australia employed public relations positioning techniques in their quest to achieve public relations goals.

The Provisional Conceptual Framework for Intentional Positioning in Public Relations (James, 2011) was applied to 21 Australian award-winning government agency/public sector organizations' communication campaigns for the period 1999–2008. All had won a Public Relations Institute of Australia Golden Target Award in their categories. There were three award entries from federal government-funded organizations, 14 from state government-funded organizations and four from local government-funded organizations. The data to which the framework was applied was that generated by textual and thematic analysis of the award entry texts and the transcripts of interviews with selected practitioners who designed award-winning government communication campaigns in recent years.

The research showed that although positioning may seem incongruous with the concept of "professional neutrality" (Althaus, Bridgman and Davis, 2007: 12) that is generally expected of government agencies' communication efforts, they did apply positioning techniques. However, James (2010) demonstrated that positioning undertaken by such government agencies and organizations is something quite different to that which is seen in marketing contexts.

Through the application of the positioning framework, evidence was presented that showed that the communication campaigns of the government agencies and public sector organizations intended to position their ideas, their offerings or their services in a particular way in the minds of target publics and that they employed a range of techniques to enact the intended positioning. The application of the Framework to these examples of practice in government communications indicated that the Framework was a useful tool for analyzing campaigns. Even in cases when there was no mention of the word "position" or a stated aim that positioning was being attempted, by applying the Framework to a particular campaign, it was found that it was possible to determine whether positioning was taking place in a public relations context, that is, a strategic attempt to stake out and occupy a site of intentional representation in a contested space where meanings are constructed, contested and reconstructed (James, 2011).

The study found that positioning activities were employed to facilitate target publics constructing the meaning that the government agency/public sector organization intended for them. These were found to have not been marketing communication campaigns but campaigns designed to construct an "interpretive potential" (Neff, 2008: 92). Evidence indicated that each was designed with a view to persuading or influencing identified target publics to view something in a particular way to undertake a certain action, thus facilitating the achievement of specific organizational goals. On the basis of the results and analysis, James (2010) concluded that the Framework offered a more comprehensive approach to positioning in public relations than approaches found in marketing models.

An analysis of positioning in national award winning PR campaigns in Australia: James (2011)

In order to test the application of the factors within the four domains of the Provisional Conceptual Framework for Intentional Positioning in Public Relations, James (2011) applied the Framework to award-winning public relations campaigns. For this project, award winning entries into the Public Relations Institute of Australia's Golden Target Awards were viewed as examples of what the public relations industry in Australia held to be best practice as judged by peers across the country. The award entries included in the data collection were 57 entries awarded a Golden Target Award between 1999 and 2007. This number of entry awards was arbitrarily selected, but represented all entries that were recorded as winners and that provided sufficient detail for the purposes of the research, these were: executive summary; situational analysis; goals and objectives; research; target publics; communication strategy; implementation; results; and evaluation.

The sample provided a good range of entries from across industry sectors including corporate, not-for-profit and government. The sample also provided a good cross section of entries across campaign types including internal communication, crisis management, marketing communication, community relations, investor relations and government communication. The award entries themselves were not unproblematic, as Jaques (2008) has stated:

> Inevitably, such "author generated" cases are prone to self-praise and wisdom after the event, and they tend to focus on successful outcomes (especially when the author is a consultant using an award program to promote work done for a client organization). More importantly, they generally lack independent review and are deficient in objective analysis.
>
> (Jaques, 2008: 195)

It was acknowledged that the award entries had constructed a retrospective narrative of the public relations activities undertaken by the entries' authors, and would be composed in a way that showed the activities in the best light in the hope of winning an award. It was clear however, that the entries would also demonstrate what was valued in public relations practice and how public relations practitioners talked about or presented their practice. The award entries were not viewed as necessarily describing accurately what "really" happened but as having used discourse as a device to construct their version of practice. The award entries were examined using primarily qualitative textual analysis to identify to what extent positioning was used in campaigns. It was noted (James, 2011) that this was a limitation of the study in that it was acknowledged that another researcher might not have categorized the factors within the four domains of the framework in the same way. However it was evident that intentional positioning was being undertaken and that the specific categorization of the factors did not detract from the evidence that positioning factors were present in each domain.

All campaign award entries were found to have positioning elements within them, with the positioning triangle domain of *position—speech act/action—storyline* being successfully applied to all campaigns. All award entries showed evidence of deliberate self-positioning (n=57) and in addition to self-positioning, 33 percent (n=19) showed evidence of forced self-positioning; 84 percent (n=48) showed evidence of the deliberate positioning of others; and, 12 percent (n=7) showed evidence of forced positioning of others. The results showed that positioning was undertaken for the purposes of self-promotion in the majority of entries (81 percent n=46) but that often this was accompanied by a second purpose such as exemplification. All award entries (n=57) showed evidence of intended positioning being related to a desire to achieve a specific strategic goal of the entity commissioning the public relations.

The overall findings indicated that positioning happened at various stages of a public relations campaign. The study demonstrated that public relations practitioners used language, symbols, knowledge, and discourse to create or influence the construction of meaning in order to position in particular ways. It was clear in the study that the use of rhetoric and the construction of "zones of meaning" (Berger and Luckmann, 1966: 55; Heath, 2001: 47–8 cited in James, 2011) through positioning and techniques such as priming and framing (e.g. Hallahan, 1999, cited in James, 2011) aimed to make it as easy as possible for targeted publics and audiences to co-construct the meaning intended by the organization commissioning the public relations. Positioning tactics, especially in the construction of storylines, were undertaken in ways that were interpretable by audiences in terms of narratives that were operating in the communities into which the messages were being sent. The results opened the door for further investigation of how the intended positioning meanings were co-constructed by both the organization commissioning public relations activity and the subjects of the public relations activity, that is, target publics and audiences. It was concluded that the Framework offered a more comprehensive approach to positioning than found in marketing models and also brought together elements identified by other public relations researchers into a single framework. It was clear that further testing and refinement was needed but this study's findings confirmed that positioning was a significant part of public relations campaign practice.

Applying positioning theory to how Russian female public relations professionals negotiated positions and manifested their identities: Tsetsura (2012)

This qualitative study sought to understand processes which were used by female public relations practitioners in negotiating their identities in the workplace in "transitional hyper-sexualized societies, such as Russia, where public relations is a relatively young field" (Tsetsura, 2012: 1). The study applied a framework of positioning theory (Davies and Harré, 1990), concepts of multiple identity negotiation (Berger and Luckmann, 1966 cited in Tsetsura, 2012) and body disciplining (Trethewey, 2000a, b, cited in Tsetsura, 2012). Specifically, positioning theory was used "to demonstrate how it can contribute to studying identity negotiation in the workplace" (Tsetsura, 2012: 15). The study collected interview data from 25 female public relations practitioners from ten agencies in Russia, with 11 women individually interviewed and 14 women joining one of the three discussion group interviews. A thematic analysis was conducted on the data. The findings showed that the practitioners "engaged in a constant process of securing their professional identities, specifically disciplining their bodies and controlling their physical presence" (Tsetsura, 2012: 1). According to Tsetsura (2012: 14), women practitioners positioned themselves as professionals primarily "by consciously controlling their appearances and disciplining their bodies". Tsetsura states:

> Because positioning allows to account for flexibility in the identity negotiation process, this study gleaned that female professionals positioned themselves and others through continuously changing discourse – and as a result demonstrated flexibility in defining advantages and disadvantages of being a female public relations professional as they discussed expectations of their employers and their own expectations toward work.
>
> (Tsetsura, 2012: 15)

Further analysis, however, suggested that these strategies might lead to reproduction of stereotypical understandings of the role and place of women in a hyper-sexualized, patriarchic environment. Tsetsura (2012) recommended further studies to further explore this phenomenon. Her research provides more insights into public relations practice but also on the further possibilities for the application of positioning theory in the public relations field.

An examination of the positioning framework as a public relations discourse analytical tool: Wise and James (2013)

This research project explored public relations positioning through an analysis of the speeches of two key political leaders in Australia during the period of polarized debate around pricing carbon in the transition to a carbon emissions trading scheme. Wise and James (2013) strove to answer the research question: What positioning intentions and supporting discourses were evident in the speeches of the Labor Prime Minister Julia Gillard, and the Liberal/National (LNP) Opposition Leader Tony Abbott, in relation to the introduction of an Australian carbon tax. The researchers developed a hybrid approach that merged critical discourse analysis approaches with the positioning framework proposed by James (2010, 2011). This approach, tentatively termed "positioning discourse analysis" (Wise and James, 2013), was used to examine the speeches with the aim of elucidating the positioning intentions and supporting discourses about the introduction of a carbon price/tax. This hybrid method, where positioning theory, the application of the Positioning Framework, and discourse analysis were brought together to provide a method of eliciting specific insights for public relations practice. The authors stressed that the method should not be viewed as a deterministic approach but that the Framework should provide an analytical guide and not limit the range of discourses that could be present in the analysis.

Using positioning discourse analysis indicated that both Gillard and Abbott held fast to their parties' positions on carbon pricing throughout the lead-up period to the legislation's introduction to Parliament. There was little evidence of straying from the basic premise that carbon pricing was good for the nation on one side, and that a carbon tax was bad for the nation on the other. The Framework approach was also useful for mapping the efforts of each side to destabilize the position of the other. It showed how the storylines further developed from the positioning enactment points through the subsequent campaign in an effort to strengthen their own position and weaken that of the opponent. Each side used discourse to enact and support positions but analysis showed that Gillard was cornered into linking all messages to investment in new technologies, leading the way forward on clean energy and so forth. Abbott, on the other hand, had literally everything at his disposal – he could talk about everything costing more and how this would make imported goods cheaper for consumers thus undermining Australian jobs.

The evidence suggested that the Gillard government's decision to position a price on carbon in the way it did might have been ill considered. This study also suggested that the Positioning Framework could be useful when planning a positioning campaign as once a position has been determined, the way it could be enacted and supported through the campaign period could be mapped. In this process the likely arguments and attempts to destabilize the position could be anticipated and a decision made as to the likelihood of the positioning to hold against such efforts. The available discourses open to the Gillard government once they had taken their position were found to be extremely limited and the authors argued that that this could have been anticipated. Had the government linked their plan to introduce a price on carbon to a different position that opened up the possibilities of different discourses, their efforts may have found more success in terms of public opinion. The study concluded that Abbott's positioning was much more strategic in terms of opening up a myriad of discourses about increased costs and the impact of this on everything and everyone in Australia. Abbott's team had the advantage of being able to position in relation to the stance taken by the government but it was argued that the Gillard team should have been able to predict such a response.

The framework approach demonstrated the dynamism of positioning efforts as each side of the debate sought to strengthen its own position and to destabilize the other's position. From a public relations theoretical perspective, the Framework was seen to offer a new method of mapping the discourses used in a public policy debate and may have wider application to analyzing discourses in public relations and other strategic communication situations. However, what was evident in this study is that no matter how Prime Minister Gillard enacted her government's position and no matter what storylines and key messages were promulgated to support this position, the position determined and taken by Gillard was in itself untenable. This seems to be related to the issue of not having earned or constructed the right to introduce and position a price on carbon pollution in Australia, post-2010 election. Having stated prior to that election that there would be no price placed on carbon under her government, she subsequently stated in 2011 that a carbon price would be introduced.

Her explanation as to her change of mind on this point was articulated as part of the supporting storyline for the position she took. However, the evidence indicated that although the position was enacted through speeches held at appropriate conferences and venues, and that the positioning was supported through reasonably consistent storylines and messages, the actual position that was determined (the first vertex of the positioning triangle domain) was unsound. Wise and James (2013) suggested that further research would be needed to explore how tenable positions were constructed by entities seeking to progress a policy debate, a project or other program or issue in a public relations sense. It was also recommended that such research should also address the ethical dimensions of position construction and what processes should inform such an exercise.

The next section of this chapter will build on the insights offered by the studies of positioning in public relations undertaken to date and offer a method of approaching a positioning analysis.

What should be researched?

One of the first methodological issues to be broached is what should be the research sample in public relations positioning analysis. To date there have been analyses of practitioner interview transcripts (James, 2011, Tsetsura, 2012), narratives of practice texts such as award entries and case studies (James 2010, 2011), self-reports of practice (James, 2012), and of public relations discourse genres such as speeches (Wise and James, 2013). It is evident that data samples could readily include public relations discourse genres (Courtright and Smudde, 2009) such as media releases, white papers, social media posts, website content and so on. The horizons for what should comprise data for positioning analysis in the context of the public relations field are broad, and wide open for exploration.

One key issue for the field is whether such data should be "naturally occurring" (Silverman, 2011: 17). Naturally occurring data enables researchers to "examine what people actually do in real life rather than asking them to comment upon it" and Silverman recommends its use over "contrivances such as interviews or focus groups" (Silverman, 2011: 166). Such decisions about data should be based on the nature of the research topic and what it is that one is seeking to find out. Silverman is in favor of using naturally occurring data in qualitative research but recognizes that other qualitative researchers see great value in research interviews. From a social constructionist viewpoint, interview data are the result of a co-construction of meaning process between interviewers and interviewees (e.g. Koro-Ljungberg, 2008) and can be conceptualized as "cultural stories" (Silverman, 2011: 188). In positioning research it can be seen that there is value in both a) gaining insights into what practitioners are "doing in real life" by observing and examining the cultural artifacts that they are producing (the naturally occurring data), and b) gaining insights into how practitioners think about/conceptualize/reflect on their positioning practices by analyzing their cultural stories (see Niska and Vesala, 2013). Positioning theorists, such as Slocum-Bradley (2007), have on occasion used a combination of naturally occurring data (e.g. public documents), along with methods such as in-situ observation and interviews with participants, an approach also used by James (2011).

The boundaries and scope of the research are also areas that require careful consideration and the boundaries of a given topic's discourse must be considered (Harré and Slocum, 2003). This also raises the question of who defines the topic being researched, which in itself may be a contested one. Actual or potential parties to public relations episodes can differ in their views as to what an issue is about and it is not unusual for there to be an array of storylines in a public relations episode, especially when the time frame extends into days, weeks and beyond. Some reported public relations episodes go on for years (e.g. Berger, 1999), or even centuries (e.g. Tilson, 2006). With the existence of multiple storylines being at the core of many conflicted situations, analytical work is often focused on where such storylines intersect and also on making distinctions between generic storylines and narrative forms (Harré and Slocum, 2003). Harré and Slocum (2003), when conducting research using a narrative analysis of a local dispute between a university and its local community, pointed out the importance of collecting data in the form of narratives that were presented to a variety of audiences:

> One must always be aware not only of the specific character of the audience, but also of other aspects of the context and the general discursive frame in which particular interventions and contributions are set.
>
> (Harré and Slocum, 2003: 130)

In the Wise and James (2013) positioning discourse analysis of the use of political speeches in a public relations context, it was found that the discourses, language and delivery style of the speeches differed significantly depending on the audience to which the speech was being delivered. This is hardly surprising from a public relations perspective as this is what would be advised in the course of practice. However, in terms of collecting data in the form of speech transcripts and videos etcetera, the research findings would not have given a sense of what was happening in the public domain if only the speeches delivered to a single type of audience, say the business community, had been included in the sample for analysis.

How should positioning analysis be approached?

A positioning analysis yields narratives that people or organizations use to position one another and themselves (Christie, 2008, n.p.). The tools used to conduct an analysis of positioning in a public relations context are closely related to those used for conducting an analysis of meaning (Bogren, 2010). How researchers approach the data in a positioning analysis varies, and there is no particular way that has emerged as a clear preference. However, most analysis centers on texts as data. For the purposes of public relations positioning analysis, the definition of texts that I believe to be most useful is that provided by Kress (2012).

In his discussion of the differences between the terms "text" and "discourse", he states that these terms are often used interchangeably. In firstly setting out a definition of discourse he draws on the writings of Foucault and states, "*discourse* as institutionally produced 'knowledge' is a *social* rather than a *linguistic* category" with our understanding of meaning generated from "the *social*" (Kress, 2012: 35). According to Kress (2012) texts can be seen as having a materiality in that they can be produced as gesture, speech, still or moving images, writing or music. Texts "realize the interests of their makers" (p. 36) but it must also be recognized that a new text can be produced as a result of someone making an interpretation of the meaning of the original text. Such thinking underpins a semiotic approach but can be seen to relate to concepts such as Bakhtin's (1987) "addressivity", discussed in the previous chapter. Coherence is also a defining characteristic of text (Kress, 2012). Whether a text is or is not coherent rests with the "socially located maker and re-maker of the text", which therefore sees power being "involved in the making, recognition and attribution of coherence in a text" (p. 36). Texts are also viewed to be, in part, "constitutive of social institutions; in part they are traces of (inter-)actions in such institutions and, in this, they provide means of 'reading' the interests and purposes of those involved in the making of *texts* in an institution" (Kress, 2012: 37). Kress states that this definition of text "makes the category of text essential and significant in discourse analysis" (2012: 37). I argue that this definition of text is also most helpful in undertaking thematic, textual and positioning analytical work.

In terms of undertaking the analytical work itself, most researchers using positioning theory generally can be seen to have taken a similar approach to that described by Walton *et al.*:

> The analysis recursively moved between, on the one hand, a global consideration of the constructions that the texts were offering and the rhetorical functions to which the texts were oriented and, on the other hand, a more

> micro-level focus on textual details…with the former being grounded in the latter.
>
> (Walton *et al.*, 2003: 49)

In positioning analysis, Harré and Moghaddam (2003) state that the "positioning triangle" can be entered at any of the vertices of position, speech act/action or storyline, but that entering at the point of storyline has "certain advantages" (p. 9). These include that the storyline can function as "a working hypothesis about the principles or conventions that are being followed in the unfolding of the episode that is being studied" (p. 9). They mention such storylines as "David and Goliath" and "doctor/patient" and immediately, for most people, certain conventions play out. For example, a mining operation seeking to expand could be seen as the Goliath and the small community action group opposing the move as the David. As readers or participants in the episode there are certain narrative conventions that stem from this storyline and these can advantage or disadvantage those organizations involved, depending on how the episode unfolds.

From an analytical perspective, researchers can examine whether the large organization undertook positioning efforts to counter the "Goliath storyline", and whether there was language used or actions evident that point to this occurring. The question can be posed whether the community group exploited such a storyline (the little guy fighting back; sustaining belief it could win against the odds and so on) to its benefit. Or whether it took action to counter such positioning, perhaps believing that to do something that countered the narrative convention of the storyline would empower them to position themselves and the mining company in different ways.

In a public relations context we often see a variety of storylines that are well known within specific societies playing out in the episodes themselves, and also in their media reporting. For example, Esrock, Hart, D'Silva and Werking (2002) report on how the company, Nabisco, was portrayed negatively in the media through the portraying of a dispute through the "David and Goliath" storyline, with Nabisco as the Goliath and a small American town being cast into the role of David. In another example, Wang and Chaudhri (2009: 247) discuss the storyline of "building a 'harmonious society'", a master narrative in China that permeates conceptualizations of corporate social responsibility now that the Chinese public and government alike have much higher expectations of Chinese companies (as well as foreign enterprises in China). In a South American context, Catellani (2011) analyzed how environmentalist NGOs built the figures of "guilty and evil businesses" in texts published on the websites of two ironic environmental prizes, and examined how the narratives were played out within the "hero/villain" storyline.

It should be noted that Bogren's (2010) assertion that "the social consequences of texts cannot be fully solved by studying texts only" points to a limitation of the analytical processes described in this chapter. Ethnographic or reception studies that explored audiences' interpretations of texts would also shed light on positioning, positioning strategies and the take up or resistance by audience members of positions offered by texts. Such studies would shed light on how public relations texts contribute to and perhaps change existing relationships of social power.

Although infrequently used in public relations, an action research approach (Rapoport, 1970; Susman and Evered, 1978) could also shed light on the way the storyline has been used as it can be considered at several steps of the research process. For example, taking a project based on the five step action research cycle (ARC) put forward by Susman and Evered (1978): a) diagnosing, b) action planning, c) action taking, d) evaluating, and e) specifying learning, the researcher/practitioner could consider storyline by firstly "diagnosing". She or he could conduct a positioning situational analysis to identify the storylines currently in use about the issue or subject, and those that had been used in the past. In "action planning" the practitioner could map how various storylines would be likely to play out through scenario planning and make recommendations for action based on likely outcomes. In "action taking", storylines would invoke the narratives and related key messages that could be promulgated as part of efforts to support the position being taken up and/or assigned.

The researcher would report on what meaning, as reported in social and traditional media, or through research conducted for the purpose, the intended and non-intended audiences constructed as a result of the storyline. The information would ideally feed into decision-making on whether the storyline or other vertices of the positioning triangle needed to be adjusted, or whether the position itself was appropriate. This work would cross over into the "evaluation" stage where more formal evaluation would be conducted on positioning efforts. Were the expected/intended meanings constructed by the audiences? Was there evidence of the position crystallizing? How closely did things that occurred in the positioning episode align with the scenarios that were worked through in the planning stage? Such questions would guide the report on the last stage, "specifying learning", in that knowledge gained would be shared with key constituents and selected stakeholders to inform future decision-making in the organization's communication programs or in future action research projects.

Conducting a positioning analysis

Adapting the analytical approach used by Harré and Slocum (2003) to a public relations context using the Framework of Intentional Positioning in Public Relations, one way of approaching a positioning analysis is as follows:

1 Texts (e.g. as defined by Kress, 2012), as the data to be analyzed, are collected from diverse sources.
2 These are read and analyzed many times, with each time being used to incorporate new insights and new information from the new materials.
3 The perceptions of the parties to the communication episode must be identified by trying to discern each party's view of what the episode is about in terms of the main issues, and the short and longer term goals.

4 Look for the answers by searching for the start and end points of specific narratives in the text, the events contained in the narrative, and "the qualitative character of the measures used to categorize and evaluate the parties involved" (Harré and Slocum, 2003: 131) and, the central issue of the narrative.
5 Identify all the parties that appear in the narratives as the main actors.
6 Are the parties identified in the narrative a group, an organization, an individual or some other entity? How are these defined? Are there parties who are excluded from the narrative? It is suggested that these parties are those who will be taking up and defending their positions, or themselves being positioned by others (Harré and Slocum, 2003).
7 The next stage is where the researcher would be using the positioning triangle domain of the Framework to guide analysis. The aim is to ascertain what parties to the episode perceive to be areas of disagreement or conflict – this is not about trying to see what is actually happening but how people are ascribing meaning to what is happening, their subjective reality. The goal of this phase, which aligns with the *positioning triangle domain* of the Framework is to identify:
   i The various storylines that constitute the collection of narratives – what storylines are being used to frame the episode in certain ways, e.g. if an organization has chosen to position itself as being exemplary, is the storyline one of "an award winner" or "going beyond the call the duty" that includes a narrative telling of exemplary proof points crafted as key messages? Are other parties' storylines indicating that they accept or reject the organization's positioning?
   ii The positionings of parties in each of the storylines: What positions are being taken and assigned by the parties? Is one party being positioned by others as a "bully"? A model member of the community? Which party has self-positioned or actively positioned others?
   iii The social forces of utterances in the storylines, that is, what social force are the words or actions having in the episode? For example, if a video shows one party kissing another on the cheek is it a kiss of greeting, affection, betrayal or something else? If a transcript reports someone saying, "Come in" is it an order, a welcome or a question?
8 The analysis then turns to examining whether any party to the episode being researched has, as the episode has unfolded through the various storylines, taken a step back and taken a position "with respect to the positionings already accomplished" (Harré and Slocum, 2003: 132). In adopting such a position, the party is claiming a right and maybe even a duty to comment on the positionings accomplished to date – the researcher can ascertain whether in the local moral order that is at work in the episode such a right or duty exists or has been constructed.
9 The researcher can then report on a catalogue of positions, storylines and speech acts/actions in relation to each of the parties involved in the communication episode. The aim here is to make comparisons between parties' positions and storylines, report on shared positions and storylines, what the various parties are doing in taking or assigning positions and what are the social forces of the speech acts that have been used.

10 From here the researcher can then ascertain what strategic framing of the position/s was undertaken by the parties, especially in terms of what rights and duties were taken up or assigned. What attributes were taken up or assigned to others in the framing or pre-positioning stage? This aligns with the *strategic pre-positioning domain* of the Framework for Intentional Positioning in Public Relations.
11 An assessment of the power relations at work in the episode can then be made. Which party/ies possessed positioning power? Harré and Slocum (2003) recommend interrogating the data to ascertain on what basis such power was allocated and what role did differences in positioning power play in the unfolding of the episode. Much of this relates to the positioning type domain, that is, were parties forced into positioning or were they proactively positioning?
12 The intention of the positioning, that is, what goals were being sought in the public relations positioning efforts in terms of specific aims but also what social constructions of reality were parties seeking to shape.

Taking this approach, largely adapted from that developed by Harré and Slocum (2003), can provide deep insights into the situation at hand and the discourses that were operating in the situation/episode being examined. This will enhance understanding of the social forces at work in positioning episodes and how organizations and publics act during such episodes. It can also shed light on why some storylines dominated the episodes. Taking this analytical approach facilitates comparison between the professed goals of the parties to the episode, and enables assessment of what is being achieved in terms of outcomes of positioning efforts. From a public relations research view, such findings provide an insight into the nature of communication power being wielded in such episodes, and furthers understanding of strategy and tactics in communication efforts. They also provide insights into how episodes unfold and this can enhance understanding that can be applied in public relations program design, especially in terms of scenario planning stages and issues management.

Positioning analysis reporting

In the research report, it is recommended that an analysis of the public relations episode in question be written from "the various points of view" (Harré and Moghaddam, 2003: 9), that is, from the perspective of the organization taking up or assigning the positions, and from the perspective of those who are positioned or repositioned intentionally or unintentionally. The recommended approach to qualitative data reporting of keeping memos throughout the analytical process (e.g. Charmaz, 2006; Saldaña, 2012; Silverman, 2011) is helpful in reporting on positioning. This is because it keeps records of key concepts and processes that emerge from the data that aid in the construction of the research narrative about the social meaning of the positioning. The arguments and central claims of the research should ideally be supported with evidence from the data being analyzed. The research report should also account for what "must be tacitly known by the participants", that is the "shared and unshared beliefs about the storylines unfolding and the rights and duties of participants" (Harré and Moghaddam, 2003: 9). To illustrate what this means we can examine a 2012 press story in the Singaporean newspaper website, *The Straits Times* (Tan, 2012) that reported on whether Singaporeans were "kind" people. This was in the wake of reports of the abuse of some foreign workers who were employed as maids. In the story, the rector of Tembusu College at the National University of Singapore, Professor Koh, positioned Singaporeans as kind people through the assertion (speech act), "most Singaporeans are kind".

The supporting storyline was one of "people living in civil society" and the narrative reported how volunteerism and philanthropy were on the increase in the country. This is an example of entering the positioning triangle at the speech act and storyline vertices. However it is evident that there is an assumption being made by the writer about Singaporeans possessing tacit knowledge about the nature of kindness. If one was unaware of what kindness looked like as an attribute, and was unaware of the rights and duties of a "kind person", such positioning efforts would not make sense. The efforts of Professor Koh to position Singaporeans as kind only works if people engaging with the story share the beliefs about the nature of kind people, that is, that kind people don't mistreat their employees. There is also other tacit knowledge assumed, that being the authority of Professor Koh to talk on such matters; the idea that according to the local moral order, as a professor, he has a right to profess certain assertions. In reporting research on public relations episodes using the Framework for Intentional Positioning in Public Relations, as well as reporting on the positioning goal, type of positioning, pre-positioning and positioning triangle domains, the assumptions relating to the tacit knowledge known by participants should be articulated wherever possible.

The domains of the Framework for Intentional Positioning in Public Relations can guide the reporting and writing up of the data analysis. This would mean that the position triangle domain vertices of storyline, speech act/action and position would be identified in the report; the strategic pre-positioning would be discussed, the positioning type addressed and the goal of the positioning efforts ascertained. The rights and duties inherent in the positions taken and assigned by the parties to the public relations episode would be reported. The implications and meaning of the positioning efforts should be discussed and the key points that the author would like readers to take away from the research highlighted.

Positioning analysis conclusion and recommendations

The recommendations and conclusion of any positioning analysis obviously relate back to what research questions were posed at the start of the exercise. Generally, the conclusion should detail what the researcher has made of the positioning analysis and relate this back to the literature and the original research questions. Recommendations could include ideas and plans for further research on the same or related areas. They could also include suggestions to be incorporated into future public relations programs. If something was found to have worked, this could be recommended for consideration in the design of a forthcoming campaign. If another area was found to be weak, the recommendation may be that further testing be undertaken prior to adopting such a strategy in future work.

Summary

The use of positioning analysis in public relations contexts is at an early stage with only a handful of studies published. The research methods used to date, namely thematic analysis, textual analysis, autoethnography and positioning discourse analysis, are all qualitative and this aligns with the large majority of positioning analytical work undertaken in other disciplines in the last two decades. Research has addressed the use of strategic positioning in public relations campaigns (James, 2010, 2011, 2012), and in political public relations (Wise and James, 2013). Positioning theory has also been used to assist in analyzing the identity work undertaken by public relations practitioners in the Russian context (Tsetsura, 2012). It is suggested that many other approaches could be considered by the field and that positioning research in other disciplines should guide researchers in this area. Approaches such as practitioner-based inquiry and action research offer opportunities for researchers to study positioning efforts in public relations practice and to work with practitioners as co-researchers. The hope is that positioning theory stimulates interest in applying a range of research methods in the field.

For the purposes of guiding researchers considering the undertaking of a positioning analysis, a way of approaching such research was outlined in this chapter. Practical considerations such as what should be researched, data sampling and research scope were discussed. The approach suggested by Harré and Slocum (2003) was adapted for a public relations context and detailed in a series of steps. It is envisaged that this approach would be further adapted by other researchers to suit particular projects and is offered as just one way of undertaking a positioning analysis in a public relations context. Chapter 8 will report on a positioning analysis that applies a version of the analytical process outlined in this chapter.

References

Althaus, C., Bridgman, P. and Davis, G. (2007) *The Australian Policy Handbook*. Crows Nest, NSW: Allen and Unwin.

Badran, D. (2010) Hybrid genres and the cognitive positioning of audiences in the political discourse of Hizbollah, *Critical Discourse Studies*, 7(3): 191–201.

Bakhtin, M. (1986) The problem of speech genres. In M. Holquist (ed.) *Speech Genres and Other Late Essays*. (Translated by V. McGee). Austin, TX: University of Texas Press, pp. 60–102.

Berger, B. (1999) The Halcion affair: public relations and the construction of ideological world view. *Journal of Public Relations Research*, 11(3): 185–203.

Berger, P. and Luckmann, T. (1966) *The Social Construction of Reality: A treatise in the sociology of knowledge*. London: Penguin.

Bogren, A. (2010) Studying social power in textual data: combining tools for analyzing meaning and positioning. *Critical Discourse Studies*, 7(1): 73–84.

Catellani, A. (2011) Environmentalists NGOs and the construction of the culprit: semiotic analysis. *Journal of Communication Management*, 15(4): 280–297.

Charmaz, K. (2006) *Constructing Grounded Theory: A practical guide through qualitative analysis*. London: Pine Forge.

Christie, D. (2008) Series foreword. In F. Moghaddam, R. Harré and N. Lee (eds) *Global Conflict Resolution through Positioning Analysis*, (n.p). New York: Springer.

Courtright, J. L., and Smudde, P. M. (2009) Recall communications: discourse genres, symbolic charging, and message design. *International Journal of Strategic Communication*, 4(1): 58–74.

Davies, B. and Harré, R. (1990) Positioning: the discursive production of selves. *Journal for the Theory of Social Behavior*, 20(1): 43–63.

Esrock, S. L., Hart, J. L., D'Silva, M. U. and Werking, K. J. (2002) The saga of the crown pilot: framing, reframing, and reconsideration. *Public Relations Review*, 28(3): 209–27.

Hallahan, K. (1999) Seven models of framing: implications for public relations. *Journal of Public Relations Research*, 11(3): 205–42.

Harré, R. and Moghaddam, F. (2003) Introduction: the self and others in traditional psychology and in positioning theory. In R. Harré and F. Moghaddam (eds) *The self and Others: Positioning individuals and groups in personal, political and cultural contexts*. London: Praeger, pp. 1–11.

Harré, R. and Slocum, N. (2003) Disputes as complex social events: on the uses of positioning theory. In R. Harré and F. Moghaddam (eds) *The self and Others: Positioning individuals and groups in personal, political and cultural contexts*. London: Praeger, pp. 123–36.

Harré, R. and van Langenhove, L. (1999) *Positioning Theory: Moral contexts of intentional action*. Oxford: Blackwell.

James, M. (2010) The use of intentional positioning techniques in government agencies' communication campaigns. In D. Verčič and K. Sriramesh (eds) *Government communication: proceedings of the 17th International Public Relations Research Symposium BledCom*. Bled, Slovenia, Ljubljana: Pristop, pp. 140–7. Retrieved from www.bled com.si/uploads/ppt2010/bledcom 2010 proceedings hi.pdf

James, M. (2011) A provisional conceptual framework for intentional positioning in public relations. *Journal of Public Relations Research*, 23(1): 93–111. http://dx.doi.org/10.1080/1062726X.2010.505120

James, M. (2012) Autoethnography: the story of applying a conceptual framework for intentional positioning to public relations practice. *Public Relations Review*, 38(4): 555–64.

Jaques, T. (2008) A case study approach to issue and crisis management: schadenfreude or an opportunity to learn? *Journal of Communication Management*, 12, 192–203.

Kerrigan, S. (2013) Accommodating creative documentary practice within a revised systems model of creativity. *Journal of Media Practice*, 14(2): 111–27.

Koro-Ljungberg, M. (2008) A social constructionist framing of the research interview. In J.Holstein and J. Gubrium (eds) *Handbook of Constructionist Research*. New York: Guilford, pp. 429–44.

Kress, G. (2012) Multimodel discourse analysis. In J. Gee and M. Handford (eds) *The Routledge Handbook of Discourse Analysis*. London: Routledge, pp. 35–50.

Lawrence, B. and Murray, L. (2000) *Practitioner-Based Enquiry: Principles and practices for postgraduate research*. London: Routledge.

McIntyre, P. (2006) Creative practice as research: "testing out" the systems model of creativity through practitioner based enquiry. In N. Bourke, B. Haseman, D. Mafe and

R. Vella (eds) *Speculations and Innovations: Applying practice led research in the creative industries*, Queensland University of Technology, 30 March–1 April 2005, Brisbane, Australia.

Neff, B. (2008) Speech act theory: an approach to public relations leadership. In T. Hansen-Horn and B. Neff (eds) *Public Relations: From theory to practice.* Boston, MA: Pearson, pp. 89–103.

Niska, M. and Vesala, K. (2013) SME policy implementation as a relational challenge, *Entrepreneurship & Regional Development: An International Journal*, 25(5–6): 521–40, doi: 10.1080/08985626.2013.798354

Rapoport, R. (1970) Three dilemmas of action research. *Human Relations*, 23(6): 499–513.

Saldaña, J. (2012) *The Coding Manual for Qualitative Researchers* (No. 14). London: Sage.

Silverman, D. (2011) *Interpreting qualitative data* (4th edn). London: Sage.

Slocum-Bradley, N. (2007) Constructing and de-constructing the ACP Group: actors, strategies and consequences for development, *Geopolitics*, 12(4): 635–55. doi:10.1080/14650040701546095

Susman, G. I. and Evered, R. D. (1978) An assessment of the scientific merits of action research. *Administrative Science Quarterly*, 23(4): 582–603.

Tan, A. (2012) "We are kind, but we could be kinder": Professor Tommy Koh. *The Straits Times.* Retrieved from www.straitstimes.com/breaking-news/singapore/story/we-are-kind-we-could-be-kinder-professor-tommy-koh-20121021

Tilson, D. (2006) Devotional-promotional communication and Santiago: a thousand-year public relations campaign for Saint James and Spain. In J. L'Etang and M. Pieczka (eds) *Public Relations: Critical debates and contemporary practice.* Mahwah, NJ: Lawrence Erlbaum, pp. 167–86.

Tsetsura, K. (2012) A struggle for legitimacy: Russian women secure their professional identities in public relations in a hypersexualized patriarchal workplace. *Public Relations Journal*, 6(1): 1–21.

Walton, C., Coyle, A., and Lyons, E. (2003) There you are man: men's uses of emotion discourses and their negotiation of emotional subject positions. In R. Harré and F. Moghaddam (eds) *The self and Others: Positioning individuals and groups in personal, political and cultural contexts.* London: Praeger, pp. 45–60.

Wang, J. and Chaudhri, V. (2009) Corporate social responsibility engagement and communication by Chinese companies. *Public Relations Review*, 35(3): 247–50.

Wilkinson, S. and Kitzinger, C. (2003) Constructing identities: a feminist conversation analytic approach to positioning in action. In R. Harré and F. Moghaddam (eds) *The Self and Others: Positioning individuals and groups in personal, political and cultural contexts.* London: Praeger, pp. 157–80.

Wise, D. and James, M. (2013) Positioning a price on carbon: applying a proposed hybrid method of positioning discourse analysis for public relations. *Public Relations Inquiry*, 2(3): 327–53.

8 A detailed study of a positioning strategy

Indonesia, "good friend" of Australia

In order to demonstrate a way of approaching positioning analysis, the research approach that was outlined in the last chapter has been adapted and applied to a specific public relations episode. The approach is that suggested by Harré and Slocum (2003) and which has been adapted for a public relations context. It is envisaged that demonstrating this approach would facilitate understanding of how a public relations positioning analysis could be undertaken. It is also envisaged that such an approach would be further adapted by other researchers to suit particular projects.

The project examines how two countries positioned themselves in a public relations context over a one-week period. It was a week when the two countries' politicians, officials and commentators were speaking publicly about the implications of a new policy. The countries involved were Indonesia, with a population of 244.5 million and GDP per capita of US$3,817 (DFAT, 2013b); and, Australia with a population of 23 million and GDP per capita US$68,939 (DFAT, 2013a). As these statistics show, the countries have vastly different populations and levels of GDP per capita. In 2013–2014, Australia's assistance to Indonesia will be worth an estimated AUS$646.8 million, making it Australia's largest bilateral aid program (DFAT, 2013a).

The policy at the center of the period of analysis was the newly elected Australian government's "Operation sovereign borders" (Coalition, 2013). This policy proposed that Australia unilaterally turn back Indonesian fishing boats, carrying asylum seekers from countries including Pakistan, Iran and Afghanistan, on the high seas. Indonesia is seen as a transit country for such asylum seekers and many of the journeys undertaken by boat are taken on Indonesian fishing boats that have been put to use by so-called people smugglers. Australia's new policy was causing consternation for the Indonesian government.

The relationship between Indonesia and Australia is changing, with White (2013) stating:

> Indonesia is emerging as one of the key powers in Asia, with a dynamic economy and growing strategic potential. The balance of wealth and power between Australia and Indonesia is shifting Indonesia's way. This makes Indonesia more important to Australia than it has ever been before. In a more

> turbulent Asia, the stronger Indonesia becomes – economically and militarily – the more Australia has to fear from it as an adversary, and the more Australia can draw hope from Indonesia as an ally.
>
> (White, 2013: 30)

It would be fair to state this one-week period of analysis was a highly politically charged communication environment. In the lead up to a 30 September 2013 meeting between Australian Prime Minister Abbott and Indonesian President Susilo Bambang Yudhoyono there was a lot of positioning evident in the communications undertaken by politicians, officials and commentators. This analysis indicated there were clear messages for the Australian government and, far from there being many voices on the policy issue, a position asserted by Abbott, this analysis indicated there was a unity in the messaging coming from Indonesia: respect our sovereignty, let's work together in partnership, regional solutions are needed, and to implement unilateral policy is offensive. Mixed messages were evident from Australia: sovereignty will be respected but we'll implement our policy nonetheless.

The other issue worth noting as background in this analysis is that the Asia-Pacific Economic Cooperation (APEC) Leaders' Meeting was due to commence in the first week of October 2013 on the Indonesian island of Bali. APEC is the premier forum for facilitating economic growth, cooperation, trade and investment in the Asia-Pacific region (APEC, 2013). APEC has 21 members, referred to as member economies, which account for approximately 40 percent of the world's population, approximately 55 percent of world GDP and about 44 percent of world trade. APEC's 21 member economies are Australia; Brunei Darussalam; Canada; Chile; People's Republic of China; Hong Kong, China; Indonesia; Japan; Republic of Korea; Malaysia; Mexico; New Zealand; Papua New Guinea; Peru; The Republic of the Philippines; The Russian Federation; Singapore; Chinese Taipei; Thailand; United States of America; and, Viet Nam (APEC, 2013). This APEC meeting was the first that the newly elected Australian Prime Minister Abbott would be attending.

This analysis is approached not from a foreign affairs policy perspective, but examines how the public relations positioning played out in the public domain. People working in foreign affairs departments and related roles would have access to much more detailed information about the diplomatic workings happening behind the public scenes. However, outside of those circles many organizations such as businesses and non-government organizations would evaluate the unfolding situation through the media. They would follow the public communication between Indonesia and Australia through the spokespeople commenting on issues in the public domain.

Many such organizations need to continue to work between the two countries and need to manage public, business and stakeholder relationships throughout periods of diplomatic uncertainty. Many organizations such as non-government organizations that work with asylum seekers around the world only see what is in the public domain and are not party to specialist foreign affairs department or commission briefings. From a public relations perspective, such organizations may carry out a communication analysis using the strengths, weakness, opportunities and threats (SWOT) approach. A positioning analysis differs from the traditional SWOT in that it attempts to capture some of the broad public discourse around the debate or issue at hand. A positioning analysis can lead to a different suite of findings that may open more opportunities for public relations interventions, or indeed, inform a decision not to proceed with an initiative at a certain time, or at all.

Research approach

The context and general discursive frame needs to be accounted for in positioning analysis and one of the most important contextual factors in the analysis is the nature of the audience for the variety of discourses. Therefore, in this analysis narratives were collected from sources that were presented to two major audiences – Australian and Indonesian domestic English-language news consumers. Harré and Slocum (2003) state that boundaries of analyses are often diffuse as often parties to the episode under analysis will differ on what they state the episode is about. The scope of the analysis was limited to those news sources where comments were made about the particular policy. The analysis began with a broad approach, looking at media reports in Indonesian and Australian media from early August 2013 through to mid September. It became evident that this was too broad and was focusing on the pre-election positioning of parties seeking to be elected by the Australian people. Given the election was held and decided upon in Australia on September 7, 2013, it seemed prudent to focus on the new government's policy and related communication of key figures in both governments.

The national news sources included in this analysis were *The Jakarta Globe* and *The Jakarta Post* online news sites (Indonesia) and in Australia, the Australian Broadcasting Corporation and The Australian newspaper/Sky news sites. Another source, which has an Asia-wide audience, was the Australian Television Network's Newsline program site. Unfortunately due to the lack of Bahasa Indonesian language skills of the author, only English news sites were included in the analysis and this is a limitation of the study. Both *The Jakarta Post* and *The Jakarta Globe* are national newspapers published in Indonesia in English. In total the sample included nine news reports and two media conference transcripts over a one-week period 12 September 2013 to 19 September 2013. The news sources included in the analysis are listed in Table 8.1.

There were also two media conference transcripts included in the analysis. They both featured the Australian Prime Minister talking on the asylum seeker policy although this was not the reason for the media conferences being called. There were no media conference transcripts in English available from Indonesian politicians' websites on this issue. Table 8.2 provides details of the two releases.

Harré and Slocum's (2003) research approach, which was adapted to a public relations context, as described in the previous chapter was broadly applied to the project. Namely:

1 Texts, as the data to be analyzed, are collected from diverse sources.

Table 8.1 News sources included in the Australia–Indonesia relationship analysis

News source	*Author/ Reporter*	*Date*	*Title*	*Spokesperson/ spokespersons*
Lateline – transcript of television interview (Aus)	Tony Jones	18/Sep/13	Australia and Indonesia should share the burden of asylum seekers	Indonesian member of parliament (MP) Tantowi Yahya is a prominent member of his parliament's Foreign Affairs Commission
The Jakarta Post website (Ind)	Bagus BT Saragih	17/Sep/13	RI 'anticipates' Aussie boat talks in upcoming meeting	Foreign Minister Marty Natalegawa, Australian Prime Minister Tony Abbott, and Presidential spokesman for foreign affairs Teuku Faizasyah
Australia News Network (Aus)	Jim Middleton	17/Sep/13	Australian military set to enter asylum seeker fold	Dewi Fortuna Anwar, a senior adviser to Indonesian Vice President Boediono.
The Jakarta Globe website (Ind)	Agence France-Presse	15/Sep/13	New Australian FM Firm on Indonesia Refugee Plans	Australia's Foreign Minister Julie Bishop, Indonesia's Foreign Minister Marty Natalegawa
The Australian newspaper website (Aus)	AAP	19/Sep/13	Indonesian anger mounts over Tony Abbott's boats policy	Mahfudz Siddiq, the head of Indonesia's parliamentary commission for foreign affairs, Australian Labor MP Matt Thistlethwaite, Indonesia's Foreign Minister Marty Natalegawa, and Australian Prime Minister Tony Abbott
ABC AM current affairs website (Aus)	Tony Eastley	17/Sep/13	Australia urged to review asylum seeker policies	Pakistan's out-going ambassador to Papua New Guinea and Indonesia, Mr. Sanaullah
ABC PM current affairs website (Aus)	Mark Colvin	17/Sep/13	Indonesia visit anticipates talks on asylum seekers	ABC Indonesian correspondent, George Roberts
The Jakarta Globe website (Ind)	Agence France-Presse	18/Sep/13	Australia's Tough Refugee Plan to Be Brought Before UN	Human Rights Law Center – Rachel Ball, Director of advocacy and campaigns, and Indonesian Foreign Minister Marty Natalegawa
The Jakarta Post (Ind)	No author	12/Sep/13	Indonesia to reject Abbott's boat people plan	Hikmahanto Juwana, an international law professor from the University of Indonesia, Indonesian Foreign Minister Marty Natalegawa

Table 8.2 Media conference transcripts included in the Australia–Indonesia relationship analysis

Type	*Place*	*Date*	*Title and Tag*	*Spokesperson*
Media conference transcript	Parliament House, Canberra	16/Sep/13	Press Conference, Parliament House "First Abbott Ministry"	Australian Prime Minister Tony Abbott
Joint Media conference transcript	Sydney	19/Sep/13	Join Press conference – various topics.	Australian Prime Minister Tony Abbott

2 These are read and analyzed many times, with each time being used to incorporate new insights and new information from the new materials.
3 The perceptions of the parties to the communication episode must be identified by trying to discern each party's view of what the episode is about in terms of the main issues, and the short and longer term goals.
4 Look for the answers by searching for the start and end points of specific narratives in the text, the events contained in the narrative, and "the qualitative character of the measures used to categorize and evaluate the parties involved" (Harré and Slocum, 2003: 131) and, the central issue of the narrative.
5 Identify all the parties that appear in the narratives as the main actors.
6 Are the parties identified in the narrative a group, an organization, an individual or some other entity? How are these defined? Are there parties who are excluded from the narrative? It is suggested that these parties are those who will be taking up and defending their positions, or are themselves being positioned by others (Harré and Slocum, 2003).
7 The next stage is where the researcher would be using the positioning triangle domain of the Framework to guide analysis. The aim is to ascertain what parties to the episode perceive to be areas of disagreement or conflict – this is not about trying to see what is actually happening but how people are ascribing meaning to what is happening, their subjective reality.
8 The analysis then turns to examining whether any party to the episode being researched has, as the episode has unfolded through the various storylines, taken a step back and taken a position "with respect to the positionings already accomplished" (Harré and Slocum, 2003: 132). In adopting such a position, the party is claiming a right and maybe even a duty to comment on the positionings accomplished to date – the researcher can ascertain whether in the local moral order that is at work in the episode such a right or duty exists or has been constructed.
9 The researcher can then report on a catalogue of positions, storylines and speech acts/actions in relation to each of the parties involved in the communication episode. The aim here is to make comparisons between parties' positions and storylines, report on shared positions and storylines, what the various parties are doing in taking or assigning positions and what are the social forces of the speech acts that have been used.

10 From here the researcher can then ascertain what rights and duties were taken up or assigned in the overall positioning. What attributes were taken up or assigned to others in the framing or pre-positioning stage?
11 An assessment of the power relations at work in the episode can then be made. Which party/ies possessed positioning power? Harré and Slocum (2003) recommend interrogating the data to ascertain on what basis such power was allocated and what role did differences in positioning power play in the unfolding of the episode. Much of this relates to the positioning type domain as whether parties were forced into positioning or were proactively positioning.
12 The intention of the positioning, that is, what goals were being sought in the public relations positioning efforts in terms of specific aims, but also what social constructions of reality were parties seeking to shape.

It should be noted that in addition to language issues, there were other limitations in this research approach and these were primarily those associated with the interpretative nature of any qualitative research project. It should also be noted that the relationship between Indonesia and Australia is complex and not limited to the brief background provided in this chapter.

The positioning analysis

In line with Harré and Slocum's (2003) advice the narratives evident in the media reports of the episode were read through numerous times to ascertain the emerging themes and insights. There were numerous views (see Table 8.3) covered in the media reports analyzed and the first stage of the analysis examines what various parties viewed the episode to "be about".

The analysis showed that there was a plethora of storylines present. However, this is not unusual and the storylines can be clustered under interrelated themes (Harré and Slocum, 2003). A catalogue of positions, storylines, and reported speech acts relative to each person or institution engaged in this episode was developed. This enabled comparison of participants' positions and storylines, shared positions and storylines and what the various participants were doing, that is, what social forces the speech acts were engendering. Five storylines were distinguished in the discourse that revolved around the public relations positioning efforts of the Indonesian and Australian governments present in the sample data. Some of the storylines were challenged by dissenting opinions that were a direct negation of the storylines. However, according to Harré and Slocum (2003: 132), "a negation does not constitute a new story line".

Storylines most offered by Indonesian government spokespersons:

1 *The bilateral partnership should be protected storyline*: Australia's new "Operation sovereign borders" policy is threatening the stability of the diplomatic partnership, and as the countries are "friends", this is not how it should be.
2 *Sovereignty cannot be violated storyline*: Australia's new "Operation sovereign

Table 8.3 Various parties' views of what the episode is "about"

Spokesperson	*View as to what the episode was "about"*
Indonesian MP Tantowi Yahya, a prominent member of his parliament's Foreign Affairs Commission	Concerned about Australia's new policy: seen as illegal; breaches sovereign rights of Indonesia; urging Australia to work with Indonesia and the region to find joint solutions.
Indonesia Foreign Minister, Marty Natalegawa	Indonesia would not accept such a policy, as it was not in line with the spirit of partnership between the two countries.
Dewi Fortuna Anwar, a senior adviser to Indonesian Vice President Boediono	Australia has to work with Indonesia and the region to solve the illegal immigrant issue and it will not go down well if Australia is using Indonesia for political campaign purposes.
Presidential spokesman for foreign affairs, Teuku Faizasyah	The solution for the boat people issue must be reached through a regional and bilateral approach, not a unilateral one.
Mahfudz Siddiq, the head of Indonesia's Parliamentary Commission for Foreign Affairs	Australian Prime Minister Abbott was urged to consider the regional ramifications of the measures.
Australian journalist, George Roberts	Speculating on how the relationship between the two countries will play out under the new Australian leadership.
Hikmahanto Juwana, an international law professor from the University of Indonesia	The policy is a humiliation to Indonesia.
Diplomat leaving post (Ambassador of the Islamic Republic of Pakistan to Indonesia, Mr. Sanaullah)	Pakistan is trying its best to address source issues; sending asylum seekers to Papua New Guinea instead of Australia is not a good outcome.
Member of Australia's opposition party, the Labor Party, Matt Thistlethwaite	Critical of Australian policy.
Australian Prime Minister, Tony Abbott	Pro-policy: it will work.
Australian Foreign Minister, Julie Bishop	Seeking Indonesia's understanding not their permission.
From the Melbourne-based Human Rights Law Center, Rachel Ball, Director of advocacy and campaigns.	Taking a statement to the current session of the UN Human Rights Council in Geneva seeking condemnation of Australia's plans for asylum-seekers who arrive by boat.
Unnamed APF journalist at Jakarta Globe	Australia doing the wrong thing according to Human Rights Law Center and UNHRC

borders" policy potentially violates sovereign rights of Indonesia and is "illegal".

3 *A regional approach is the only solution storyline*: All countries involved in this issue must work together to find a solution.
4 *Playing for the domestic political advantage storyline*: Australia is taking this position not because it offers a real solution but because it plays well with conservative voters domestically.

In many of the examples, the storylines were woven together by the government spokespersons. Such storylines can be seen to open up certain narratives and positions and contribute to the overall positioning triangle.

Storylines most offered by Australia government spokespersons:

1 *The policy will be implemented storyline*: Australia is not seeking permission from Indonesia, it's "a stand or fall issue".
2 *The bilateral partnership is important storyline*: Australia sees its partnership with Indonesia as one of the most important and will seek to work cooperatively and respect Indonesian sovereignty.
3 *There are many voices on this issue storyline*: there are many views on this issue in Indonesia and we'll endeavor to work cooperatively.
4 *The problem is the people-smugglers, not the government storyline*: sets up a dichotomy between the government and a segment of the Indonesian population.

Storylines most offered by external commentators from both countries:

1 *The policy is inhumane storyline*: the Australian policy neglects obligations under the United Nations Human Rights Council and is treating needy people without compassion.
2 *The humiliation of Indonesia storyline*: that Australia has unilaterally announced the policy and that detail was only conveyed to the Indonesian government through the media.

Storylines, speech acts and associated positions

Indonesia

The storylines offered by the Indonesian government spokespersons can be seen to be embedded in an overarching "We are good friends" meta-storyline. Of course, when people are good friends there are certain rights, obligations and duties associated with the friendship. Good friends would expect to be consulted on matters that directly impacted on each other, they would talk through any problems that were arising, they wouldn't expect to be kept in the dark about important issues relating to the friendship and they'd care about each other, looking out for the interests of each other. Good friends could also be seen to have a duty to talk to each other when something arises that threatens the friendship, or to alert one another when there is unacceptable behavior within the friendship. It is evident that Indonesia is acting in accordance to this overarching storyline through the period of analysis.

In the interwoven narratives reported in the Indonesian and Australian media, Indonesian ministers and officials, who are conveying the views of the president and vice-president, are all working within the meta-storyline. There are affirmations of the strength of the partnership between Indonesia and Australia, for example:

> Indonesian MP Tantowi Yahya: Indonesia and Australia are very good neighbors, despite our up-and-down relationship, but then I think we have homework to deal with, we have homework that we have to solve together. And I do believe that the new administration will be a good partner of Indonesia in overcoming all issues that come up in this region. We are friends.
>
> (www.abc.net.au/lateline/content/2013/s3851845.htm)

This speech act is an "assertive", that is, it is asserting the subjective reality of the situation from the Indonesian perspective. Within the meta-storyline of "good friends" the spokesperson positions the two countries as good neighbors. It invokes the rights of such a position, such as the right to be party to the development of a solution. It invokes the duties of Australia in such a relationship, that is, that Australia under the new government will be "a good partner". Within the positioning triangle perspective, the three vertices of position, speech act and storyline are aligning in a dynamic stability. From a public relations strategic perspective, it puts the onus on Australia to act within the local moral framework that such a position invokes. If the Australian government's messages fall outside the positioning triangle being used by the Indonesian government, Indonesia may be able to position Australia as acting outside the parameters of "good friends".

The narrative also indicates that there is the expectation that Indonesia will be consulted on the asylum seeker policy issue:

> Presidential spokesman for foreign affairs, Teuku Faizasyah: The solution for the boat people issue must be reached through a regional and bilateral approach, not a unilateral one.
>
> (www.thejakartapost.com/news/2013/09/17/ri-anticipates-aussie-boat-talks-upcoming-meeting.html)

This is also an assertive speech act in that the spokesman is asserting what must happen according to the local moral order in which the positioning is taking place. That is, a good friend does not go off unilaterally and do something that would potentially cause harm to their friend. However it appears that such consultation on the new policy may not have happened, which is clearly breaching the "good friends" storyline, as reported in this exchange between Australian journalist, Tony Jones, and Indonesian MP, Tantowi Yahya:

Tony Jones: So to your knowledge, were either of these policies discussed with the Indonesian government or with your Foreign Affairs Commission before they were announced in Australia?

Tantowi Yahya: It's very offensive.

Tony Jones: So they were not discussed with you?

Tantowi Yahya: No. As far as I remember, no. We just know everything from the newspaper (www.abc.net.au/lateline/content/2013/s3851845.htm).

The Indonesian MP, Tantowi Yahya, uses an expressive speech act in this exchange to express an attitude or feeling, that of offense. This again is not what a good friend would be expected to do and it works within the positioning triangle of positioning Australia as acting as something other than a good friend to Indonesia. Australia is thus positioned by Indonesia as potentially threatening the friendship storyline. This is further strengthened with comments such as:

> Senior adviser to Indonesian Vice President Boediono, Dewi Fortuna Anwar: If that policy came about simply as a political campaign within Australia against a previous government and in which Indonesia is used as a whipping boy I don't think this is going to go down very well.
>
> (www.abc.net.au/news/2013-09-16/australian-milltary-set-to-enter-asylum-seeker-fold/4961604)

This is also an expressive speech act used to shape understanding of the episode. It alerts audiences that Indonesia is likely not to tolerate being positioned in a way not aligned with being a good friend to Australia. That is, good friends don't "use" each other for singular benefit. There were even stronger comments made by Indonesia's Foreign Minister,

> Indonesia's Foreign Minister Marty Natalegawa: Jakarta would reject the plans as not in the spirit of partnership between the two countries.
>
> (www.thejakartaglobe.com/news/new-australian-fm-firm-on-indonesia-refugee-plans/)

This speech act could be seen as an expressive (an attitude) or perhaps even a commissive in that it commits Indonesia to rejecting Australia's policy plan on the basis that it contravenes what should happen between good friends. This can be seen as forced self-positioning by Indonesia in that Australia's actions have forced Indonesia to assert a position that it will not be party to something that is not "in the spirit of partnership". Had Australia not indicated that it would implement its new policy, Indonesia would not have needed to undertake any specific positioning activity in the public domain on this issue.

These speech acts were supported by others, for example:

> Indonesian MP Tantowi Yahya: I think the policy [of Australia] will be very offensive [to Indonesia] and we in the parliament fully support what was said by our foreign minister, that we will fully reject the policy.
>
> Head of Indonesia's Parliamentary Commission for Foreign Affairs, Mahfudz Siddiq: They [Australia] should be more careful when it comes to another country's sovereignty.
> (www.theaustralian.com.au/national-affairs/policy/indonesian-politician-warns-of-rift-over-offensive-boats-policy/story-fn9hm1gu-1226722486024)

Again we see a combination of speech acts, expressives and commissives, that are expressing views in an attempt to shape the way social reality is perceived by audiences and committing to support the views of the Foreign Minister. In the analysis of the messages within the storylines it is clear however that Indonesia wants to work collaboratively with Australia in a wider regional context. It keeps reiterating this, seemingly giving Australia every opportunity to take up such an option:

> Head of Indonesia's Parliamentary Commission for Foreign Affairs, Mahfudz Siddiq: This issue is a regional issue and it's not something that the new elected [Australia] prime minister and new foreign minister can solve by themselves.
> (www.theaustralian.com.au/national-affairs/policy/indonesian-politician-warns-of-rift-over-offensive-boats-policy/story-fn9hm1gu-1226722486024)
>
> Indonesian MP Tantowi Yahya: What Australia should do right now in relations with the asylum seekers is sitting together with any countries that will be involve in this issue. So the country of origins, the country of transfer and the country of destination should be sitting together and we have to fight against it in a spirit of friend, in a spirit of togetherness…we open to all propositions that lead toward solving the issues in a very peaceful way in the spirit of sharing the burden.
> (www.theaustralian.com.au/national-affairs/policy/indonesian-politician-warns-of-rift-over-offensive-boats-policy/story-fn9hm1gu-1226722486024)

In fact, in a single interview on Australian television current affairs program, Lateline, Indonesian MP, Tantowi Yahya, repeatedly stated versions of this message throughout (www.abc.net.au/lateline/content/2013/s3851845.htm `18 Sept 2013), for example:

- "This case should be settled in a very modest and a very peaceful way."
- "The spirit is sharing the burden. I mean we have to settle this case together."
- "We have to sit together and find a great way out that might be useful for each and every one."
- "I think there are still room for us to open up discussion in order to find a very respectful and a very peaceful result out of this issue."

- "We are open for any cooperation that might be possible in making this issue end in a very peaceful way."
- "We have to work together, so the platform is cooperation."
- "Your government in this very case, again, should discuss it with our side and we are willing to help."

It is very evident that Australia is positioned by Indonesia as having an obligation or duty to sit down in the spirit of cooperation and partnership, and to work out a solution to the asylum seeker issue with both Indonesia and other regional countries involved. Indonesia has positioned itself as a good friend and diplomatic partner to Australia but has asserted the right, associated with such a position, to be treated with respect and to be consulted in matters impacting on its sovereignty.

Australia

The storylines offered by the Australian government spokespersons do not fall neatly into a single overarching meta-storyline; in fact there are quite disparate storylines playing out and this could be seen to be destabilizing the overall positions Australia is attempting to claim for itself, and to assign to Indonesia. There is some play into the "We are good friends" meta-storyline through the use of speech acts such as:

> Australian Prime Minister Tony Abbott: In many respects, this is our most important single relationship.
>
> (www.thejakartapost.com/news/2013/09/17/ri-anticipates-aussie-boat-talks-upcoming-meeting.html)

> Australian Prime Minister Tony Abbott: I am very confident that this government will be able to work effectively with the Indonesian government.
>
> (www.abc.net.au/pm/content/2013/s3850768.htm)

> Australian Foreign Minister Julie Bishop: We have policies that we wish to implement as soon as we're sworn in, and we will be working with Indonesia through a series of bilateral meetings and broader meetings that will occur as soon as I'm sworn in.
>
> (www.thejakartaglobe.com/news/new-australian-fm-firm-on-indonesia-refugee-plans/)

The above speech acts are assertives, that is, attempts to assert the way the social world is constructed from an Australian perspective. It seems clear from such examples that the new Australian government envisages itself working bilaterally with the Indonesian government. There is no doubt in the assertions and indeed, Prime Minister Abbott specifically asserts that Australia is keen to be seen as a good partner in the bilateral diplomatic relationship.

However, the moral rights and duties that are associated with the "good friends" storyline are seemingly violated by statements such as:

> Australian Foreign Minister Julie Bishop: I point out we're not seeking Indonesia's permission to implement our policies, we're seeking their understanding.
>
> (www.thejakartaglobe.com/news/new-australian-fm-firm-on-indonesia-refugee-plans/)

This assertive speech act seems more aligned to a "We're doing what we have to do" storyline than a "good friends" one, although seeking understanding is what friends do. With a "We're doing what we have to do" storyline, when people do what they think they have to, there are sometimes unfortunate consequences along the way. Within such a storyline however, these consequences sometimes can't be helped, and it's just hoped somewhere down the path there will be some understanding of why things had to go that way. This storyline is associated with having a higher purpose, with having to take what are sometimes viewed as unpopular decisions for the greater good. The gravity of the situation for Australia was reiterated in Prime Minister Abbott's first media conference after being sworn in to office on 16 September 2013:

> Prime Minister Tony Abbott: This [stopping the boats] is one of those stand or fall issues. It really is. It's a stand or fall issue. We will make a difference. We will start from day one.
>
> (www.pm.gov.au/media/2013-09-16/press-conference-parliament-house)

There are two speech acts in this statement. Firstly an assertive, stating the status of the issue as one on which his government will stand or fall; this issue is obviously, in the view of the government, extremely serious. Secondly a commissive, committing the government to making a difference and starting on that course from the first day of office. It is apparent that working a strategic positioning effort within this storyline is somewhat at odds with the "good friends" storyline. Prime Minister Abbott's subsequent attempt to work within both storylines is evident in this statement:

> Prime Minister Tony Abbott: I have no argument with anyone in the Indonesian establishment or parliament. My argument is with people smugglers and my point to the people smugglers is the game is up. We absolutely totally respect Indonesia's sovereignty.
>
> (www.pm.gov.au/media/2013-09-19/transcript-joint-press-conference)

This suggests Prime Minister Abbott is trying to establish a positioning situation where he is on good relationship terms with the Indonesian government; that is, there is no argument with government members and his speech act (an assertive) aligns with the storyline of "good friends". The statement then expresses that his argument is with the "people smugglers". Obviously he doesn't want to be "good friends" with them. However, this raised the vexed question of whether a group of citizens of a country can be excised, at both a public perception and policy level, from those for whom the government represents.

Indonesia, during the week under analysis, were very moderate and at times even conciliatory in their political rhetoric in this episode. In a positioning theoretical context, the study of the concept of mutual radicalization, "which stems from the interdependence of escalatory and aggressive political rhetoric" (Konaev and Moghaddam, 2010: 168), can shed light on such a communication strategy. Mutual radicalization works on the premise that, "by channeling negative energies onto external 'enemies', aggressive leadership will be able to solidify internal support and gain international leverage" (Konaev and Moghaddam, 2010: 168). Indonesia had expressed no real need to shore up internal support on the issue of people seeking asylum in Australia. However, the new Australian government had sought to score points on the political board as quickly as possible to maintain the strong support shown toward them in the election.

Konaev and Moghaddam's (2010) work indicates that the stronger a politician's rhetoric is towards the perceived "enemy", the stronger the support from that politician's internal constituents. This could conceivably be one of the primary reasons behind the Australian government's use of a) the "We're doing what we have to do storyline, b) the assertion that "it's a stand or fall issue" and c) the position taken on going forward with the policy's implementation (the three vertices of the positioning triangle). This helps to explain why Prime Minister Abbott needed to differentiate between not having any argument with the Indonesian government but having his argument with the Indonesian people-smugglers.

However, Konaev and Moghaddam (2010: 168) warn that aggressive leadership is placed in a precarious position when the external "enemies" do not play a hostile role. Although Indonesia has expressed concern and flagged that it would reject Australia's new policy, it maintained its position using the "good friends" storyline; and "good friends" are not generally hostile to one another. As described above, Indonesia played out the rights and duties that aligned with their position. They seemingly did not buy into the most aggressive or offensive tones of the Australian government.

The other storyline used by the Australian government, the "There are many voices on this issue" storyline, did not fit into the two meta-storylines discussed so far. Prime Minister Tony Abbott:

> There are many voices in Indonesia but I am very confident that this government will be able to work effectively with the Indonesian government as former coalition governments have done.
>
> (www.pm.gov.au/media/2013-09-19/transcript-joint-press-conference)

This appears to be an effort by the Australian government to position the Indonesian government's voice as just one of many Indonesian voices on the issue. This was in spite of a comment three days earlier by a senior adviser to Indonesian Vice-

President Boediono, Ms. Dewi Fortuna Anwar, pre-emptively negating a "many voices" storyline, stating that "illegal migrants" were not much of a domestic issue in Indonesia and that there was, "very much a united consensus position in Indonesia [on the need for a regional approach to the policy] whether in the government or parliament" (www.abc.net.au/news/2013-09-16/australian-milltary-set-to-enter-asylum-seeker-fold/4961604). There appears to be no evidence in the media reports on this issue during the analysis period that indicates Prime Minister Abbott is correct about there being multiple Indonesian voices. If there was dissent in Indonesia, the Indonesian government spokespeople did not acknowledge it and the journalists were not reporting it. This casts doubt on whether the Australian government has the right, according to the local moral order in which this public relations episode is occurring, to position the Indonesian government as one of many voices in the country on this issue. Positioning theory indicates that if Prime Minister Abbott was serious about such positioning he would need to back up the assertion. This would need to be done with examples within a narrative about the other voices and which views on the policy they held. This did not occur.

The audience for both governments' statements on Australia's "Operation sovereign borders" policy during the time of analysis shed further light on communication strategies. Interestingly, Prime Minister Abbott stated:

> We aren't going to conduct discussions with Indonesia through the media. Too much damage has been done in the past by megaphone diplomacy and it's never going to happen under this government.
>
> (www.pm.gov.au/media/2013-09-19/transcript-joint-press-conference)

However, it appeared that Indonesia was quite keen to position in a public relations sense through the media, both in Indonesian and Australian media outlets. Prime Minister Abbott's statement suggests that Australia would be loathe to play out their positioning efforts through the media given their seemingly contradictory positions of wanting to be "good friends" with the Indonesian government but wanting to appear for Australian domestic audiences to be strongly addressing the issues of asylum seekers.

Other commentators

The media reports of four commentators on the unfolding episode between Indonesia and Australia were examined:

- the outgoing Pakistani ambassador to Indonesia and Papua New Guinea reported on the Australian Broadcasting Corporation's AM Current Affairs news site;
- the Director of advocacy and campaigns for Melbourne-based Human Rights Law Centre as reported on *The Jakarta Globe* news site;
- the Australian Broadcasting Corporation's Indonesian Correspondent, and;
- an Indonesian professor in law reported on *The Jakarta Post* news site.

The "Policy is inhumane" storyline is evident in the speech acts of outgoing Pakistani ambassador to Indonesia and Papua New Guinea, Mr. Sanaullah. According to Australian Broadcasting Corporation's Indonesian Correspondent, George Roberts, now that Mr. Sanaullah was leaving his post he was free to speak, as the following on-air exchange indicates:

Mr. Sanaullah: Those who are reaching Australian waters by boat or by any other means are a desperate lot.
George Roberts: Now he's leaving the post, he's free to give his view on what Australia's asylum seeker policies appear to be aimed at.
Mr. Sanaullah: Just to ensure electability with the domestic politicians and voters. That is my concern.

(www.abc.net.au/am/content/2013/s3850125.htm)

Mr. Sanaullah's first speech act is an assertive in that he is asserting that this is the state of the social reality, that is, that asylum seekers are "a desperate lot". His second speech act is an expressive in that he is expressing his view/attitude about the Australian policy. Within a positioning triangle domain context, Mr. Sanaullah's remarks can be seen as positioning the Australian policy as inhumane and being used for domestic political purposes.

The journalist, George Roberts, went on in his story to report that Mr. Sanaullah's reading of the situation was that Indonesia wouldn't like Prime Minister Abbott's policies. He reported that Mr. Sanaullah stated that Indonesian officials were confused and jittery about the new Prime Minister's approach to asylum seekers, but that it would be up to the two countries to work them through. This provides some indication that behind the scenes in Indonesia, not all officials of the government were comfortable with the positions being taken and assigned by the two countries in a public relations sense. Although such a view occurs within the discourse of concerns about the inhumanity of Australia's policy, it is unclear whether this is behind the source of "jitters" in Indonesian officials.

The rights associated with Mr. Sanaullah's position are linked to his recently occupying a senior diplomatic post in the vortex of the asylum seekers' issue: Pakistan is a source country for people seeking refuge in Australia and Indonesia is the transit country. He would be seen, according to the local moral order, to have the right to comment and to have such comment taken seriously. What is interesting is the question of what duties came with his position. It could be argued that Mr. Sanaullah did not have a specific duty within a diplomatic framework to comment on the unfolding episode between Indonesia and Australia. It would be fascinating to explore further the rationale behind his decision to comment, although from the context of the full interview with the Australian journalist, the goal of the exercise was to position Pakistan as not shirking its own responsibilities in regard to the issue. Pakistan has not been specifically mentioned by either Indonesia or Australia as being required to take action in the unfolding episode under analysis. The positioning by the outgoing diplomat may well have been a pro-active attempt by

Pakistan to be considered as being prepared to be part of future regional discussions about a possible solution, as mooted by Indonesia in the media coverage.

The views of the Director of advocacy and campaigns for Melbourne-based Human Rights Law Center, Rachel Ball, were reported on *The Jakarta Globe* news site via Agence France-Presse. These also articulated a narrative within the "Policy is inhumane" storyline. It was reported: "Ball said her organization hoped member states of the UN Human Rights Council would urge Australia to stop shirking its responsibilities and comply with international law". The story went on to state:

> Tough plans by Australia's new conservative government to deter asylum-seekers, including towing back their boats, will be raised at the UN's Human Rights Council, lawyers said Tuesday. The Melbourne-based Human Rights Law Center (HRLC) said it intended to deliver a statement to the council's current session in Geneva seeking condemnation of prime minister-elect Tony Abbott's plans for asylum-seekers who arrive by boat.
>
> (www.thejakartaglobe.com/international/australias-tough-refugee-plan-to-be-brought-before-un/)

Ball's speech act is an expressive, which is conveying hopes for the United Nations Human Rights Council to take action, and expressing a view about the deficiencies in Australia's policy. The positioning triangle sees the dynamic stability of the three vertices being maintained throughout the episode, that is: a) the "inhumane" storyline, b) the expression of the hope of censure (speech act) and c) the positioning itself of the policy as being wrong.

The other storyline present in the commentary was "The humiliation of Indonesia" storyline and this was firstly evident in media reports that Australia had unilaterally announced the policy and that detail was only conveyed to the Indonesian government through the media as described by Indonesian MP, Tantowi Yahya.

It was secondly seen in the reports of *Australian Broadcasting Corporation's* Indonesian Correspondent, George Roberts. He suggested that for Indonesia, having taken the position it had, it was then also about Indonesia losing face if it was to back down and allow the things in the Australian policy such as:

> going to send people in to start buying up boats and also to do other things such as put more Australian Federal Police on the ground in Indonesia, as was also suggested, and start paying locals effectively to spy for Australian authorities.
>
> (www.abc.net.au/pm/content/2013/s3850768.htm)

Finally, an international law professor from the University of Indonesia, Hikmahanto Juwana, said in his interview with *The Jakarta Post* that he despised Australia's plan, calling it "humiliating" as it made Indonesian fishermen "look like mercenaries who do dirty jobs" (www.thejakartapost.com/news/2013/09/12/indonesia-reject-abbott-s-boat-people-plan.html)

Discussion

Given that the "good friends" storyline is common to both the Indonesian and Australian governments' communication, it is clear that certain aspects of the discourse are contributing to the way this episode has unfolded. In the case of Indonesia, the positioning of the relationship between the two countries as one of strength and cooperation is holding from their perspective. In taking up the position as a good friend to Australia, they are indicating that they are willing to cooperate in working together to find a solution that addresses the asylum seeker issue from within a wider Asian regional context. In essence, they are taking the moral high ground, which could be seen to be a position of power. In assigning the position of good friend to Australia, Indonesia is positioning Australia in a way that opens up certain courses of actions (such as cooperation, working collaboratively) and closes down other actions within the position (such as keeping the other side uninformed of intentions, working unilaterally). As such if Australia does things that do not align to the rights and duties of being a good friend to Indonesia, the position of friend will not hold and Indonesia would be in a position to claim that Australia was no longer a good friend to their country.

Secondly Indonesia, in both taking up and assigning the good friend position has the right to warn of things that could damage the friendship between the two nations. It is essentially a position where one friend is reminding the other that they are in fact friends, and to remain so requires that they act in the manner of good friends. That is, that they don't breach the idea of friendship that is held within the local moral order in operation. Australia, on the other hand, is also playing its position of friendship with Indonesia in stating that the nation is seeking Indonesia's understanding, not its permission, in planning to proceed with the controversial policy. It could be interpreted to be perhaps overplaying its position of friendship in this circumstance. In the responses of Indonesia, it is evident that this approach is not in line with the good friend storyline. This is evident as there were assertions made that Australia's plans would be rejected, as they were not in the spirit of partnership between the two countries. This is a clear indicator that if Australia were to continue its course of unilateral action, Indonesia would see that as breaching the current status of the relationship.

Thirdly, Australia's positioning could be seen to reflect confidence in flirting with the idea that it still holds the position of strength in its relationship with Indonesia. This position is debatable (White, 2013). However, in thinking that it held the "power card", Australia's new government might have felt confident to flex a little muscle over Indonesia. It might have also felt sufficiently comfortable in the partnership to assume that Indonesia would let the Australian government step over the line a little in order to play to its domestic audience.

Fourthly, Indonesia's positioning of itself and Australia may indicate that it is feeling confident with its position within the partnership. Indonesia may well be happy to have let Australia have some room to play to internal domestic audiences. It should be noted that the speech acts expressing some concern about Australia's approach also indicate that Australia's "room to play" might in fact be quite limited.

The other interesting aspect of the analysis was to identify which parties were largely absent from the episode when viewed through a public relations lens. The asylum seekers themselves were largely absent in the written texts and commentary. However, it is worth noting that on the Indonesian news sites, one picture of an asylum seeker behind a wire fence in detention, and two pictures of asylum seekers on fishing boats were used. There were no reported comments from Indonesian boat owners or village residents.

In a wider context, the analysis suggests that although public relations in a diplomatic context could be seen to focus on the storylines of building and maintaining relationships and partnerships, there may have been an Indonesian concern that was not being conveyed publicly. One interpretation is that Indonesia was either giving Australia every opportunity to work things out cooperatively, or, it knew that Australia had to position in a way that was sympathetic to domestic political pressures and was setting up a new Australian government to be unsuccessful in implementing its new policy. Indonesia could be seen to be positioning itself as the more reasonable country; seeking new ways on partnership and regional solutions. This then would position Australia as something less than a regional player, less than reasonable. Going into the October 2013 APEC with such a positioning assigned by Indonesia, Australia could be seen as being at a disadvantage.

Further insights for public relations positioning

Given that Australia was less than wholehearted in taking up the position as collaborative partner as part of the "good friend" meta-storyline, Indonesia could be viewed to have had the right to issue statements that had the social force of rebuke, chastisement or warning. In the period under analysis, it issued such statements only in the context of a friend warning another friend that it was potentially approaching the territory of jeopardizing the friendship. In rejecting the full ramifications of the "good friend" meta-storyline, Australia was seen to appear as somewhat morally defective, e.g. as arrogant or even a potential bully.

In planning a public relations approach for future dealings between the two countries, it could be seen that the analysis and findings provided insights that a regular SWOT analysis would have been likely to miss. If a practitioner was working in a non-government organization in an area such as refugee advocacy, for example, this analysis would provide insight into where a communication intervention could have been most appropriate. The absence of advocates, apart from a single human rights law agency, could have been highlighted. There could have been more criticism of the Australian government's position by such advocates based on the contradictory storylines that were being used by the government's spokespeople. There could have been more advocacy for a bilateral or regional solution by NGOs based on the Indonesian positioning of being so keen for this to happen.

The fact that during the period of analysis, Indonesia stayed within the "good friends" storyline was potentially significant for those watching the episode. It provided good intelligence on what kinds of public relations initiatives would have been welcomed by Indonesian organizations working to position their own profiles or programs in either country. It also provided similar intelligence to Australian organizations seeking to work in either country. For those organizations working in other regional countries, the positioning analysis would have provided initial insights into how the countries were adjusting to a new Australian government. For those countries attending APEC, or for those businesses on which APEC forum outcomes had an impact, it provided insights on where Australia's positioning was weak.

For researchers interested in positioning and discourse more generally, the analysis provided insights into positioning strategy and tactics and allowed close examination of the discourses that were operating in the episode. It explored the social forces at work in the positioning episode and how parties acted. It shed light on why the "good friend" storyline dominated the episode and provided context for examining the statements of the parties to the unfolding situation. Taking this analytical approach facilitated comparison between the professed goals of the parties to the episode, and enabled assessment of what was being achieved in terms of outcomes of positioning efforts. From a public relations research view such findings provided insight into the nature of communication power being wielded between the parties, and furthered understanding of strategy and tactics in communication efforts. It also provided more insight into how episodes unfold and this may enhance understanding that can be applied in wider public relations program design, especially in terms of scenario planning stages and issues management.

Summary

This chapter applied the analytical processes recommended by Harré and Slocum (2003) and demonstrated how they could be adapted to an analysis of a public relations episode.

The project examined how two countries, Indonesia and Australia, positioned themselves in a public relations context over a one-week period. It was a week when the two countries' politicians, officials and commentators were speaking publicly about the implications of a new policy proposed by Australia relating to asylum seekers.

The exercise shows that positioning analysis in "real time", that is, as the episode is unfolding, helps to reveal the topics around which public relations episodes emerge. It also helps to identify where public relations interventions may be applied. Positioning analysis undertaken retrospectively sheds light on how positioning was undertaken, how positions were constructed and what if any impact certain public relations actions had on the episode. Such an analysis furthers understanding of public relations positioning but can also guide practitioners and students in learning to understand how a positioning strategy could be developed. From a public relations perspective, the issue at the episode's center can be challenged more effectively if the premises of the episode and the legitimacy of the issue are challenged through a positioning analysis.

The following chapter provides an in-depth examination of the design of a positioning program.

References

APEC (2013) *What is Asia-Pacific Economic Cooperation?* Retrieved from www.apec.org/About-Us/About-APEC.aspx. Accessed 18th November 2013.

Australian, The (2013) Retrieved from www.theaustralian.com.au/national-affairs/policy/indonesian-politician-warns-of-rift-over-offensive-boats-policy/story-fn9hm1gu-1226722486024

Coalition (2013) *Operation Sovereign Borders*. Retrieved from www.nationals.org.au/Portals/0/2013/policy/The%20Coalition%E2%80%99s%20Operation%20Sovereign%20Borders%20Policy.pdf. Accessed 18th November 2013.

DFAT (2013a) *Australia Fact Sheet.* Australian government, Department of Foreign Affairs and Trade. Retrieved from www.dfat.gov.au/geo/fs/aust.pdf. Accessed 18th November 2013.

DFAT (2013b) *Indonesia Fact Sheet.* Australian government, Department of Foreign Affairs and Trade. Retrieved from www.dfat.gov.au/geo/fs/indo.pdf. Accessed 18th November 2013.

Harré, R. and Slocum, N. (2003) Disputes as complex social events: on the uses of positioning theory. In R. Harré and F. Moghaddam (eds). *The self and Others: Positioning individuals and groups in personal, political and cultural contexts*. London: Praeger, pp. 123–36.

Konaev, M. and Moghaddam, F. (2010) Mutual radicalization: Bush, Ahmadinejad, and the "universal" cycle of out-group threat/in-group cohesion. In F. Moghaddam and R. Harré (eds) *Words of Conflict, Words of War: How the language we use in political processes sparks fighting*. Santa Barbara, CA: Praeger.

White, H. (2013) Northern exposure: what the rise of Indonesia means for Australia. *The Monthly*, June 2013, 30–7.

9 Utilizing the framework for intentional positioning in designing public relations strategies

Positioning extreme poverty

Approaching public relations program design through strategic positioning considerations can provide clarity for practitioners and students of public relations. Concepts or practices that seemed to have stemmed from "gut" feelings, or from adapting something that had been seen to work previously, are often unclouded when examined through positioning theory. Specifically, the ideas of storyline and speech acts/actions, and the rights and duties that operate within locally operating moral orders, can provide valuable guidance in program design. In this chapter, such an approach will be demonstrated through working through the Framework for Intentional Positioning in Public Relations, as detailed in Chapter 3, which was adapted for public relations from the work of positioning theorists (e.g. Harré and van Langenhove, 1999; Slocum-Bradley, 2007).

Working with the Framework, we can define the goal of engaging in positioning efforts. Are we endeavoring to position our own organization or client (or its personnel, products, services, actions or ideologies), or those of others? Have we been forced to position in some way? Or is this proactive positioning? What pre-positioning is being undertaken? Which audiences and publics are being targeted? What rights can we claim to position in certain ways and not others? What is the position being taken or assigned? Is there a statement of the position? Is there more than one? Is positioning different for different audiences? How will we enact the position? Will this be done differently for each audience/public? What are the language and behavioral choices? How will we support such choices; for each audience? What is the overarching storyline and what narratives and messages will be developed: the underdog story; the innovator; the backbone of the country? Such decisions are culturally influenced and this will often determine what will be seen as the conventional description of events and cast of "characters" in an unfolding public relations episode.

To demonstrate how positioning theory can inform a large-scale global public relations program, this chapter will utilize the brief supplied as part of the 2013 "Cannes Chimera Challenge". Cannes Chimera is an initiative by the Cannes Lions International Festival of Creativity and the Bill and Melinda Gates Foundation that aims to use the creativity of communication professionals around the world to help solve global problems (Cannes Chimera, 2013). The 2013 challenge was as follows:

> The world is making incredible progress against extreme poverty. Over the last two decades, the number of people living on less than $1.25 per day has been cut in half to 1.1 billion. Now the world is coming together to get this number down to as close to zero as possible, by 2030. It's a huge goal. All of us can play a role. The Cannes Chimera is looking for perception-changing communication strategies which will help towards this goal. This is an opportunity to do the most important work of your life:
>
> - Make this long-term goal feel possible, and personal.
> - Give people a voice and a way to take action.
> - Make it matter until it's achieved.
>
> *The problem*: In 2000, international leaders committed to the Millennium Development Goals (MDGs), a set of targets to improve the lives of the world's poorest by alleviating extreme poverty, hunger, gender inequality, illiteracy and disease by 2015. The MDGs recognized $1.25 a day as the global poverty line – a threshold for supporting basic human needs. The world has made incredible progress at reducing the number of people who live below this line. In fact, the goal to cut extreme poverty in half was achieved five years early. But there's more work to do. That's why the world is coming together around a new, ambitious agenda to help ensure that by 2030, extreme poverty is virtually eliminated from the planet.
>
> *The challenge*: We need the best and most innovative communications ideas in the world to help bring this long-term goal to the forefront and build public awareness and support for the policies and investments that will be required to make progress against it. We need your help. Competition winners will be eligible to apply for a grant to implement their concept in partnership with the Bill and Melinda Gates Foundation and its global partners.
>
> *Our audience*: People who believe that global development problems are important but aren't acting on that interest, as well as people who may not know enough about development to understand what it is and what it has achieved. We are interested in reaching people who already participate in some kind of social action, such as: consuming media content on development issues and sharing it with their social networks, donating money or volunteering their time for causes. These are people who can catalyze the perceptions and behaviors of others and help create change.
>
> (Cannes Chimera, 2013)

Applying a positioning framework approach to help eradicate extreme poverty by 2030

This public relations strategy aims to purposefully reconstruct long-term social reality in the minds of the target audience. Audience members will be positioned as having a duty to act to condemn and eradicate extreme poverty. It will highlight how they are personally involved in the issue and how they can contribute to ending it. Research (Pinazo and Nos Aldas, 2013: 3) supports moving to a conceptually different "protest scenario" emphasis from the traditional "donor scenario". Many current campaign storylines build on these donor-centric scenarios, that is, the need for donations, or the positive results of making a donation. Pinazo and Nos Aldos (2013) suggest these are serving to inhibit rather than strengthen audiences' moral sensitivity because even if audience members do make a donation, this assuages their guilt and they move on without further worry. The "protest scenario" has been shown to be more likely to activate people to be motivated to take action and to condemn extreme poverty:

> When a donation has only been solicited by direct guilt, the person avoids the moral condemnation of the causes of poverty, particularly if he or she bears some feeling of involvement with it. In contrast to this donor scenario, the protest scenario provides a communication structure in which the audience judges that a moral norm is being violated in a certain situation. In this way, the audience can assess their own participation in the injustice and the possibility of acting to resolve the problem by pressing the liable agents to prevent the conditions that lead to the problem...These judgments will be associated with emotions of condemnation such as indignation over the harm caused, without impeding compassion for the suffering.
>
> (Pinazo and Nos Aldos, 2013: 5–6)

Many storylines in current campaigns do not strongly activate this sense of social injustice. They do not construct audiences' perceptions with sufficient intensity to stimulate these "condemnation emotions" like being indignant or angry. There is a focus on asking individuals to click on a website or to buy certain merchandise rather than focusing on the need to change structural issues which contribute to extreme poverty (Wilkins and Enghel, 2013). Such campaigns just encourage "clicktivism" (Wilkins and Enghel, 2013: 168). This results in people feeling useful and worthy, encouraging others to feel useful and worthy. Such measures seem doomed to failure in terms of moving towards the eradication of extreme poverty because "the click" is the end of engagement for many.

With this in mind, in this public relations positioning exercise, a new space where other ways of talking about poverty and encouraging engagement will be created. Through this, a new social norm can come into existence where the eradication of extreme poverty can be achieved. This new strategy will encourage condemnation so that people will judge the injustice and obscenity of extreme poverty more severely. They will be more willing to undertake actions but in such a way that it does not impact on their willingness to make a donation. Such a strategy brings the extreme poverty problem closer to target audience members. This will trigger their motivation to act based on condemnation emotions, that is, on their sense of responsibility instead of ego (Pinazo and Nos Aldos, 2013).

Messages within this strategy will center on taking a position on extreme poverty, and on the rights and duties that come with that position. Such messages will be mostly unfamiliar to target audiences. They will not be geared up to respond in a set way, as they do with donor-centric messages. People can construct new moral meaning around extreme poverty and this has been shown to impact their judgment and their consequent responses (Pinazo and Nos Aldos, 2013). This can have long-term ramifications as it fundamentally changes their social reality and can't be put out of mind with a click. Results of recent research (e.g. Pinazo and Nos Aldos, 2013; Thomas and Louis, 2013; Wilkins and Enghel, 2013) indicate this approach is well worth putting to the test on a large scale.

The positioning strategy

The first three domains of the Framework for Intentional Positioning in Public Relations have been shown to set the strategic context for public relations programs, and the positioning triangle domain has been shown to guide the tactical considerations. This differentiation in the Framework was first shown by James (2012) in an autoethnographic study into designing a positioning public relations plan for an environmental organization. Table 9.1 shows the positioning strategy.

The positioning tactics

Within the broad strategic concept there can be several positions taken. This program will work with three key positions:

1. Extreme poverty is obscene and should be condemned and eradicated.
2. People have a duty to condemn and eradicate extreme poverty.
3. People or institutions must stop contributing to the continuation of extreme poverty.

At this tactical design stage, there will be a positioning triangle for each of the positions to be established. The positions will sit at the first vertex of the positioning triangle, "position determined". At the second vertex of the triangle, the "speech acts/actions" will work to enact the positioning for the target audience. In this approach the five categories of speech acts (Searle, 1979) will be applied: assertives, expressives, directives, commissives and declaratives.

At the third vertex of the positioning triangle, "storyline", a master plotline for each of the positions will be used. There are various approaches that can be taken, as described in Chapter 6, however to further demonstrate the way this idea of storyline can be applied, the work of Tobias (1993) will be used. Tobias (1993) suggested 20 master plotlines which are: quest, adventure, pursuit, rescue, escape, revenge, the riddle, rivalry, underdog, temptation, metamorphosis, transformation, maturation, love, forbidden love, sacrifice, discovery, wretched excess, ascension and descension. These are essentially examples of the storylines that can be used

Table 9.1 The positioning strategy

Framework domain	*Description*
Goal	To position the ongoing existence of extreme poverty as both socially unjust and immoral, in fact it is obscene (i.e. offending social and moral principles; repugnant); to move focus from audience awareness to action-taking by changing people's perceptions and positions, and highlighting personal responsibility.
Positioning type	Deliberate self positioning of: 1 poverty as an issue 2 people living in extreme poverty 3 people who have a duty to assist Deliberate positioning of others: 1 people and organizations doing the right things 2 people and organizations doing the wrong things Forced self-positioning in the face of criticism: 1 poverty as an issue 2 people living in extreme poverty 3 people who have a duty to assist Forced positioning of others in the face of criticism: 1 people and organizations doing the right things 2 people and organizations doing the wrong things
Strategic pre-positioning	The pre-positioning strategy names the ongoing existence of extreme poverty as both socially unjust and immoral, in fact it is obscene (offending social and moral principles; repugnant). It is structured to support the taking up and allocation of rights and duties, namely: • I have the **right** the speak out and position extreme poverty as obscene – I've been there, I am there, I speak on behalf of, I've seen it, I've worked with it and I condemn that it continues to exist. • I have the **duty** to speak out and position extreme poverty as obscene – I am aware, I am part of humanity, I live on this earth, I cannot ignore it and I condemn that it continues to exist.

in public relations positioning programs within which narratives can be formulated and framed, and messages developed. Table 9.2 shows how the strategic positioning aspects of the Framework inform the tactics as determined within the positioning triangle.

Public relations positioning program execution

Positioning extreme poverty would need to happen at the local, regional and global level. This strategy aims to get audience members who are aware, or who become aware, of the goal to eradicate extreme poverty by 2030 to:

Table 9.2 Strategic positioning concept informs tactics – the positioning triangle

Strategic concept: The ongoing existence of extreme poverty as both socially unjust and immoral, in fact it is obscene (offending social and moral principles; repugnant)			
Positions	i) Extreme poverty is obscene and should be condemned and eradicated	ii) People have a duty to condemn and eradicate extreme poverty	iii) People or institutions must stop contributing to the continuation of extreme poverty
Speech acts	Assertive Expressive Directive Commissive	Assertive Expressive Directive Commissive	Assertive Expressive Directive Commissive
Possible storylines	Quest Metamorphosis Transformation	Quest Sacrifice (time, money, etc.: donor-centric)	Transformation Discovery (protest-centric) Rescue Wretched excess

1 assert that the situation with extreme poverty is obscene in the context of the world's resources so everyone knows about it and condemns it (assertive);
2 direct people to action (tell people what they can do to help and to harness the feelings of anger, indignation and injustice – what they can do varies with audiences and locales) (directive);
3 make commitments to act on achieving the 2030 goal (e.g. informing, educating, amplifying, protesting, donating, researching) (commissive); and,
4 express through word and action that extreme poverty is obscene and must be eradicated by 2030 (expressive).

Three key positioning focuses are:

1 Changing the extreme poverty storyline – aligns with the position that extreme poverty is obscene and should be condemned and eradicated.
2 Moving on from "clicktivism" – aligns with the position that people have a duty to condemn and eradicate extreme poverty.
3 Dismantling repugnant positions – aligns with the position that people or institutions must stop contributing to the continuation of extreme poverty.

The following section demonstrates the application of a master plot (Tobias, 1993) storyline to each of these positions. These storylines provide an arc for the trajectory of the public relations program. Although this may seem an unusual way to approach planning, applying different storylines to an issue can assist in developing more options for a public relations program. It can also tease out where programs may split and have different approaches to address different audiences or aspects of the situation. Such options can feed into the scenario planning that should be undertaken as part of the research phase of public relations planning, as outlined in Chapter 4.

Changing the extreme poverty storyline

The creation of new positions on extreme poverty begins by people living and using the new storyline. This means that the old donor-centric storylines need to be dropped. They will be replaced by a new storyline that is about positioning people in extreme poverty as people who are an integral part of humanity and the societies in which they live. These people will be positioned as having a right not to live in extreme poverty. Target audiences will be positioned as having a duty to ensure that these people do not live this way. People experiencing extreme poverty will not be positioned as powerless. By articulating their right to not live in extreme poverty, their power to unleash emotion in targeted audiences will be activated. Audiences will then have a duty to speak out and act. People who are identified as having no right to speak on extreme poverty, that is, people who speak falsely about the situation and its causes, will be challenged as part of this duty and falsehoods will be exposed.

This exercise will utilize the storyline of "metamorphosis" (Tobias, 1993: 146). It is evident that if extreme poverty is to be positioned through the storyline of metamorphosis there are positions and speech acts that are opened up, and others that are closed down. For example, if people living in extreme poverty are positioned as living under a "curse" in this storyline (positioning vertex), there is no right for someone to assert that those people should pick themselves up and get a job; such an assertion would be incongruent with living under a curse, according to the storyline. In the metamorphosis storyline (Table 9.3), it is the antagonists (that is, the people causing the poverty or those that can help alleviate poverty) who must act to remove the curse (Tobias, 1993). As Tobias (1993) stated, "the cure of the curse…is always the same: love. Love can correct wrong; it can heal the wounded and strengthen the weak at heart. Love can take many forms. It can be…the love of people for one another" (p. 147).

This exercise reveals possibilities for a narrative and message development based on the storyline of metamorphosis that could be used over a lengthy period of time. It provides the scaffold for campaign elements within a longer program of raising awareness, protesting and condemning the conditions of extreme poverty and reporting on changes that occur due to action or inaction. Through the attribution of rights and duties that accompany the positioning efforts, the exercise provides a "moral" code against which an audience's moral sensitivity can be monitored. It provides an expected trajectory of resolution against which progress could be measured. Such measures could contribute to indicators against which decisions on whether a campaign element needed to be recalibrated could be assessed. This same exercise could be undertaken using one of the other master plotline checklists (Tobias, 1993) and a different set of possibilities for the program would emerge. The next section shows how the plotline of "discovery" (Tobias, 1993: 201) can be applied.

Table 9.3 The metamorphosis storyline

Storyline/master plot elements (Tobias, 1993)	*Storyline elements applied to position extreme poverty*	*Rights/duties inherent in ensuing narratives/messages*
"Metamorphosis is usually the result of a curse" (Tobias, 1993: 151).	People in extreme poverty are cursed by societal, political and cultural structural conditions, natural disasters, climatic conditions and so on.	People living in extreme poverty have the right to be free of the curse. People causing the poverty, or those that can help alleviate poverty, have a duty to remove the curse.
"The cure for the curse is generally love" (Tobias, 1993: 151).	If people turned their love for humanity towards people living in extreme poverty they could be cured of the curse of poverty.	People living in extreme poverty have the right to be cared about. People causing the poverty, or those that can help alleviate poverty, have a duty to care.
The form of love is "people's love for each other" (Tobias, 1993).	The form of love is caring for humanity, being humane.	People living in extreme poverty have the right to be cared about. People causing the poverty, or those who can help alleviate poverty, have a duty to care.
The "metamorph" is usually the protagonist (lead character) (Tobias, 1993: 152).	People in extreme poverty are the lead characters. Sub characters: – people who can help; and – those who cause extreme poverty.	People living in extreme poverty have the right to be at the center of the story. People causing the poverty, or those who can help alleviate poverty, have a duty to focus on the people.
Plot shows "transformation back to humanity" (Tobias, 1993: 152).	Must show the transformation back to a humane state of being.	People living in extreme poverty have the right to live in a humane state. People causing the poverty, or those who can help alleviate poverty, have a duty to facilitate this.
"Metamorph is a character plot" so "we care more about nature of the people than their actions" (Tobias, 1993: 152).	Focus on the people living in extreme poverty.	People living in extreme poverty have the right to highlight the nature of their plight. People causing the poverty, or those who can help alleviate poverty, have a duty to listen.
Metamorph is "innately sad" (Tobias, 1993: 152).	People living in extreme poverty are in a sad state.	People living in extreme poverty have the right to get out of this state. People causing the poverty, or those who can help alleviate poverty, have a duty to facilitate this.

Table 9.3 Continued

Storyline/master plot elements (Tobias, 1993)	*Storyline elements applied to position extreme poverty*	*Rights/duties inherent in ensuing narratives/messages*
"Metamorph's life is usually bound by rituals and prohibitions" (Tobias, 1993: 152).	Highlight the structural and cultural bonds that restrict the agency of people living in extreme poverty.	People living in extreme poverty have the right to get out of this state. People causing the poverty, or those who can help alleviate poverty, have a duty to facilitate this.
"Metamorph generally wants out of the situation" (Tobias, 1993).	People don't want to live in extreme poverty.	People living in extreme poverty have the right to get out of this state. People causing the poverty, or those who can help alleviate poverty, have a duty to facilitate this.
"There is usually a way of out the predicament, which is called release" (Tobias, 1993: 152).	People living in extreme poverty can be released from extreme poverty.	People living in extreme poverty have the right to be released from extreme poverty. People causing the poverty, or those who can help alleviate poverty, have a duty to facilitate this.
"The terms of the release are nearly always carried out by the antagonist" i.e. the principal character in opposition to the protagonist (Tobias, 1993: 152).	Highlight who can help to orchestrate the release of people from conditions of extreme poverty.	People living in extreme poverty have the right to be released from extreme poverty by those who contribute to or cause the condition. People causing the poverty, or those who can help alleviate poverty, have a duty to facilitate this.
"If the curse can be reversed by the antagonist performing certain acts, the protagonist cannot either hurry or explain the events" (Tobias, 1993: 152).	The power rests with those not living in extreme poverty to facilitate the metamorphosis.	People causing the poverty, or those who can help alleviate poverty, have both a right and a duty to remove the curse of extreme poverty.
"In the first dramatic phase, the metamorph usually cannot explain the reasons for his curse. We see him in the state of his curse" (Tobias, 1993: 152).	The state of extreme poverty must be shown; extremely impoverished people have no explanation as to why they are not helped; why they cannot be released from the curse.	People living in extreme poverty have the right to have their living conditions shown and explained on their behalf. People causing the poverty, or those who can help alleviate poverty, have a duty to release people from extreme poverty and to explain to people why they are not helped/or are helped.

Table 9.3 Continued

Storyline/master plot elements (Tobias, 1993)	*Storyline elements applied to position extreme poverty*	*Rights/duties inherent in ensuing narratives/messages*
Begin the story at the point prior to the resolution of the curse (release) (Tobias, 1993).	Story starts with the people living in extreme poverty.	People living in extreme poverty have the right to have their plight shown. People causing the poverty, or those who can help alleviate poverty, have both a right and a duty to see the plight.
"The antagonist should act as the catalyst that propels the protagonist toward release" (Tobias, 1993: 152).	The people and structures causing extreme poverty should act as the catalyst to release people from the curse.	Once the plight is known, people causing the poverty, or those who can help alleviate poverty, have both a right and a duty to act.
"The antagonist often starts out as the intended victim but ends up as the 'chosen one'" (Tobias, 1993: 152).	The people and institutions causing extreme poverty often start out as those being criticized for lack of action but will end up as the ones that save the day.	People causing the poverty, or those who can help alleviate poverty, have a right to be portrayed as having the ability to act, and as having a duty to do so.
"The second dramatic phase should concentrate on the nature of evolving relationships between the antagonist and the metamorph" (Tobias, 1993: 152)	Focus on how thing are changing between those living in extreme poverty and those who can change things.	People causing the poverty, or those who can help alleviate poverty, have a right to be portrayed as doing the right thing when this is occurring. The opposite also applies.
"The characters will generally move toward each other emotionally" (Tobias, 1993: 152).	Mutual understanding will be portrayed as the situation evolves.	People causing the poverty, or those who can help alleviate poverty, have a right to be portrayed as helping and changing things for the better.
"In the third dramatic phase, the terms of release should be fulfilled and the protagonist should be freed from the curse. The metamorph may either revert to his original state or die" (Tobias, 1993: 152).	Extreme poverty is overcome and people formerly living in the state of extreme poverty live in a state where things are humane. If the transformation does not happen, people will die from a preventable cause.	People living in extreme poverty have the right to live in humane conditions. People causing the poverty, or those who can help alleviate poverty, have both a right and a duty to see this maintained or improved.
"The reader should learn the reasons for the curse and its root causes" (Tobias, 1993: 152).	People should learn the reasons of the curse of extreme poverty and its root causes so as to ensure the transformation out of extreme poverty is permanent.	People who have escaped extreme poverty have the right to never descend into extreme poverty again. People causing the poverty, or those who can help alleviate poverty, have both a right and a duty to never let it occur again.

Moving on from clicktivism

Clicking "like" on a website to support the eradication of extreme poverty is counterproductive as it makes people feel engaged when they aren't (Wilkins and Enghel, 2013). It could be the surest way to encourage irresponsible awareness. In this new strategy, a click will mean audience members commit to condemning extreme poverty and to taking culturally appropriate action to move towards the achievement of its eradication. There is not one single correct action to take but a series of actions that will be designed and implemented at local, regional and global levels. This exercise will utilize the storyline of "discovery" (Tobias, 1993: 201) for positioning someone as having a duty to condemn extreme poverty and work towards its eradication (Table 9.4).

Dismantling repugnant positions

Some people and governments hold the position that they cannot afford to donate monetarily towards to the eradication of extreme poverty, or that they cannot condemn extreme poverty when and where it occurs. Such positions have roots tied up in a knot of language and inaction. The storylines used by people and governments who are acting like this help to cement their arguably flawed positions into place in people's minds. These words and actions work to shape people's social reality so the flawed positions become even more fixed, entrenching inaction on extreme poverty. Attacking the bonds that tie up this knot can unpack the rhetoric, publicly demonstrating that whatever is holding them back can be readily overcome. Taking this approach positions people and governments as being *able* to act. Positioned this way, they then have a duty to act accordingly or to be challenged by now activated audiences. Opening up the tightly woven fabric of these fixed positions offers hope of finding a place where public relations interventions have good chances of succeeding.

One can imagine positioning members of an autocratic inhumane government as supporting the structures that contributed to extreme poverty (as imposing the curse). Then, imagine if these same members were subsequently positioned as those who could alter the structures and thus alleviate extreme poverty. There would be a right assigned with such positioning for the autocratic government to change its ways and act more positively. If it failed to do so, the duties that came with being positioned as being able to help could be highlighted through public relations techniques. Such techniques would pressure the government members to act on extreme poverty. This could be aligned to a "rescue" (Tobias, 1993: 86) storyline (Table 9.5).

Working though just three storyline options indicates that there are situations where all storylines could work within an overall position of extreme poverty being obscene and needing to be eradicated.

Table 9.4 The discovery storyline

Storyline/master plot elements (Tobias, 1993)	*Storyline elements applied to position people as having a duty to condemn extreme poverty and work towards its eradication*	*Rights/duties inherent in ensuing narratives/messages*
"Remember that the discovery plot is more about the character making the discovery than the discovery itself. This is a search for understanding about human nature. Focus your story on the character, not on what the character does" (Tobias, 1993: 208).	This focuses on the change within the audience members as they change their opinions, attitudes and actions to help condemn and eradicate extreme poverty.	People causing the poverty, or those who can help alleviate poverty, have a right to information about people living in extreme poverty, its causes and what actions they should take to condemn and eradicate it. They have a duty to help once they are aware.
"Start your plot with an understanding of who the main character is *before* circumstances change and force the character into new situations" (Tobias, 1993: 208).	Describe the characteristics and nature of the intended audiences for the program before the public relations interventions commence in order to position potential helpers and the phenomenon of extreme poverty itself.	People causing the poverty, or those who can help alleviate poverty, have a right to be positioned as those who can help the situation, and as having a duty to do so.
"Place the character on the cusp of change. Start the action as late as possible but also give the reader a strong impression of the main character's personality as it was before events started to change her character" (Tobias, 1993: 208).	This gives focus to the intended audience for the program, i.e. "People who believe that global development problems are important but aren't acting on that interest" (Cannes Chimera, 2013).	People have a duty to act once they are aware of how they can help people living in extreme poverty.
"Make sure the catalyst that forces the change…is significant and interesting enough to hold the reader's attention" (Tobias, 1993: 208).	The nature and causes of extreme poverty are the catalyst.	Public relations practitioners have the right and duty to work to position extreme poverty as a catalyst for change.
"Move your character into the crisis (the clash between the present and the past) as quickly as possible, but maintain the tension of past and present as a fundamental part of your story's tension" (Tobias, 1993: 208).	Bring the nature and causes of extreme poverty as the catalyst into the positioning narrative.	Public relations practitioners have the right and duty to work to do this.

Table 9.4 Continued

Storyline/master plot elements (Tobias, 1993)	*Storyline elements applied to position people as having a duty to condemn extreme poverty and work towards its eradication*	*Rights/duties inherent in ensuing narratives/messages*
"Maintain a sense of proportion. Balance action and emotion so that they remain believable. Make sure your character's revelations are in proportion to the events" (Tobias, 1993: 208).	Balance the nature and causes of extreme poverty and the anticipated and actual responses of the audience in terms of awareness and action to be taken, including the personal responsibility for causes and actions.	Maintain balance between rights and duties.
"Don't exaggerate either your character's emotions or the actions of your character to 'force' emotions from her. (This maintains proportion.) Avoid being melodramatic" (Tobias, 1993: 208).	Let the situation of people living in extreme poverty speak for itself; let the people in extreme poverty themselves speak.	People living in extreme poverty have the right to speak for themselves where possible. Others have a duty to speak of the situation when people are unable to speak for themselves.

Next steps

Who could possibly develop and implement such a global public relations program? Who would be in a position to do so? One possible approach to implementing this ambitious global program would be to activate a global action research project (Rapoport, 1970; Susman and Evered, 1978) that does not reside with any single organization or enterprise. It would instead be managed by senior public relations academics, working through the already established global network of public relations researchers and professors, and an agreed project management system.

Why propose such an academic network as being such a strong possibility for overseeing the project? Because it can be shown that their expertise in public relations scholarship, management and relationship building situates them as having a right to undertake the action research project management. Many public relations academics are past or current senior level practitioners, and are invariably enmeshed in local, regional and international networks of communication industry leaders, professional associations and NGOs. They can often harness the power of keen undergraduate and postgraduate public relations and wider communication studies students on projects in partnership with industry.

This approach enables the use of people, organizations, channels and so on that are best suited to particular aspects of the program's implementation at the various levels. It also prevents having all program resources and initiatives tied

Table 9.5 The rescue storyline

Storyline/master plot elements (Tobias, 1993)	*Storyline elements applied to position people as having a duty to condemn extreme poverty*	*Rights/duties inherent in ensuing narratives/ messages*
"The rescue plot relies more on action than on the development of characterization" (Tobias, 1993: 92).	Focuses on rescue of people from their circumstances on extreme poverty.	Right to rescue. Duty to undertake rescue.
"Character triangle should consist of hero, villain and victim. The hero should rescue the victim from the villain" (Tobias, 1993: 92).	People living in extreme poverty (victims) rescued by helpers (heroes) from the villain (that is extreme poverty or those who cause it).	Right to undertake rescue. Right to rescue. Duty to rescue. Duty to stop causing poverty.
"Moral argument tends to be black and white" (Tobias, 1993: 92).	Extreme poverty is obscene – no argument about this.	Right to position poverty as obscene and duty to eradicate it.
"Focus of story should be on the pursuit of the hero of the villain" (Tobias, 1993: 92).	Focus would be on those seeking to eradicate extreme poverty, on the poverty itself, or the causes of it.	Right to pursue eradication of poverty. Duty to pursue eradication of poverty.
The "hero should go out into the world to pursue the villain, and usually must contend with the villain on the villain's turf" (Tobias, 1993: 92).	Those who seek to eradicate extreme poverty (heroes) must take the fight to the villain's turf – where is this? UN level, governments, regional, country, village, personal?	Duty of helpers to fight extreme poverty on the villain's turf.
The "hero should be defined by the relationship with the villain" (Tobias, 1993: 92)	Those who seek to eradicate extreme poverty (heroes) seek to define relationship with the villain (cause) – part of the problem or solution?	Right to define relationships. Duty to do so.
"Use the antagonist as a device whose purpose is to deprive the hero" of what is believed to be rightfully theirs (Tobias, 1993: 92)	The solution to the eradication of extreme poverty is rightfully with the heroes, and the villain stands in the way.	Right to find the solution. Duty to do so.
"Make sure the antagonist constantly interferes with the hero's progress" (Tobias, 1993: 92).	Constantly show that it is the villain that causes the poverty, not the victim.	Duty to fight the villain.

Table 9.5 Continued

Storyline/master plot elements (Tobias, 1993)	*Storyline elements applied to position people as having a duty to condemn extreme poverty*	*Rights/duties inherent in ensuing narratives/ messages*
The victim is generally the weakest of the three characters and serves mainly as a mechanism to force the hero to confront the antagonist" (Tobias, 1993: 92).	People living in extreme poverty are the social force that is driving the people who can help to take on the causes of extreme poverty.	People living in extreme poverty have the right to elicit the response from helpers.
"Develop the dramatic phases of separation, pursuit and confrontation and reunion" (Tobias, 1993: 92).	Attempts to help people are thwarted by the villain (i.e. causes of extreme poverty); helpers must fight poverty wherever the villains are in action; confronting the causes until the helpers win and people are freed from extreme poverty.	Claiming the right to help; the duty to help.

up with a single entity and thereby largely mitigates the risk of program collapse. Such a structure could be set up through the establishment of regional nodes based through universities in partnerships with NGOs, government agencies, philanthropic organizations and industry. Having university-based nodes is innovative as it could contribute to changing the social norms and create the new spaces for new conversations about extreme poverty. Many academic institutions have community and humanitarian goals embedded in their constitutions and this, in one way, attributes a duty to this academic network to undertake such a program.

The structure of an action research project managed by a network of academics working with practitioners and local organizations might be helpful in overcoming audiences' resistance to charitable messages, or what has been called "compassion fatigue" (Moeller, 1999: 1). Seu (2010) highlighted in her research how the language used when appealing for donation or action is not "neutral" but highly significant in terms of a) how it is structured, b) who is communicating and, c) the nature of the request action. The action research model, which sees the public relations program being developed and implemented through the partnerships between academics and practitioners from across a range of organizations, could provide the necessary circuit breaker to audiences who operate within a "discursive machinery of denial" (Seu, 2010: 454).

Seu (2010) describes this machinery as including audiences not responding to appeals for help by justifying themselves as being cleverly resistant to manipulative messages by charitable organizations. These same audiences can be seen to undermine the credibility of the messenger to weaken the impact of the appeal (Seu, 2010). Finally, Seu's (2010) research showed audiences positioning themselves as "savvy" assessors of the success or failure of charitable organizations' appeals strategies. Audience members can avoid moral criticism for not engaging with the recommended action because the action itself can be deemed to be failing.

The "project nodes" could work to coordinate tailored public relations initiatives to position extreme poverty, and to position those who could help to condemn or alleviate it. As action research "aims to contribute both to the practical concerns of people in an immediate problematic situation and to the goals of social science by joint collaboration within a mutually acceptable ethical framework" (Rapoport, 1970: 499), such an approach may be the way to overcome that "discursive machinery of denial" (Seu, 2010: 454).

A suitable name for such project nodes would need to be agreed, like Poverty Eradication Action Research Sites (giving the acronym of PEARS), Poverty Eradication Action Centre Hubs (giving the acronym of PEACH) or Poverty Eradication Action for Change and Equity (giving the acronym of PEACE). The node title would obviously need to work across cultures and languages and so on. Such a project would require extensive funding along the lines of that which winners of awards such as Cannes Chimera Challenge have opportunities to gain. That particular program opens doors to funding from the Bill and Melinda Gates Foundation, but there would also be other avenues of funding for such a large-scale action research exercise, or at least pilot testing of the project.

In a funding proposal, one way of proceeding could be based on the five-step action research cycle (ARC) put forward by Susman and Evered (1978): a) diagnosing, b) action planning, c) action taking, d) evaluating, and e) specifying learning. The proposal would outline that academics would be working alongside industry professionals and NGO practitioners, with all parties working in dual researcher/practitioner roles in line with the action research approach. Through the newly established project nodes, the network members would firstly undertake step one of the action research cycle: *research*. We would identify who is currently speaking on extreme poverty, how they are positioning the issue, and the rights and duties associated with the positions they take. We would identify what actions people in a position to condemn or help eradicate extreme poverty are currently being asked to take. We could identify what storylines are functioning in the local moral orders operating in the regions around the project nodes.

Step two of the action research cycle is *action planning* and at this point we could identify how best to tailor the strategy to work for diverse audiences at the different levels such as local, regional, country and so on. Working within the project node network we could map how various storylines would be likely to play out through scenario planning and make recommendations for action based on likely outcomes. We could work out what channels would be most suitable, how traditional and social media would be used (e.g., recognizing that some places in the world don't even receive radio), what materials are needed, what skills are required, what talent would be necessary, and, how programs could best be structured to work in specific locations. Budgeting and administrative details would be attended to and translation from planning to action would begin.

Step three is *action taking* and it is here that the narratives and related key messages could be promulgated as part of efforts to support the position being taken up and/or assigned. As the program proceeded, we would report on what meaning was being constructed by intended and non-intended audiences as a result of the public relations efforts. The information would ideally feed into decision-making on whether the storyline or other vertices of the positioning triangle needed to be adjusted, or whether the strategic pre-positioning efforts were appropriate for particular local moral orders that were in operation. It is envisaged that as some project nodes would be better situated in terms of network expertise and resources, that there would be resource and idea sharing at each point throughout the action research cycle.

The work undertaken at the third step would cross over into the *evaluation* stage (step four) where more formal evaluation would be conducted on positioning efforts. Did the audiences construct the expected/intended meanings? How closely did things that occurred in the positioning episode align with the scenarios that were worked through in the planning stage? Such questions would guide the report for step five, *specifying learning*, in that knowledge gained would be shared with the project node members, the wider node network and other key constituents and stakeholders. This knowledge would inform future decision-making in the public relations programs or in recommencing the action research project cycle until extreme poverty was eradicated in line with the Millennium Development Goal.

The actions that would need to be undertaken to make such a project happen are:

- Map the network of people that could be activated – identify the key communication academics and their networks in order to define local and regional networks and personnel across universities, communication and creative industries and NGOs.
- Identify regional project coordinators and calculate capabilities and areas where there is over or under supply of capacity.
- Audit local, regional and global positions on extreme poverty being taken and assigned.
- Collate current dominant storylines operating at each level and map to spokespeople and influence measures.
- Report on who is speaking and acting in positive and negative ways on extreme poverty.
- Assess the rights and duties associated with positions taken and assigned, as this determines power differentials and exposes where concentration of communication effort is required.
- Work with partners to design interventions based on the new storylines for each level so that specific positions are taken up, dismantled or assigned.
- Implement, monitor, reassess, recalibrate as required through the network of project coordinators.

Summary

This chapter demonstrated how the Framework for Intentional Positioning in Public Relations could be used to guide the design of a large-scale public relations program. It used as a program brief the material from a global communication initiative award scheme, the Cannes Chimera, in order to show the Framework's application to a real world situation. The overall strategy was developed using the first three domains of the framework, namely the goal domain, the positioning type domain and the strategic pre-positioning domain. This exercise indicated that there would be several different types of positioning as part of the program including positioning the phenomenon of extreme poverty itself, positioning people who live in extreme poverty, positioning those who could help to condemn or eradicate extreme poverty, and finally, those people and institutions that could be identified as being part of the cause of extreme poverty.

The next section demonstrated how the positioning triangle domain worked to guide tactical decisions related to the position to be taken, the way positions would be enacted and what storylines could be used to support the positioning. Tobias' (1993) checklists for 20 master plots were drawn upon to expand how different storylines could inform the development of campaign narratives and messages. It also served to highlight the rights and duties that were associated with the various positioning efforts. Finally, one approach to how such a global public relations program could be implemented was suggested. The possibility for an extensive action research project was outlined that saw public relations academics and practitioners working together on project elements in the dual roles of researcher and practitioner. It is hoped that this overview provided readers with some insights into the possibilities of taking a positioning approach to public relations program design.

References

Cannes Chimera (2013) 2013 challenge brief: lead the fight against extreme poverty. Retrieved from www.canneschimera.com/challenges/2013/brief/

Harré, R. and van Langenhove, L. (1999) *Positioning Theory: Moral contexts of intentional action*. Oxford: Blackwell.

James, M. (2012) Autoethnography: the story of applying a conceptual framework for intentional positioning to public relations practice. *Public Relations Review*, 38(4): 555–64. http://dx.doi.org/10.1016/j.pubrev.2012.05.004

Moeller, S. D. (1999) *Compassion Fatigue: How the media sell disease, famine, war and death*. New York: Routledge.

Pinazo, D. and Nos Aldas, E. (2013) Developing moral sensitivity through protest scenarios in international NGDOs' communication. *Communication Research*, 1–24.

Rapoport, R. (1970) Three dilemmas of action research. *Human Relations*, 23(6): 499–513.

Searle, J. (1979) *Expression and Meaning: Studies in the theory of speech acts*. Cambridge: Cambridge University Press.

Seu, I. B. (2010) "Doing denial": audience reaction to human rights appeals. *Discourse and Society*, 21(4): 438–57.

Slocum-Bradley, N. (2007) Constructing and de-constructing the ACP Group: actors, strategies and consequences for development. *Geopolitics*, 12(4): 635–55, doi:10.1080/14650040701546095

Susman, G. I. and Evered, R. D. (1978) An assessment of the scientific merits of action research. *Administrative Science Quarterly*, 23(4): 582–603.

Thomas, E. F. and Louis, W. R. (2013) Doing democracy: the social psychological mobilization and consequences of collective action. *Social Issues and Policy Review*, 7(1): 173–200.

Tobias, R. (1993) *20 Master Plots (and how to build them)*. Cincinnati: Readers Digest.

Wilkins, K. G. and Enghel, F. (2013) The privatization of development through global communication industries: living proof? *Media, Culture and Society*, 35(2): 165–81.

10 Future directions for positioning theory in public relations

Positioning theory has been used in this book to examine and articulate strategic positioning in public relations. To re-cap, positioning theory, according to Harré (2012) is:

> ...based on the principle that not everyone involved in a social episode has equal access to rights and duties to perform particular kinds of meaningful actions at that moment and with those people. In many interesting cases, the rights and duties determine who can use a certain discourse mode – for example, issuing orders, giving grades, remembering a past event. A cluster of short-term disputable rights, obligations, and duties is called a "position".
>
> (Harré, 2012: 193)

Taking account of the work of Berger (1999) and Motion (1997), together with the perspectives of positioning theory, I proposed that the definition of a public relations position is: a point of intentional representation discursively constructed for the purposes of achieving an intended outcome, and from where possibilities for action are established, or in some cases denied, in terms of the local moral order/s wherein the public relations activity is taking place. Positioning is comprised of those actions taken to achieve the position.

Until this book, positioning theory had not been explored deeply in terms of its application to public relations. The hope is that readers will agree that the theory offers a different lens through which to examine and design public relations practice. This book was always seen as a catalyst to beginning a wider discussion of intentional strategic positioning in public relations. It was never intended to be a definitive treatise on the subject. In examining my own efforts to position my work in the field of public relations I can apply the Framework for Intentional Positioning in Public Relations in the following way:

> *The positioning goal domain*: My goal is to further the field's understanding of public relations practice, and the way it shapes and is shaped by society and social contexts, by exploring the possibilities offered by positioning theory. My previous research had indicated that positioning was a prominent area of practice but that it was under-researched outside of the marketing context. My motivation in pursuing this goal was to examine whether there

was a better way to theorize and account for the strategic practice of intentional positioning in public relations.

It is important to identify the goal of the positioning effort to gain an understanding of what is trying to be achieved, and what motivation may lie behind such efforts. In addition it provides clues for researchers and analysts as to what impact such a goal may have in a wider context. It raises questions on what the repositioning effects on others may be when such efforts are played out. For example, if I am to position my theoretical work in a particular way, does this exert a social force that may reposition someone else's work either positively or negatively? What repercussions would such an outcome have? What reactions would be likely to play out? Would a group of scholars who felt I had somehow negatively positioned their work begin efforts to reposition their own work more positively, and mine more negatively? Such questioning is the beginning of a positioning analysis. From a public relations perspective, the work identifying the positioning goal is part of helping to develop possible scenarios that might play out and to help anticipate how issues may emerge and develop.

The positioning type domain: It is clear that my efforts are an exercise in deliberate self-positioning. I am striving to position my work and myself in a particular way. This is deliberate. My academic role in a university is one in which I am expected to be actively researching in my field, and publishing my findings. However outside these broad expectations, there is no one forcing me to position my work or self in a particular way. I am not under attack, or immediate threat of being removed from my job, if I do not publish this work on positioning theory. Examining the type of positioning that is occurring highlights factors such as intention, power relations, social context and so on.

For example, the fact that I am deliberately self-positioning my work, and myself, is indicative that my intention is to position in a way that makes others take notice of and engage with my work. The power relations at play are multilayered but are centered on the actual sayings/actions of each of the parties that are part of this positioning episode (author, publisher, reviewers, readers and so on). They have the power to shape certain aspects of the social world, namely the positioning of my work in the public relations field, and myself as one of its scholars.

The strategic pre-positioning domain: This is where I had to make the decision how to strategically pre-position what I was doing in order to position it in a particular way. My current employment as a university academic, the question of where my research sits in the field, and my standing in the professional practice community are seen as my attributes. These serve to underpin and justify the rights and duties I am claiming in positioning my scholarly work. In essence these attributes determine what position I am entitled to take up, that is, what I have the right to do and say within the context of the local moral order (e.g. academic publishing norms of track record, citations, and standing).

My current position affords me the right to put forward my work for the consideration of the field in the form of a book published by a reputable academic publisher. It affords me the right to argue the case for considering positioning theory as a way to analyze and design public relations practice. However my current position does not afford me the right to, for instance, trash all other theories in the field and hold up my own as the best. If I was to position my work in this way I would be viewed very negatively, and my work would be likely to be disregarded in large part. I have no right, according to the local moral order within which I am operating to take up such a position. It is at the point of pre-positioning that the concept of rights and duties first comes into play for public relations. This is because the attributes I am assigned by others, or those that I choose to take up for myself, help to construct the cluster of rights and duties my actual positioning affords me.

The positioning triangle domain: I am positioning my work as offering a different lens through which to examine and design public relations (the position vertex of the triangle); I am enacting this position through speech acts and actions such as making assertions, publishing findings of research and publishing them in an academic text; and, I am supporting my position through the storylines used throughout this text that aim to prove or demonstrate specific aspects of my theoretical work. This positioning strategy is one that I have taken after examining the terrain of practice within the academic public relations field. It is one that I have determined that I have the "right" to take on. In my estimation, it seems to optimize the likelihood of my text being noticed and being engaged with. I also realize that with this comes the duty to argue, to the best of my abilities, the case for positioning theory.

One can see how such strategic positioning as described above maps quite closely to what happens in much public relations practice. When someone, or an organization, takes a position on something it opens up possibilities for action. However, taking a position can also close down options for action. Positioning theory provides a way to explore this as it is concerned with the way the actions of participants in social interactions are constrained by an understood framework of rights, duties and obligations, that is, a local moral order (Tan and Moghaddam, 1999). Positioning theory focuses on how the rights and responsibilities, duties and roles of organizations, aiming to position themselves or others, influence positioning outcomes. Positioning theory explicates why an organization's desired positioning may not be viable. It indicates why positions need to be negotiated through discursive practices in the contested space where public relations takes place.

In this final section, an overview will be provided of possible future directions for positioning theory to be applied in public relations and wider communication areas. This is not a finite list of suggestions but highlights areas of interest or concern that could potentially be illuminated through applying positioning theoretical approaches.

Research relating to roles, rights and responsibilities in positioning

It remains to be examined whether Smudde and Courtright's (2010) descriptions of hierarchical, social, and rhetorical power are adequate to explicate how positioning power operates in public relations contexts. It seems that as a field, public relations scholars are only beginning to scratch the surface of the work of scholars such as Foucault and Bourdieu on power, and how such work could inform further scholarship in public relations.

For example, Motion (2000) suggested that morality and truth in the Foucaultian sense of moral code form a foundation for examining personal public relations. I suggest that scholars revisit Motion's paper and examine how her proposed framework for personal public relations, which draws on the power in truth, and moral codes, can guide research in networked and social media contexts. The focus on what comprises truth and authentic positioning in personal public relations as articulated by Motion could focus on emerging roles for public relations practitioners. Adapting Motion's work to current contexts would see practitioners not only working as advisers to clients but also as working to actively constitute public relations personas for individuals and organizations, and devising platforms for the construction and exchange of such meanings. I argue that Motion's framework, which is based on Foucault's technologies of the self (in Motion, 2000), although designed for personal public relations should be tested to ascertain whether it could be adapted for organizational contexts, or melded in some way to the Framework proposed in this book. Motion's (2000) framework for personal public relations, which involves the "technology" of positioning, may be ideal to analyze the way personal public relations and personal branding are undertaken through social media.

Ethical contexts of public relations positioning also remain under-examined. It has only been in recent years that a public relations model has been developed that offers a step-by-step process that integrates ethics with existing campaign activity. This enables practitioners to, measure, clarify, communicate, and manage an ethical compliance strategy at micro and macro levels, transforming ethics from an abstract concern into a standard reporting line, alongside financial, behavioral, attitudinal, sales, inquiry levels, or any other measurable outcomes in typical public relations campaigns (Tilley, 2005).

For example, intentionally undertaking a kind of "character assassination" in a public relations context can be seen in terms of positioning theory as a way of "deleting" the right of the claims of that organization to be believed (Harré, 2012). Positioning theory can be used to study the discursive processes by which such organizations took up, refused, contested, and so on, the rights and duties they found were ascribed by the local moral order (Harré, 2012). This would be a way of researching the components of such positioning and examining their ethical dimensions. It is envisaged that positioning theory may provide the insights into processes and techniques used in public relations that could indicate where ethical models, such as that proposed by Tilley (2005), could be more readily integrated into the processes and techniques of practice.

Research relating to the Framework for Intentional Positioning in Public Relations

The Framework has already undergone several iterations since it was first presented as a "Provisional Conceptual Framework" (James 2010, 2011). The first iteration had a positioning purpose domain, which included the five positioning purposes of self-promotion, exemplification, ingratiation, supplication and intimidation. However, since 2009, there has been significant work amongst positioning theorists on the concept of pre-positioning. Lee (2010) writes that there has been a major refinement of positioning theory that differentiates it into two phases. Phase one is now being referred to as pre-positioning. This involves the attribution of qualities such as character, intellect or temperament and can be seen to be supported by evidence of past behavior (Lee, 2010). This pre-positioning can be seen to set the stage for assigning or refusing rights and duties, which is the pivot of phase two positioning (Lee, 2010). Lee suggests that further research into the relationship between pre-positioning and phase two positioning will assist in furthering understanding of the "local moral order that sustains those speech acts as meaningfully distributing rights and duties" (2010: 204). This would be particularly pertinent research in a public relations context to further examine the strategic aspects of such pre-positioning efforts.

Another area for research would be to examine whether positioning theorists' ideas around pre-positioning may in fact relate more to the idea of priming. Priming has been previously explored in public relations research (e.g. Danowski, 2008; Hallahan 1999, 2000; Wang, 2007). Priming involves people using schematic processes that entail them "using association and expectation to make inferences about events and to impute meaning not manifested in the message itself" (Hallahan, 1999: 208). "It can influence the standards by which a particular issue is judged" (Wang, 2007: 124). Such priming provides context "wherein the information environment surrounding a message provides cues for its interpretation" (Hallahan, 2000: 472). As pre-positioning discourse involves listing and sometimes justifying attributes deemed relevant to whatever positioning is going forward, the link to priming seems to warrant further investigation. The main rationale behind the concept of pre-positioning could be priming for the attribution or denial of rights and duties. These rights and duties "are shorthand terms for clusters of moral (normative) presuppositions which people believe or are told or slip into and to which they are momentarily bound in what they say or do" (Harré, Moghaddam, Pilkerton Cairnie, Rothbart and Sabat, 2009: 9).

As such the Framework, I expect, will continue to evolve until research shows that it has reached a point where it is truly useful for positioning strategy development and positioning research. It may of course be shown through research that this point of attainment is not possible and there may be different frameworks suggested. I believe the current strength of the Framework for Intentional Positioning in Public Relations is that it provides a way to apply a social constructionist approach to theory and practice. One can see that this relates to Bourdieu's (1991) concept of field in terms of having sufficient symbolic capital to position in a particular way, that is, in accordance with the local moral order. The Framework may be a practical way to apply such thinking to public relations. Until now, the work of Bourdieu has perhaps been seen as too abstract to have much application. I see possibilities in future research to map positioning theory more closely to the work of Bourdieu, bringing together the linguistic and the social scientific aspects of public relations scholarship, and to use such work in making necessary iterations to the Framework.

The other avenue for future research using the Framework would be to apply the idea of the "enacting organization" (Gilpin and Murphy, 2006: 386) in order to ascertain the extent to which working through the Framework in the design of public relations strategy delivered benefit. This could especially lead to research into whether organizations could do positioning simulations and scenarios for training and mapping communication strategy in much the same way they do training for crisis management. The Framework for Intentional Positioning in Public Relations has shown to have the potential to guide the determination of a viable position. Further research could help confirm its usefulness in meeting both the challenge of demonstrating to senior management why positions taken need to be viable within the local moral order and, of guiding the development and implementation of viable positioning strategies for organizations.

The significant implication for practice of applying positioning theory, and in particular the Framework, is that it may assist practitioners to analyze why past campaigns have or have not worked. The Framework provides an heuristic for practice but importantly, makes positioning, one of the key methods and techniques used in public relations, more transparent, breaking the techniques down into component parts. Just as marketing has a "marketing mix", the positioning framework may see public relations developing a "public relations mix". This may make the design of campaigns more streamlined but may also deliver benefits by way of being able to explain to clients/internal stakeholders the steps through which practitioners work to deliver desired outcomes. This could help break down misconceptions from those outside of the public relations field that "PR" is not underpinned by practical, proven theory and is somehow a poor cousin to marketing. This is not just about the reputation and understanding of the public relations field but also relates to the way public relations work is credited to the workload of employees and billed to clients.

Research relating to the positioning triangle: determining the position, the first vertex of the triangle

A public relations position was defined as a point of intentional representation discursively constructed for the purposes of achieving an intended outcome, and from where possibilities for action are established, or in some cases denied, in terms of the local moral order/s wherein the public relations activity is taking place. Further research would help confirm whether this definition stands in a public relations context or whether further refinement is needed. The relationship between other public relations theories such as coorientation theory and contingency theory is also an area for further exploration, as current work indicates that the theories can work together well to explicate and inform practice.

The public relations environments in which intentional strategic positioning is undertaken are often complex. The initial work on positioning theory in conceptualizing public relations practice within ideas of emergent strategy, complexity absorption, and risk management seems promising in reflecting the realities of dynamic positioning practice. However, there is a strong argument for further exploring the relationship of emergent strategy (e.g. King, 2010) and positioning, and how this can assist in managing complexity.

The idea of crystallizing and liquidating positions was introduced as a way of encapsulating the way much public relations practice was conceptualized (Henriksen, 2008). Whether this way of viewing public relations positions is useful in terms of research and practice has yet to be confirmed. It seems to hold promise, firstly when public relations is viewed in a more functional, theoretical perspective. One can imagine that in a plan driven by "a management-by-objectives" style approach, aiming for position crystallization may form the basis for developing a specific objective. Secondly, when viewed through a discursive lens, there is clearly a case for shoring up certain discourses to assist in the crystallization, and in unsettling current discourses if one is seeking to liquidize a position.

Research relating to the positioning triangle: enacting the position, the second vertex of the triangle

A possible future research direction at this vertex of the positioning triangle is related to Bazerman's (2012) work on genre. From a theoretical perspective, what role does genre play in public relations positioning? Could the selection of genre be part of the speech act, or is it part of the public relations skill in promulgating the speech act in an appropriate way? Applying Bazerman's (2012) work, it could be seen that a public relations practitioner might ascertain that a particular situation requires the kind of speech act that has worked in previous situations, not just in terms of language used but also the genre used. For example, a practitioner wouldn't send a journalist the information about a new initiative as a poem, but would send it as a media release. Perhaps research that "played" with genre in public relations could result in some interesting findings!

Genres are interesting in the public relations context, with some being more fixed than others in the local moral orders in which we operate. The media release once functioned purely as a media information tool but with the advent of changing technology, such as websites and social media, now also can function as a general alert to publics and audiences. Such releases also function as a corporate narrative on a newsroom website page, Facebook page, and so on. The nature of the genre might change over time, such as when we have seen components added to media releases such as tags and keywords, and search engine optimized content. However, all this does is optimize the chances that a web searcher will find the organization-initiated text about a situation rather than fundamentally changing the nature of a genre.

The system of activity that the genre is part of provides communication stability (Bazerman, 2012: 230). In the context of media relations there is a certain system that operates and the media release remains part of the system. It is notable that the elements of the genre still need to all be present for the release to have the desired outcome. A confused lead paragraph, a failure to include key aspects of the story or contact details will lead to the release failing to comply with the genre requirements, and the intended social effect will not be achieved. This seems to lend weight to the argument that genre may work as a speech act in itself and may fit within the positioning triangle. This is obviously fertile ground for further research.

Speech act theory is not without critics and further research is needed to address these critiques to ascertain whether they weaken the concept of the "positioning triangle" (Harré and van Langenhove, 1999: 12). For example, Bourdieu, in criticizing speech act theory as put forward by Austin in 1962, stated that Austin "has found in discourse itself – the specifically linguistic substance of speech, as it were – the key to the efficacy of speech" (1991: 109). In countering Austin's assertions, Bourdieu suggests (1991) that a spokesperson's "speech concentrates within it the accumulated symbolic capital of the group which has delegated him and of which he is the *authorized representative*" (p. 111). Bourdieu (1991) claims that it is this that gives the words their effect, not the words or utterances themselves. The whole idea of Bourdieu's "authorized language" is centered on his view that:

> It is clear that all the efforts to find, in the specifically linguistic logic of different forms of argumentation, rhetoric and style, the source of their symbolic efficacy are destined to fail as long as they do not establish the relationship between the properties of discourses, the properties of the person who pronounced them and the properties of the institution which authorizes him to pronounce them
>
> (Bourdieu, 1999: 111).

Further research is needed to investigate this view and to determine whether the situating of the speech act in the positioning triangle of "position, act and storyline" addresses Bourdieu's concerns to any degree.

Research relating to the positioning triangle: supporting the positioning through storylines, the third vertex of the triangle

Future directions for researching storylines in public relations positioning relate to the way narrative works in public relations. As narrative has the ability to reach out and connect with audiences, it is effective for engagement with internal and external stakeholders (Gill, 2009). It remains to be seen whether the works of Gergen (2005), Bakhtin (1986) and Tobias (1993) are the most appropriate for guiding the development of storylines in public relations positioning.

A further challenge for storytelling in public relations is the fragmentation of media and communication platforms. Questions as to how stories are told to support public relations positioning on such a platform as Twitter, in which we are limited to posts of 140 characters, have yet to be answered. Is a platform like Twitter simply an augmentation to other storytelling platforms or can it be a positioning platform in its own right? Could exercises such as that seen in the book, *Twitterature* (Aciman and Rensin, 2009), which claims to have "distilled through the voice of Twitter to its purest, pithiest essence" the works of "over sixty of the greatest works of western literature", provide insights as to how public relations positioning efforts could make use of the platform? The visual aspects of storytelling are also projected to grow with the uptake of increasingly accessible online film and photography sites. Of course, it is not only the sites and platforms but the way they can be integrated with other platforms and networks that provides never before seen opportunities to integrate sound, written text and image. Positioning theory may well provide an analytical approach that can accommodate an emerging communication and engagement landscape.

Research relating to analyzing positioning strategies in public relations

The use of positioning analysis in public relations contexts is at an early stage with only a handful of studies published prior to this book (e.g., James, 2010, 2011, 2012; Tsetsura, 2012; Wise and James, 2013). The research methods used to date, namely thematic analysis, textual analysis, autoethnography and positioning discourse analysis, are all qualitative and this aligns with the large majority of positioning analytical work undertaken in other disciplines in the last two decades. Research has addressed the use of strategic positioning in public relations campaigns (James, 2010, 2011, 2012), and in political public relations (Wise and James, 2013). Positioning theory has also been used to assist in analyzing the identity work undertaken by public relations practitioners in the Russian context (Tsetsura, 2012). Different approaches to research may be needed, as stated by van Ruler (2005: 171):

> In the community of management scholars, anthropological methods and action research are emerging as important and valuable research methodologies for certain practical questions. In view of the kind of problems that confront public relations practitioners, we also might need to reconsider our methodology and find methods that are more in line with public relations planning than the normal, classical social-sciences methods.

Approaches such as practitioner-based inquiry and action research offer opportunities for researchers to study positioning efforts in public relations practice and to work with practitioners as co-researchers. As detailed in Chapter 9, I believe that action research such as seen in the recent work of Piezcka and Wood (2013), and methods such as practitioner-base inquiry, have much to offer in furthering understanding of public relations positioning.

The hope is that positioning theory stimulates interest in applying a range of research methods in the field. Harré (2006: 229–30) tells us:

> positioning analysis can be applied to episodes of different scales – from individual persons face to face, to rival scientific teams, up to nation-states – whenever there is an issue of the distribution of rights and duties among the participants. What people do is draw from what they believe they may do, which is itself drawn from what they believe they can do.

Positioning analysis allows the public relations scholar to examine the relations between what organizations "do", "may do" and "can do" in specific social and cultural circumstances.

It should be noted that some scholars using positioning theory in their research work are critical of some aspects of the theory, and these criticisms may be relevant for public relations research. For example, Wilkinson and Kitzinger (2003) point out that their research into everyday conversational positioning revealed "a number of distinctively different practices and actions, all of which are sometimes glossed by use of the term 'positioning'" (p. 174). They call for more work on how positioning works to reproduce and reinforce (and sometimes resist) social categories, and for analysts to be more precise in their unpacking of what they refer to as "positioning" in their data. They propose three ways of doing this:

1 *Naming or indexing a category*: on naming or indexing a category, a person is subsumed into a category and positioned as a "presumptive representative (or, sometimes, as an exceptional member) of that category" (p. 174). The category itself may be named such as "young people today" or may not be named and instead is indexed, meaning that it might be quite an oblique reference such as "you can never tell with that lot" (Wilkinson and Kitzinger, 2003: 174).
2 *Invoking categorical membership*: a category may not be named or indexed but may be invoked through the orientation of a storyline, for example through the things that are assumed in the storyline (such as having a primarily heterosexual audience; or, that parties in a particular conversation have had similar experiences with something) (Wilkinson and Kitzinger, 2003: 174).
3 *Invoking attributes*: where people display in their exchanges the kind of person they are through displaying what attributes they possess as individuals. This can be seen to be pertinent in a professional communication context where organizations speak through an organizational voice and attempt to position themselves through such invocation (Wilkinson and Kitzinger, 2003: 174).

Wilkinson and Kitzinger (2003) also called for more work to examine how individuals are produced as members of social categories, how inferences about such social categories are mobilized and for what ends this takes place. This can be seen to relate to strategic public relations practice and the exercise of power in positioning efforts by organizations. Wilkinson and Kitzinger (2003) point out that many positioning episodes take place and are researched from a perspective of a relatively stable backdrop of normative cultural assumptions. Further research into such normative positioning, they state, is "important for the theoretical development of positioning theory… and for understanding how oppression works in ordinary, everyday interactions" (p. 177). From a public relations perspective it would be fascinating to examine what normative backdrops for organizational positioning efforts are assumed by practitioners (and audiences).

Conclusion

I have not built an original theory but I hope to have added value to existing ideas, pushed forward hitherto unexplored questions, and challenged conventional thinking. These are the elements that Kilduff (2006) states are intrinsic requirements to making an original contribution to a research field. Positioning theory for public relations application can be viewed as potentially both a positive, or explanatory theory, and a normative theory. It is a positive or explanatory theory as it sheds light on the nature of the phenomenon of public relations positioning practice. Positioning theory also has the potential to be a normative theory if it was applied to drive more ethical practice by organizations.

Corley and Gioia (2011) state that revelatory thinking doesn't necessarily require introducing new concepts but is much more often accomplished "by offering a novel approach to integrating prior thought and research into some model or framework that constituted a different way of understanding some phenomenon" (p. 19). I trust this is what I have done in this book. I have aspired to address aspects of public relations practice and research that are not just significant at the current time but that will only increase in their significance in years to come.

I see positioning theory's strength in its capacity to help conceptualize and understand future practices. With the rise of social media, mobile technologies, networked communication, and the increasing ability for monitoring and recording what all institutions are doing, the local moral order in terms of the idea of rights and duties becomes paramount. This theory seems to be one that is both currently relevant but that could take the field forward as it grapples with notions such as control and dialogue, and co-creation and "produsage" (Bruns, 2012). Corley and Gioia (2011: 23) state that:

> Widely influential theorizing should also hold the potential for trying to identify domains that will soon be in need of theorizing (e.g. virtual societies, sustainability, accelerating globalization, new models of management not based on the preeminence of economic factors).

How much influence positioning theory will have on the field of public relations remains to be seen. Perhaps it will be positioning theory that has what Corley and Goia (2011: 24) call "theoretical prescience" in that it will be able to give meaning to "ambiguous informational cues" and be able to articulate "viable interpretations and actions to cope with coming organizational and environmental demands". I see positioning theory as robust in that it links the cultural and social aspects of public relations practice and research, can be readily used to assist practice design, and can guide management decision making.

In completing this book I hope that I have contributed to the body of knowledge in the public relations field in a way that will help advance future research amongst the global community of scholars. My work, I trust, contributes to the foundations on which new approaches to examining and practicing public relations can be built in the future.

References

Aciman, A. and Rensin, E. (2009) *Twitterature: The World's greatest books retold through Twitter*. London: Penguin.

Bakhtin, M. (1986) The problem of speech genres. In M. Holquist (ed.) *Speech Genres and Other Late Essays*. (Translated by V. McGee). Austin, TX: University of Texas Press, pp. 60–102.

Bazerman, C. (2012) Genre as social action. In J. Gee and M. Handford (eds) *The Routledge Handbook of Discourse Analysis*. London: Routledge, pp. 226–38.

Berger, B. (1999) The Halcion affair: public relations and the construction of ideological world view. *Journal of Public Relations Research*, 11(3): 185–203.

Bourdieu, P. (1991) *Language and Symbolic Power.* Cambridge: Polity Press.

Bruns, A. (2012) Reconciling community and commerce? Collaboration between produsage communities and commercial operators. *Information, Communication and Society*, 15(6): 815–35.

Corley, K. G. and Gioia, D. A. (2011) Building theory about theory building: what constitutes a theoretical contribution? *Academy of Management Review*, 36(1): 12–32.

Danowski, J. A. (2008) Short-term and long-term effects of a public relations campaign on semantic networks of newspaper content: priming or framing? *Public Relations Review*, 34(3): 288–90.

Gergen, K. (2005) Narrative, moral identity, and historical consciousness: a social constructionist account. In J. Straub (ed.) *Narration, Identity, and Historical Consciousness*. New York: Berghahn, pp. 99–119.

Gill, R. (2009) Building employee engagement and reputation through storytelling. In T. Flew (ed.) *Communication, Creativity and Global Citizenship: Refereed proceedings of the Australian and New Zealand Communication Association Conference 2009*, Brisbane. Retrieved from www.proceedings.anzca09.org

Gilpin, D. and Murphy, P. (2006) Reframing crisis management through complexity. In C. H. Botan and B. Hazelton (eds) *Public Relations Theory II*. Marwah, NJ: Lawrence Erlbaum, pp. 375–92.

Hallahan, K. (1999) Seven models of framing: implications for public relations. *Journal of Public Relations Research*, 11(3): 205–42.

Hallahan, K. (2000) Enhancing motivation, ability, and opportunity to process public relations messages. *Public Relations Review*, 26(4): 463–80.

Harré, R. (2006) Positioning theory. In V. Jupp (ed.) *The Sage Dictionary of Social Research Methods*. Sage, pp. 229–30. Retrieved from http://srmo.sagepub.com/view/the-sage-dictionary-of-social-research-methods/SAGE.xml

Harré, R. (2012) Positioning theory: moral dimensions of social-cultural psychology. In J. Valsiner (ed.) *The Oxford Handbook of Culture and Psychology*. New York: Oxford University, pp. 191–206.

Harré, R., Moghaddam, F., Pilkerton Cairnie, T., Rothbart, D. and Sabat, S. (2009) Recent advances in positioning theory. *Theory and Psychology*, 19(1): 5–31. doi: 10.1177/0959354308101417

Harré, R. and van Langenhove, L. (1999) *Positioning Theory: Moral contexts of intentional action*. Oxford: Blackwell.

Henriksen. T. (2008) Liquidating roles and crystallising positions. In F. Moghaddam, R. Harré and N. Lee, (eds) *Global Conflict Resolution through Positioning Analysis*. New York: Springer, pp. 41–64.

James, M. (2010) The use of intentional positioning techniques in government agencies' communication campaigns. In D. Verčič and K. Sriramesh (eds) *Government Communication: Proceedings of the 17th International Public Relations Research Symposium BledCom*. Bled, Slovenia, Ljubljana: Pristop, pp. 140–7. Retrieved from www.bledcom.si/uploads/ppt2010/bledcom 2010 proceedings hi.pdf

James, M. (2011) A provisional conceptual framework for intentional positioning in public relations. *Journal of Public Relations Research,* 23(1): 93–111. http://dx.doi.org/10.1080/1062726X.2010.505120

James, M. (2012) Autoethnography: the story of applying a conceptual framework for intentional positioning to public relations practice. *Public Relations Review*, 38(4): 555–64. http://dx.doi.org/10.1016/j.pubrev.2012.05.004

King, C. (2010) Emergent communication strategies. *International Journal of Strategic Communication*, 4(1): 19–38. doi: 10.1080/15531180903415814

Lee, N. (2010) Afterword. In F. Moghaddam and R. Harré (eds) *Words of Conflict, Words of War: How the language we use in political processes sparks fighting*. Santa Barbara, CA: Praeger.

Motion, J. (1997) Technologising the self: an art of public relations. *Australian Journal of Communication*, 24(2): 1–16.

Motion, J. (2000) Personal public relations: the interdisciplinary pitfalls and innovative possibilities of identity work. *Journal of Communication Management*, 5(1): 31–40.

Pieczka, M. and Wood, E. (2013) Action research and public relations: dialogue, peer learning, and the issue of alcohol. *Public Relations Inquiry*, 2, 161. doi: 10.1177/2046147X13485955

Smudde, P. M. and Courtright, J. L. (2010) Public relations and power. In R. Heath (ed.) *The Sage Handbook of Public Relations*. Thousand Oaks, CA: Sage, pp. 177–90.

Tan, S. and Moghaddam, F. (1999) Intergroup positioning. In R. Harré and L. van Langenhove (eds) *Positioning Theory: Moral contexts of intentional action*. Oxford: Blackwell, pp. 178–94.

Tilley, E. (2005) The ethics pyramid: making ethics unavoidable in the public relations process. *Journal of Mass Media Ethics*, 20(4): 305–20.

Tobias, R. (1993) *20 Master Plots (and how to build them)*. Cincinnati: Readers Digest.

Tsetsura, K. (2012) A struggle for legitimacy: Russian women secure their professional identities in public relations in a hypersexualized patriarchal workplace. *Public Relations Journal*, 6(1): 1–21. Retrieved from www.prsa.org/intelligence/prjournal/documents/2012tsetsura.pdf

van Langenhove, L. and Harré, R. (1999) Introducing positioning theory. In R. Harré and L. van Langenhove (eds) *Positioning Theory: Moral contexts of intentional action*. Oxford: Blackwell, pp. 14–31.

van Ruler, B. (2005) Commentary: professionals are from Venus, scholars are from Mars. *Public Relations Review*, 31(2): 159–73.

Wang, A. (2007) Priming, framing, and position on corporate social responsibility. *Journal of Public Relations Research*, 19(2): 123–45.

Wilkinson, S. and Kitzinger, C. (2003) Constructing identities: a feminist conversation analytic approach to positioning in action. In R. Harré and F. Moghaddam (eds) *The Self and Others: Positioning individuals and groups in personal, political and cultural contexts*. London: Praeger, pp. 157–80.

Wise, D., and James, M. (2013) Positioning a price on carbon: applying a proposed hybrid method of positioning discourse analysis for public relations. *Public Relations Inquiry*, 2(3): 327–53.

Index

For Product Safety Concerns and Information please contact our EU
representative GPSR@taylorandfrancis.com
Taylor & Francis Verlag GmbH, Kaufingerstraße 24, 80331 München, Germany

www.ingramcontent.com/pod-product-compliance
Ingram Content Group UK Ltd.
Pitfield, Milton Keynes, MK11 3LW, UK
UKHW022037061126
477531UK00008B/390
* 9 7 8 1 1 3 8 4 9 7 3 6 8 *